the
second
cooperative

SPORTS

&

GAMES

---

book

OTHER BOOKS BY TERRY ORLICK

The Cooperative Sports & Games Book
Every Kid Can Win (with Cal Botterill)
Winning Through Cooperation
In Pursuit of Excellence

the
second
cooperative

SPORTS
&
GAMES
book

Terry Orlick

PANTHEON BOOKS / NEW YORK

Library of Congress Cataloging in Publication Data
Orlick, Terry.
The second cooperative sports and games book.
1. Games. 2. Sports. I. Title.
GV1201.0723   794   81-18965
ISBN 0-394-51430-0   AACR2
ISBN 0-394-74813-1 (pbk.)

Grateful acknowledgment is made to the following for permission to reprint previously published material:

Alberta Recreation and Parks: Paraphrased descriptions of modified rules for Volleyball, Field Hockey, and Water Polo from *Senior Citizens Sports and Games Manual*, 1978. Reprinted by permission of Alberta Recreation and Parks, Edmonton, Alberta, Canada.

Jim Deacove: Paraphrased descriptions of Touch Blue, Collective Marathons, Cooperative Meets, Handball, Badminton, and Football, mostly from *Sports Manual of Cooperative Recreation*. Copyright © 1978 by Jim Deacove. Reprinted by permission.

Harper & Row, Publishers: Text of "Hug O' War" from *Where the Sidewalk Ends: The Poems and Drawings of Shel Silverstein*. Copyright © 1974 by Shel Silverstein. By permission of Harper & Row, Publishers, Inc.

Impact Publishers: Paraphrased versions of Magic Number II, Incorporations, Imaginary Ball Toss, and Wonderful Circle from Matt Weinstein and Joel Goodman, Ed.D., *Playfair: Everybody's Guide to Noncompetitive Play*. Copyright © 1980. Impact Publishers, Inc., San Luis Obispo, California. Reprinted by permission of the publisher.

Prentice-Hall: Paraphrased versions of Four Square, Team Juggle, Car and Drive, and Alaskan Baseball from *Follow Me* by Marianne Torbert. Copyright © 1980 by Prentice-Hall, Inc. Published by Prentice-Hall, Englewood Cliffs, New Jersey 07632. Reprinted by permission of the publisher.

Yachting and David Perry: Excerpts from David Perry's two-part article, "Improving Your Junior Sailing Program," *Yachting*, April 1978 and May 1978. Reprinted by permission of *Yachting* and the author.

TO ANOUK

for bringing in the sunshine

HUG O'WAR

I will not play at tug o'war,
I'd rather play at hug o'war,
Where everyone hugs
Instead of tugs,
Where everyone giggles
And rolls on the rug,
Where everyone kisses,
And everyone grins,
And everyone cuddles,
And everyone wins.

—Shel Silverstein

preface
where are you taking me?

The first *Cooperative Sports & Games Book* was published in 1978. The response to that book from concerned people working with children around the world has been overwhelming. Almost everyone who contacts me is excited about the concept and is looking for more cooperative games. My first reaction is to ask them to look within themselves and to those they engage in play for new directions, which lots of them are doing. But many people also feel a need for additional cooperative games from which they can draw and adapt. To help them along, I have put together *The Second Cooperative Sports & Games Book*. It is in no way a repetition of the first book. Almost all of the several hundred games are completely different; a few are modified or refined versions of previous cooperative games.

Since 1978 I have traveled extensively in search of more cooperative games, from the frozen ice packs of the Canadian Arctic to the deserts of the Australian outback to the jungles of Papua New Guinea. I have also conducted hundreds of workshops on cooperative games, all over the world. In this book I share with you not only the wonderful games I've found around the world but the practical ramifications of these experiences as well.

It has become clear to me that people who are looking for cooperative games are also searching for paths to more peaceful and fulfilling life-styles for their children. Many want to understand fully the concept behind the games. Many ask about how it applies to raising cooperative and self-confident children and how it relates to harmonious versus violent coexistence. As a result of this interest, you will find interspersed throughout this book my attempt to respond to some of these broad concerns.

It is my sincere hope that these additional thoughts translated into action will strengthen your capacity to provide humanizing experiences for the children with whom you live, work, and play.

acknowledgments

I would like to thank those many people from around the world who contributed to this book, particularly those people from aboriginal cultures who opened their hearts and freely shared their traditional games, as well as many others who continue to help the cooperative-games concept move forward.

Special thanks are extended to Sally Olsen, who has played an integral part in our Ottawa-based cooperative-games movement, for her vaulable contributions to this book, including writing the sections on cooperative parachute activities and party games. The continued excellent work of other members of our Ottawa-based Games Co-op—Cathi Foley, Roberta Haley, Michel Villeneuve, Pierre Provost—is greatly appreciated.

Sincere appreciation is also extended to Jim Deacove for Touch Blue and collective teen-age activities; Lucie Joannette and Annette Spirators for co-op games for handicapped children; Marianne Torbert for Co-op Four Square, Team Juggle, Car and Driver, Clap Together, and Alaskan Baseball; Matt Weinstein and Joel Goodman for Magic Number 11, Incorporations, Imaginary Ball Toss, and Wonderful Circle; Darrilyn Wood for Balloons Over and Under and Water Slide; Katherine Linsley and Ralph Ingleton for ecological games; David Moses for Adopt-a-Friend and Sucker's Creek; Mollie Elie for cooperative fitness activities; Margaret Mulac for Swiggle Sticks; Pensa Roleasmalik, Naomi Martin, Audrey Aarons, and Graeme Kemelfield for access to New Guinea games; Ian Robertson and Neil Hammond for access to Australian aboriginal games; Wang Min Qi for Chinese games; Elsdon Best and Wharepapa for Maori games; the Malaysian National Unity Board for Malay games; Martin Strube for Alternative Hockey and Alternative Monopoly; Susan Kalbfleisch for Magic Number and Running to the Olympics; Harry Sawchuck for cooperative-game strategies for high-school students; the Saskatchewan Department of Cooperation and Cooperative Development for Internal Cooperation, Jug-Band, Pot Luck, and Recreation Places; David Perry for Cooperative Sailing; Alex Bavelas and Elliot Aronson for Broken Squares; Maria Witt for Ten-Second Parachute Formations; Gayle Hughes and Skip Kutz for Saskatchewan Cooperation; Alberta Parks and Recreation and Kathy O'Connor for senior citizen games; Bob Wiele for Sports Collage; Jack Donohue for Point to the Passer; Kate O'Connor and Donna Lowe for Human Obstacle Course; Lucie Coté, Robert Cronier, and Mario Lapointe for Log Walk; Shiro Tanaka for Hug and Roll; Jack Coberly for Co-op Golf; Bernie Swords for Cooperative Musical Desks; Nic Nilsson for mentioning Three-Sided Soccer; Cal Botterill for Multiball Games; Dan Smith for Grapefruit Cup; John Partington for children's perspectives; Bill Michaelis for his thoughts on "it" power; Susan Buck for Bandaids and Belly Buttons, Three-Part People, the turnip book, and lovely visits; the Social Sciences and Humanities Research Council of Canada for assistance toward cross-cultural research that contributed to the content of this book; Ann Hyland for an excellent review of the rough manuscript; Wendy Wolf for doing a super editorial job; and Sylvie Lavoie, who continues to bring joy and spark to my life.

contents

the
second
cooperative

SPORTS
&
GAMES

---

book

the magic realm of play

The play world is the child's natural medium for personal growth and positive learning. Young people are the masters of this magic realm—they play the most and are most influenced by play. Their play is both serious business and pure fun. At its heart, it signifies nothing less than how they will be in this world.

Play is an ideal medium for positive social learning because it is natural, active, and highly motivating for most children. Games constantly involve people in the processes of acting, reacting, feeling, and experiencing. They can be a beautiful way to bring people together. However, if you distort children's play by rewarding excessive competition, physical aggression against others, cheating, and unfair play, you distort children's lives.

In cooperative sports, we are actually going back to an ancient form to help more children blossom into happy and fully functioning human beings. Cooperative play and games began thousands of years ago, when tribal peoples gathered to celebrate life.

The concept behind cooperative games is simple: People play with one another rather than against one another; they play to overcome challenges, not to overcome other people; and they are freed by the very structure of the games to enjoy the play experience itself. No player need find himself or herself a bench warmer nursing a bruised self-image. Since the games are designed so that cooperation among players is necessary to achieve the objective(s) of the game, children play together for common ends rather than against one another for mutually exclusive ends. In the process, they learn in a fun way how to become more considerate of one another, more aware of how other people are feeling, and more willing to operate in one another's best interests.

People of every size, shape, age, and ability—from infants to the aged—can enjoy these games, and they can be played virtually anywhere with almost no equipment. When the right games for a specific age or ability are chosen, they almost always result in total involvement, feelings of acceptance, cooperative contribution by all players, and lots of smiling faces.

One of the things we hope to teach the children of the future is to become more receptive to *sharing* both human and material resources (for example, ideas, talents, concerns, feelings, respect, possessions, equipment, time, space, and responsibility). Our studies assessing the social impact of well-designed cooperative-games programs have consistently shown an increase in cooperative behavior in games, in free play, and in the classroom for children involved in these programs. The change does not occur overnight; but over a period of several months, the children seem to become more considerate and caring human beings.

Cooperative learning can also enhance a child's capacity to create or excel by freeing her to do so within a less threatening framework. In addition, cooperative games can satisfy the desire to engage in enjoyable, self-paced leisure activities for the sheer fun of it. The feelings generated in many little people can best be summed up in the words of one who said "In cooperative games I feel left in."

Cooperation, Creativity, and Choice

The "magic" of cooperative games revolves around several real freedoms that help nurture cooperation, good feelings, and mutual support. To understand how the games "work" a little better, think about these aspects of cooperative activities.

FREEDOM FROM COMPETITION

The distinctive feature of cooperative games that separates them from all other games, old and new, is their structural makeup. For example, in the traditional game King of the Mountain, the rules dictate that one person be king while all others are to be shoved down the mountain. The game has a competitive structure in that it demands that players act against one another and excludes all but one from attaining the object of the game. In the cooperative version, People of the Mountain, the structural demands of the game are completely reversed. The objective is to get as many people as possible to the top of the mountain, and children play together to accomplish it. This frees them from the pressure to compete, eliminates the need for destructive behavior, and by its very design encourages helpful and fun-filled interaction.

When you place people in competitive King of the Mountain structures *and* you make them feel as if their personal acceptability or self-worth is dependent on being on top, you create problems. These problems surface in the form of high levels of distress, dropping out, destructive aggression, and depression. If the outcome is made to seem important enough, people will deceive, cheat, hurt, and even kill to get to the top. And the rules they learn as children will affect them all their lives. By accepting the competitive goal as all-important, people not only become more willing to destroy others but may also destroy themselves and their families in the process.

FREEDOM TO CREATE

Children are creative largely because they have not yet learned that their world *must* be viewed or acted out in certain narrow or preset ways. Their refreshing visions will continue to grow if they are given the freedom to create and adapt and are encouraged for their creative endeavors. Why is this important? Because children who are free to develop their creativity not only get a great deal of personal satisfaction but also gain experience in working out solutions to their own problems. If we destroy children's curiosity, creativity, and originality of thought, we risk destroying the future of humankind. As pointed out by Sir Herbert Read, "Destructiveness and creativity are opposed forces. . . . To create is to construct, and to construct cooperatively is to lay the foundation of a peaceful community."

Cooperative games have grown out of many people's creative thought and will continue to do so. They should never become so rigid or static that they are resistant to creative and sensitive input from participants. No rule—in this or any other book—

should be seen as hard and fast. Let's keep on freeing children to create in a truly cooperative atmosphere.

FREEDOM FROM EXCLUSION

Games in which players are put out or removed are particularly brutal because they punish those who are less experienced or less skilled, fostering feelings of rejection and incompetence. Worse yet, the elimination effectively removes the opportunity to gain additional experience and improve skills. Games that are truly cooperative eliminate the elimination and reject the entire concept of dividing players into winners and losers.

Do you like pressured situations in which you have to worry about being accepted or achieving some numerical score? Most kids—like most adults—prefer self-paced activities in which they don't have to worry about failure, criticism, or rejection. They like to be with friends, to meet personal challenges, and most of all, to have fun.

If smiles are any indication of joy, you will quickly observe that highly organized competitive sport is not for joy. It is simply another area of specialized work, aimed at achievement.

FREEDOM TO CHOOSE

Providing children with choices (even small ones) demonstrates respect for them and confirms the belief that they're able to be responsible for themselves. When you treat children like responsible human beings, rather than like pawns, they will begin to behave in a responsible way. Try asking your children how they think a game should be played or how a game could be made more fun or how they can ensure that no one is left out or feels bad. When a particular problem arises, ask them how to solve it. They will almost always come up with humanizing suggestions.

When children are given the freedom to offer suggestions, make decisions, and choose for themselves, their motivation is greatly enhanced. It makes them feel important, gives them a sense of personal control, solves many problems, and helps them learn to make decisions for themselves. The initial choices can be within realistic limits, such as deciding how to make a number or shape by using their bodies, selecting a few cooperative games to play, or choosing a fun activity with which to end the games session. From a modest beginning their input can increase to the point where they have complete control over themselves and their play.

I cannot overemphasize the importance of listening to children's feelings and perspectives. However, in order for children to express their true feelings in your presence, you must first establish a genuine sense of mutual acceptance and trust. We spend too much time getting children to nod their support for our views rather than helping them to express their own. Once children are familiar with various kinds of activities and various ways of playing together in constructive ways, they are in a better position to choose from among cooperative, competitive, and individual options. Early experience with cooperation, creativity, and choice will enable more people to become happier through cooperation and healthier in competition.

FREEDOM FROM HITTING

At a cooperative games workshop for a group of teachers at a large city high school one Saturday, we were all outside playing together joyfully with parachutes billowing and beach balls flying. In the midst of our carefree play, a group of seven-year-olds trotted onto the field dressed in full armor for a football war. They looked more professional than the pros. I watched their faces closely as they trotted past us. They paused momentarily, glancing over, with a wishful look in their wide-open eyes. But it didn't last for long. The bellowing holler of the coach across the field quickly silenced any thoughts of playfulness; they were there to do battle. There was something ironic about the whole situation, especially when the command "Hit! Hit!" penetrated through the laughter of our adjoining play space.

Do you see children playing games that involve hitting and sometimes hurting one another with their bodies, fists, forearms, helmets, or even rolled-up newspapers or padded sticks? If so, someone is teaching them that pushing, shoving, hitting, and perhaps even hurting is OK and that other people's feelings don't count.

Hitting "sports," war games, war toys, and other types of actual or ritualized violence teach similar lessons. By promoting physical aggression or requiring it in the rules of a game, you teach children that it is perfectly acceptable to hit, push, shove, and otherwise mistreat other human beings.

Why in the world do we want to encourage young children to act out the hurting or killing of others in war simulations, shoot-outs, and so on? Why organize children into competitive games or leagues that by their very rules necessitate pushing, shoving, or hitting (for example, boxing, tackle football, full-contact hockey)?

There is not a single shred of evidence to support the position that aggressive tendencies are reduced "harmlessly" by engaging in physical aggression against others. Through physical activity children release energy and may become fatigued. However, if physical aggression is promoted in the process, the likelihood of that child's engaging in destructive or dehumanizing behavior is increased. Children in peaceful societies are not nurtured on games of aggression or destruction.

Balloon Balance

WHAT ARE OUR ALTERNATIVES?

We can play within cooperative People of the Mountain structures—cooperative games and cooperative outdoor pursuits.

We can play within competitive structures in less stressful ways (for example, placing less importance on the outcome and eliminating physical contact of a destructive nature through noncontact games).

We can engage in self-paced activities that are not assessed or scored.

We can choose serious, goal-oriented play in some situations and light-hearted play in other situations.

finding and creating
your own play equipment

Something magical happens to children when they create their own playthings. Starting with what seems like nothing, they can generally produce imaginative inventions that rival any sophisticated toy manufacturer's efforts—and enjoy themselves thoroughly in the process. Such an activity promotes self-reliance, creativity, and in many cases, cooperation among playmates.

As you read on in this book, you'll find that we actually call for very little "traditional" sports or game equipment and in almost every case suggest ways to invent, create, or improvise your own from readily available materials. That's one of the beauties of cooperative sports and games: They draw almost everything they need from within the players themselves. Again, this goes back to old-fashioned ideas of play. Fifty years ago, children in almost all cultures created their own playthings, often with their parents or friends. One of the most impressive qualities about children in contemporary nonindustrialized societies is the ease with which they still make their own toys and play equipment. For instance, a group of village children in Papua

New Guinea consented to show us some of their traditional dances. The little boys who provide the musical accompaniment dashed off into the jungle, wielding large machetes like skilled adults. They sliced down bamboo saplings and cut them into flute-size sections with a lengthwise slit in each. Every child, even the tiniest boys, made a flute. It took only about a minute or so to complete one flute, but because all the children shared the few knives available, the overall process took about a half an hour. No one left the flute-making area until the last child had completed and tooted his flute. They returned as a unit to begin the dance, testing out their flutes along the way. The boys also made their own bows from young hardwood trees, their arrows from the mid rib of dried sago palm leaves, and their bowstrings from dried and twisted strands of wood, bark, or vines.

When I asked a group of young girls if they would show me some of their string-figure games, without a second thought they ran up the bank of the river to some nearby ferns. They broke off the ferns at the bottom of the stem, stripped off the leaflike fronds, and peeled back the outer layers of the stem, leaving a white central core. This white core, which resembles a string, was simply tied together at the ends and the cat's cradle game commenced.

The Inuit of the Canadian Arctic made their own " beach balls" by blowing up seal bladders and "softballs" by stuffing caribou hides with hair or moss. They turned light stones and animal bones into juggling balls, caribou antlers into bats, and animal hides into tossing blankets, skipping ropes, whips, leather high bars, and gymnastic rings. They made their own harpoons, bows, and arrows, and they carved their own toys out of materials that were readily at hand. They even made bouncing balls out of animal joints and shelled very-hard-boiled eggs, easily available in their environment. Play included the preparation for play, which involved children in the creation and adaptation of their own playthings.

In the province of Quebec, where I live, children used to make their own skipping ropes by weaving a yarn through the center hole of a spool of thread. They also fashioned balls from the bladders of pigs, skis from the slats on wooden barrels, marbles from clay, spinning tops from chunks of wood, and literally hundreds of other playthings. They played hockey outdoors with mail-order catalogs or telephone books wrapped around their shins for protection. Frozen balls of horse manure were the prize pucks of the day.

Today toys are born in department stores, and factory-made equipment can be found by the boxload in living rooms all across the industrialized world. But it doesn't have to be that way. Think back to your own childhood—what did you do when the equipment wasn't there or broke or had to be improvised? Ask your parents or grandparents if they've got other memories and ideas. What did they play with and how did they make or find their playthings? Now get started rekindling that creativity with your own children.

Spinning homemade tops in Papua New Guinea

Creative Beginnings

The outdoors with all its splendor is a beautiful playground because it is alive and can be experienced in so many different ways. It moves of its own accord and can also be moved by a little person's touch.

Children love to explore, manipulate, transform, and create. They love to turn one thing into something else. Conversely, they tire quickly of toys or materials that can only be used in one way. Perhaps this is why natural materials invite such stimulating play. Young children delight in stomping around in puddles of water largely because they can produce a direct effect on a puddle. It is very responsive and therefore an exciting medium for play. For indoor play, moist clay (or a substitute such as Play-do) also provides an excellent medium for manipulation that can be enjoyed by almost all age groups.

A first step in helping young children to create their own playthings is probably to encourage them (or at least allow them) to discover natural items for play that are readily available in their immediate environment (such as puddles, mud, sand, clay, earth, sticks, logs, wood, pebbles, rocks, leaves, grass, water, snow, ice, holes, and caves). Even normal household items—pots and pans, bowls, cardboard boxes, old clothing, towels, sheets, hats, shoes, ropes, wooden blocks, and paper—will prompt creativity. Did you ever notice that very young children prefer to play with the boxes and paper in which their presents were wrapped rather than with the presents

Boxes equal instant great toys

themselves? That's often because they are free to explore and manipulate the wrappings, turning them into whatever they please. Sophisticated toys, including expensive mechanical and electronic versions, exist more to fill the profit motives of manufacturers than the play needs of children.

What then should I buy my one-and-a-half-year-old daughter or my five-year-old nephew for Christmas? How about an empty cardboard box or roll of toilet paper (wrapped, of course) for the toddler and a pig's bladder or inner tube for the five-year-old? Both are usually free for the asking and can provide for hours of creative fun for your children and their friends.

Children are not only capable of creating their own play and simple playthings, they can also contribute to the creation of more complex sports equipment and exciting "child-oriented" play areas or playgrounds. Ten years ago in the People's Republic of China, I observed nine- and ten-year-old children making wooden toys and conducting homemade puppet shows for their younger peers in kindergarten and nursery school. Elementary-school children made much of their own play equipment; groups of teenagers built ping-pong tables, gymnastics equipment, basketball courts, and even swimming pools for school and community use. For some excellent ideas on how to help children create simple pieces of sports equipment such as bats, balls, rackets, batting tees, and pucks, see "Making Equipment at Little or No Cost" in *Follow Me* (this and many other books you'll find useful are listed in the bibliography on pages 249–53).

When children and adults join together to create and construct community play areas or sports equipment, both the process and the product of creation provide valuable and enjoyable learning experiences. In *Playgrounds for Free*, Paul Hogan presents some excellent ideas on how to transform readily available materials that can be found lying around the neighborhod (old boxes, crates, cable reels, planks, logs, tires, inner tubes, blocks, and so on), into creative play equipment. If you inject a little cooperative thinking into the vital creative process, the play equipment itself will encourage cooperative social interaction among the children. Some homemade examples extracted from Hogan's book include tire swings upon which two or three children can swing at once; bench swings that hold half a dozen kids; circle swings made of a series of connected tires, which can be swung on by a dozen or more kids at the same time; child-powered merry-go-rounds; horses, giraffes, turtles, camels, and cars that can be ridden by several children at once; seesaws that spin in a circle as well as go up and down; and bucking broncos that can be powered by a friend.

In creating play equipment, it is important to remember that the most inspiring, durable, and valuable play element of all cannot be bought. It comes in the form of other children—playmates.

Rethinking Traditional Play Equipment

If we want children to learn to get along better, we can help by providing equipment conducive to positive interaction. Why not make beach balls (or air mattresses) with two or three spouts so that several people can blow them up? Why not have swings on which many children can sit side by side, pumping together? Why not have baby carriages and strollers built for two or tricycles built for three (with three seats and three sets of pedals) or slides wide enough for children to go down in pairs or groups? Why not have a giant ping-pong paddle (the circumference of a small table) with two or three handles? Why not have stilts for walking three-legged-race-style, with two people sharing three stilts—two conventional ones on the outside and a central one with two footholds, one for each person. It's fun to take a walk together in the high country and more challenging than walking alone. We tried it and it works.

In Papua New Guinea I saw three small children all drinking together out of one coconut. There are three little holes that can be penetrated quite easily in the top of every coconut. I wonder if the coconut had anything in mind? At any rate, these three little kids sauntered down by the river and cut three sturdy reeds to use as straws. The coconut became a cooperative piece of equipment, providing a taste of enjoyment for all three.

Another New Guinea group known as the Red Bowmen makes its own musical instruments out of bamboo and assorted other woods. Each instrument can play only one note; thus the musical harmony depends on each player to come in with her note

Anyplace is fine for co-op play

at the right time. This equipment creates a need for interdependent functioning. One note does not a song make, but many notes mixed together create harmony.

My good friend Wang Min Qi from the People's Republic of China relayed to me one of the classical Chinese stories on the virtues of cooperation:

> Once upon a time there was an old man who had ten sons. When he was dying, he called his ten sons over and took out ten chopsticks. He gave each son a chopstick and asked him to try to break it. Each son broke one chopstick without any difficulty. Then the old man took out another ten chopsticks. This time he bundled them up and asked each son to try again to break them. None of them could break the ten chopsticks tied together, no matter how hard he tried. They looked at each other in blank dismay. Then the old man said, "See, each of you is just like one chopstick: One chopstick is easy to break. If you unite and cooperate, your strength is so great that no one can easily destroy you."

My first exposure to a country that made extensive use of specially designed cooperative-play equipment for preschoolers was during an educational tour of the People's Republic of China in 1972. I saw young children playing together on rocking horses built to support two, three, or four children at a time. I saw swings on which two children could sit, facing each other, and by mutual action pump themselves high into the air. I saw preschoolers stringing beads onto opposite ends of the same string. It seemed such a natural and playful way to help children come together.

Other impressive adaptations for children that I viewed in China included the scaling-down of equipment to child size. Five-year-olds played on miniature basketball courts with a five-foot-high basketball net. If dunking a ball through a ten-foot-high-hoop is exciting for a six-footer, why not allow a three-footer to experience the same kind of enjoyment with a five-foot-high basket? Besides lowering the net, we could enlarge it to the size of a bushel basket. In fact, we could quite easily adapt all kinds of play equipment, as well as everyday household items, for better use by children. For example, a one-year-old can control a light, open a bedroom door, and use a sink if the switch or handle is within reach. I put an extended string on the fluorescent light in my office for my daughter, and she really appreciated that; it allows her to feel that she is shaping a small part of her world. If everything is out of reach, life can be pretty frustrating.

When I worked at a day camp in my late teens, it always seemed a bit ludicrous to take these little kids to a bowling alley (a scheduled activity). They picked up these great big heavy balls and tried to roll them all the way down the alley as if the children were full-grown adults. The balls usually ended up in the gutter or came crashing down to the ground, sometimes behind (or on top of) the child. Perhaps I began recognizing there the need to adapt games to meet the specific needs and capabilities of children. Why don't we provide them with lighter bowling balls, shorter alleys, bigger bowling pins, and lanes without gutters? At least we could let them walk closer to the target pins or allow two children to roll the big balls together.

Bats, balls, pucks, hurdles, and a variety of other sports equipment can be adapted for kids. In 1979 John Salmela, a good friend and colleague, headed a Canadian gymnastic delegation to China. He reported many adaptations in gymnastics equipment for young children, including the use of a miniature gymnastics horse that sat right on the ground. It was about 8 inches (20 cm) high and about 16 inches (40 cm) long. The point isn't to get rid of challenge—just frustration and nearly ensured defeat!

The Chinese do some very exciting things with animal "props" such as dragons and lions. These props are made out of various kinds of material, and when donned by two or more human beings, make the people look like big stuffed toy animals. To make a lion, one person controls the head and front feet and the other person controls the back feet and tail; working together, they can make the beast roll, walk, jump, and even stand on two feet. Dragons usually require more people to move but can do similar stunts. Very simple soft-construction props, like one resembling the shell of a giant turtle, can be used with young children to promote cooperation, creativity, and fun. Creative demands can be steadily increased to challenge the skills of any group, as can readily be seen by watching Chinese acrobats perform as lions and dragons.

When Michel Villeneuve, a fellow promoter of cooperative games, recently visited China, I asked him to be on the lookout for cooperative-play equipment. At a children's play center in Canton he saw a seesaw (teeter-totter) built for four, complete with four sets of handles. Just outside Shanghai he saw kindergarten children playing on rocking horses built for two. These horses had two heads, one facing in each direction; the children sat on the horses and began a rocking motion together. He also saw children engaged in what might best be described as a collective log roll. A hollow wooden cylinder, the size of a short, thick wooden log, was suspended on an axle a few inches off the ground. Several children could stand together on the log and roll it while holding onto a railing that extended across the apparatus at chest level.

One other interesting piece of equipment Michel saw in China was a carousel-type apparatus on which I remember playing as a youngster. Perhaps you'll remember it too. A pole extends from the ground and a series of chains hang down from a cap at the top of the pole. On the end of each chain is a handle, which children grab onto as they run around the pole to get the whole thing spinning. Once the contraption is spinning they can lift their feet off the ground and glide through the air between spurts of running. The spinning apparatus on which I played as a youngster had eight or ten handles, all hanging from equal lengths of chain. The Chinese version had a complete range of lengths of chain, thus allowing (and encouraging) big people and little people to play together on the same piece of equipment.

The Koreans have a very popular teeterboard activity that is cooperative in structure. A plank or sturdy piece of board (resembling a diving board) is used to propel partners into the air by turns. A mound of sand or earth about 12 inches (30 cm) high is made on the ground. The center of the plank rests on this mound, which acts as a fulcrum. One person stands on one end of the board while her partner jumps onto the other end. This sends the first person straight up into the air. She tries to come back down onto the board where she started, which in turn sends her partner into the air. The objective is to keep this seesaw bounding going for as long as possible.

For beginners, the mound of sand can be reduced in size so that it is just high enough to send a "bounder" a few inches into the air. Spotters can be stationed behind and on either side of the bounder to catch her if she leans off balance. Big soft mats are also a good idea, especially if the activity takes place indoors.

For young children I have replaced the bounding with simple balancing activities. For example, one child can stand on each end of the board and together the children attempt to keep the board and themselves in balance. Very short balance boards can also be used to facilitate some balancing activities. With a board about 36 inches (91 cm) long, partners can face each other and lean together so that their arms are in contact. They can then try to balance the board or move it up and down in seesaw fashion. This can also be done with two people on each end of the board. Seesaw activities for four allow more sharing, more equal distribution of weight (by switching partners), more challenge, and more fun.

To do either balancing or bounding activities indoors, a piece of wood that is rounded at the bottom can be attached to the center of the balancing plank. This takes the place of the mound of sand used outdoors.

Co-op playground equipment in Montreal

I was pleased to see that Le Parc Lafontaine in Montreal recently added two pieces of equipment to its playground area, both of which encourage cooperative play. The park now has an interesting long horse that sits on springs and is very low to the ground. The horse can be mounted and "ridden" by eight to ten preschoolers at once. Each child straddles the horse and holds onto a separate handle. To get the big horse rocking, all the children must lean forward and then backward in unison. Older children or adults can also join in on the ride. Lafontaine also has a piece of equipment resembling a large swing that is suspended by a chain at each of the four corners. Five to ten children playing together on the swing can get it moving freely in an end-to-end direction.

The concept of cooperative-play equipment may also be turned into something very functional for adults. Some innovators in Japan have devised what looks like a little train rolling around on thin bycicle wheels. It holds twenty-five people, each of whom has a set of foot pedals directly in front of his seat. By pedaling together, they can easily power the minitrain around large buildings and through long corridors. It's ideal for massive conference or shopping centers with connecting buildings, large airports with many terminal buildings, and so on. It is fuel efficient and pollution free, provides a community spirit, and is good for your health. Those who like a little diversion en route can read a paper while pedaling along the way.

We are just beginning to recognize the value of cooperative-play equipment. In the Resource section, starting on page 248, you'll find a list of suppliers who can provide some of the raw materials for redesigning playgrounds and play. But don't stop there: The possibilities for equipment design are endless—as are the potential benefits.

cooperative games for the tiniest tots

Learning to Share

I consider myself a very fortunate father. For the first fifteen months of my daughter's life, I was with her for a good part of her waking hours. We traveled around the world together and made up lots of cooperative games along the way. I have grown to a fuller understanding of the nature and needs of children as a result of my opportunities to soak in various cultures. However, nothing to date has had more impact on my recognition of the universality of certain traits than living with my daughter during this time. She has taught me about joyful play and about little people's capacities for love and sharing.

I believe that every child is capable of the same kind of responsiveness as I saw in Anouk. Observant parents who are willing to focus some energy in a well-planned cooperative direction can help ensure that their children develop into warm and loving human beings. This path is certainly not free from obstacles, but with your persistence the most cherished human values will win out in the end. The games that fill the latter part of this chapter are written primarily for parents who are seeking constructive ways to play with very young children. I hope my experiences with Anouk can help you find new ways to communicate with your own kids.

For more information on raising healthy young children, see Appendix A.

I am convinced now more than ever that cooperation and sharing surface naturally in young children and that the only reason those qualities fade is that they are not nurtured. No doubt babies demand a tremendous amount of their parents, but they also give much in return; sometimes we just have to look harder, and with more open eyes. For example, my daughter began food sharing when she was three months old. We accepted her offers and shared in return. We played simple sharing games by passing blocks, balls, sticks, earth, flowers, and other things back and forth.

At eight months old she was sharing her food with some regularity, taking some off her plate while she was eating and feeding it to me. It didn't always reach my mouth (more often my beard, shirt, or eye), but her aim improved over time; her intent, not her skill, was the point.

By ten months old she was pressing her cup to my lips and raising the bottom so that I could drink. At this age she also quite clearly shared her playthings by taking turns. One of the first times this happened was with a small container with seeds inside, which makes a noise when shaken. We sat on the floor one morning, and after she rattled it, I put my hand out in a receiving manner. She gave me the toy; I rattled it and handed it back. This was actually a very early form of cooperative play, and it went on for some time, holding both our interests.

By eleven months old Anouk was playing cooperatively with other children. She shared playthings with her cousin Alex, who is two months her elder. She also smothered him with kisses, much to his dismay. Now and then she batted him on the head too. This first occurred when she got very excited, as they chased each other back and forth playfully on all fours. I think that she wanted to express her happiness at being with him but didn't quite know how. It seemed as if she wanted him to feel the full weight of her touch and affection. Perhaps it was simply exploration. We helped turn her gesture into something more gentle, not by separating the two of them but by taking her hand and moving it softly and gently over his head and face. At the same time we said "*doux*," the French word for "gentle" or "soft." (Actually this was the first word she learned.) Often a young child is rough because he has not yet learned how to express his gentleness or been applauded when he does.

Before long, batting on the head had been replaced with more affectionate hugs and kisses. Anouk and her cousin shared their toys spontaneously. They played together most of the time in a beautiful manner, like little bear cubs, and they began doing this before they were one year old.

At the ripe old age of one year Anouk was directing her mother and me through a sharing ritual for drinking juice or milk in the morning. She drank, then offered me a sip, then her mother a sip, then she took a sip, and then back to me. Responding to this kind of giving gesture takes a little more time than shoving the bottle (or cup) back into her mouth and saying, "Drink!" However, the extra time is well spent. By accepting, acknowledging, and nurturing the simple gestures that surfaced naturally (and that surface naturally with many other children), she developed into a very empathetic and very giving child.

While watching Anouk direct a simple cooperative game, I've thought about the developmental psychologists who describe children as egocentric, incapable of taking another's point of view, incapable of taking turns in games, unable to develop a concern over other people's feelings, and "pre-cooperative" until about seven years of age. It's hard for me to believe that these psychologists' own children never engaged in any sharing gestures during the first few years of life. Perhaps they were so busy focusing on other sorts of development that they didn't take time to respond to natural sharing gestures.

I know that their "nonsharing" views of children do not hold up in the light of cross-cultural analysis. Clearly, very young children share and cooperate with great regularity among the Inuit, Australian aboriginals, Siwai from Papua New Guinea, Chinese from the People's Republic of China, Israeli living on kibbutzim, Tasaday, Zuni Indians, Mountain Arapesh, and so on. Young children in North America share in similar ways when they are encouraged to let these natural tendencies grow.

Why would a young child want to share? Parents give a tremendous amount to their infants; I think that most infants are happy to be able to give a little in return. Sharing may give them a sense of control, a sense of pleasure in being able to give something, a sense of importance, and a feeling of playing an equal part in the action. Or perhaps they want to share, as Gregory Bateson says, because doing so is part of the genetic makeup that ensures the survival of the human species.

Sometimes, of course, your child's idea of a gift may not be the same as yours; but think before you react! The other day after a steak cookout, Anouk ended up parading around with a large greasy T-bone in her hand. She looked as if she had walked right out of a cave as she waddled over to me offering the new toy. The last thing I wanted was that greasy old bone, but I accepted it, admired it, and gratefully returned it to her, and she waddled off on her merry way. If I had responded "No—dirty!" and had thrown the bone in the garbage, I would have been rejecting her sharing gesture rather than the bone itself. It's too simple to reject without thinking. We have to make a special effort to accept.

COOPERATIVE GAMES FOR THE TINIEST TOTS

Moving from sharing with parents to sharing with others seems to occur naturally. Anouk had been sharing her bottle with us for several weeks when, just after her first birthday, she began to share it with her cousin Alex. She sat next to him on the floor, drank a little herself, then stuck the bottle in his mouth for about an equal length of time, then took a sip herself . . . back and forth for several minutes. Gestures of sharing and giving come early and often in life; we simply don't tune into them and nourish them.

If you share some of your own activities and interests with very young children, you can enhance their social development. For example, if I read the newspaper when Anouk is around, I sit on the floor with her and give her a section to "read" (that is, to play with or tear up). Often it is a section of yesterday's paper, but she hasn't complained yet.

When an infant is giving, accept her offerings, show appreciation, demonstrate your affection, and give again in return. Give her hugs, accept her hugs, and give them in return. Play her game of give and take and give—whether it be with a teddy bear, a book, or a bone. If you make the effort to accept your baby's offerings and then return those same offerings, you may lose a little time in the short run, but you will certainly both gain in the long run.

At fifteen months old Anouk was feeding Alex with a spoon and giving freely of her playthings, to me and to little friends we encountered here and there. She often played a little with an object and then offered it as a part of her play. She seemed to

Sharing a treat

enjoy the other child's acceptance of the toy. If he did not return the object after a few gestures on her part, she simply turned her attention to another item. Sooner or later the original object would come back. When we visited a little girl three weeks younger, not only did Anouk offer her playthings but she helped her friend climb a set of stairs by placing her open hand on her friend's behind. She also consoled her friend when she began to cry by gently stroking her head.

When Alex hurts himself or cries, Anouk shows a genuine concern. She puts her arm around him in a consoling way, as if to say, "It's OK, you'll be all right." He sometimes pushes her away with an abrupt no between tears. But she seems to understand his temperament and tries to console him again the next time he appears in distress. The more we show our appreciation for these kinds of actions, the more common they become.

A sense of peace settles over you when you see your child play joyously with other children. When Anouk was sixteen months old, she joined in the play of two older children, aged seven and ten, whom she'd never met before. They were playing with a box of Scrabble letters. She sat down, observing their play for a few minutes, and then reached into the box and handed the older girl one of the letters. The girl bypassed her outstretched hand and reached for another letter. Anouk persisted, and the older girl finally responded when she recognized the gesture was one of giving.

At about twenty months Anouk began to share her new discoveries with me. The first time this happened was when she began to leaf through a little book that involved various sensory organs in touching, smelling, and so on. When she came to a page of flowers that smelled, she sniffed them, smiled, and put the page in front of my nose for me to sniff. She grasped my hand so that I could feel the texture of a soft bunny and the sandpaper beard on a man's face.

The desire to share experiences with loved ones seems to me an important first step in developing a healthy and open relationship. Many times doing so takes rethinking on our own part about what actions mean and about how we can communicate so many different messages to our children through gestures, touch, and voice; we have to stop to listen and *hear* children, not just correct "bad" behavior.

During the first two years of Anouk's life we actively promoted cooperation and sharing. Now they seem to happen all by themselves. She has carried her sharing orientation with her into a variety of mediums. Take cats, for example. Anouk has loved cats ever since she first laid eyes on a "Minou." The first time a cat let her get close enough for intimate interaction, she sat on the floor right next to him and watched carefully as he ate and drank. She offered him her bottle, nipple first. Who could refuse that? He turned and walked away. She persisted by offering him her crayons, her coloring book, his sleeping box, her full-body hugs, and finally pieces of food. He accepted the latter, and they became friends. Her sharing orientation had transferred to interaction with her fuzzy little friend.

COOPERATIVE GAMES FOR THE TINIEST TOTS

Cooperative-Game Beginnings

Most of the games outlined here for the tiniest tots grew out of spontaneous playful interactions between Anouk and her little friends. The games illustrate the kinds of cooperative activities that can be successfully introduced with children under two years.

- *Simple Exchanges.* Some of the simplest games of sharing for babies involve the exchange of objects between adult and infant. Any kind of object (for example, shakers, bottles, toys, balls, food, pieces of wool, flowers, and leaves) can be passed back and forth in a variety of ways: hand to hand, foot to hand, hand to mouth, mouth to mouth, and so forth. Anouk used to enjoy passing a cork back and forth—mouth to mouth.

- *Bear Hug.* Hug your child's cuddly little teddy bear and then hand it back to her. See if she hugs it. Ask for the bear back again with an open-hand gesture, hug it, and then return it again. End this simple game of sharing with a loving hug for both your child and her bear.

    Teddy bears, along with other similar kinds of creatures, give children an opportunity to act out the caring for others that is so important for both boys and girls. They can cover their miniature friends with a blanket, put them to sleep, feed and cuddle them, and so on.

    Anouk once walked out of her room with one teddy bear tucked under each arm. She had decided it was time for a two-teddy exchange. She gave me one bear so that we could each hug one, and then she gestured for an exchange in bears. We ended with a four-sided hug: two bears, my daughter, and me.

- *Teddy Bear Cradle.* After a bath, lay a towel down on the living room floor, then place a teddy bear in the center of the towel. Pick up two corners of the towel and hand your child the other two corners. Swing the towel gently back and forth to rock the teddy bear in the "cradle."

    When Anouk and I began this game, she wanted first to swing the bear in the towel, then toss him, then replace him with a necklace, and then give both the bear and the necklace a ride together. When her mother peeked around the corner to see what crazy things I was up to, my daughter crawled into the towel and handed her mother the ends to swing. We rocked her right into bed.

- *Peek-a-Boo.* Little kids love Peek-a-Boo games. You can begin by momentarily covering your eyes with your own hands and gradually move to hiding your face behind a paper or under a sheet. Gradually your baby will begin to do the hiding herself; this is best left for her to do at her own pace. One way to get very young children started with the Peek-a-Boo concept is to draw a happy person on a piece of paper. Then attach a small piece of paper or cloth to the drawing so that it covers the figure's face. Attach the cloth only at the top so that it can be raised and lowered by the child.

For a long time my daughter enjoyed playing Peek-a-Boo through a hole in the back of a chair. We stationed ourselves on opposite sides of the chair and took turns looking for each other through the hole. As she got slightly older, she enjoyed taking turns "hiding" behind a couch or cabinet and then peeking out.

Peek-a-Boo can be tied into crawling activities by crawling after your baby and then turning and encouraging her to crawl after you. As you crawl out of sight, perhaps around a corner, you stop, turn around, and sing "Peek-a-Boo" as soon as she comes into view. It's a good way to bolster the playful spirit.

- *Splish-Splash.* Young children love for you to play with them. They beam when you get down on the floor so that they can look you in the eye or when you climb into the bathtub with them. Splish-Splash is a game that works best when soaking in the bath with your little one. Use a soft plastic cup to pour water over him; then let him use the cup to pour water over himself and you. As he scoops up water in the cup, you can cup your hands together for him to pour the water into them. Then you can pour the water over his body, and so on.

- *Co-op Trucking.* There's more than one way to keep a truck on the move. To begin this game, attach a string to a little truck. Pull the truck toward you with the string, and then turn the truck around so that it faces your child. Hand him the string. Let him pull the truck toward him, help him flip it around (if necessary), and reach your hand out for the string. Let him put the string in your hand and repeat the whole process. You can play it on the bed or on the floor, sitting, kneeling, or with both people stretched out on their stomachs. My daughter loved this game at thirteen months.

- *Walking with a String.* This is a game that my daughter and I discovered a few weeks after she began walking. She was wearing one of those hooded sweatshirts that has a string threaded through the hood. She had pulled the string halfway out so that it was dangling by her knees. I pulled it the rest of the way out. When she sat down on a nearby log, I offered her one end of the string, which she held onto as I pulled her to a standing position. We then walked along the grass together, connected by the string. Now and then she tugged on the string to maintain her balance. At one point I sat down and she attempted to pull me up by the string.

• *Pot Hat Exchange.* At sixteen months Anouk was playing with those wonderful kitchen toys: pots and pans of various textures and sizes. I sat down on the kitchen floor and joined her. Before long I popped a pot onto my head. Intrigued by my dapper appearance, she wanted to try it on for size. Together we moved the "hat" to her head. Then she put it back on my head, and finally we began to exchange pot hats of all sorts.

Bowls and dampened facecloths work well too, as do all kinds of real hats. Before long Anouk and her little cousin were playing Pot Hat Exchange on their own. With your help, slightly older children can create their own hats out of newspapers, paper bags, or other materials, and then walk or skip around exchanging them.

• *Boxcar.* A large empty cardboard box or plastic laundry basket provides the means of locomotion for this game. Each child takes a turn sitting inside the box while another child or two (maybe with your help, too) provides the engine power by pushing on the back of the box. When we first played this game, Anouk and Alex also enjoyed putting a teddy bear in the boxcar and pushing him around with a two-kidpower engine. I even figured out a way to take a turn in the box myself. I simply ripped out one of the ends so that my feet could stick out, and then motioned my two little playmates to push me. Of course, I helped by extending my legs, digging my heels into the floor, and pulling myself and the box forward.

If you tie a string on the box, children will also enjoy pulling it around, either empty or bear-filled. Roaring sounds and changes in direction add some spice to the game. Slightly older kids (two and a half to five years old) can usually provide their own power for their friends, especially if they team up to push. They also enjoy painting their "cars" or putting numbers on them.

Old industrial mop buckets with casters on the bottom also make delightful boxcars, but they are not the easiest things to find. If no boxes or mop buckets are in sight, a blanket, a towel, or a small rug can be used as a substitute. They all slide well on a smooth wooden floor when other children push or pull. The kids can imagine they are whatever vehicles they might like them to be.

An interesting variation to Boxcar that some kids love involves slowly tipping the boxcar backward toward you and then gently setting it down again. That's sure to get a squeal or giggle.

• *Anouk's Water Ball Pass.* We discovered the beautiful little game of Water Ball Pass while playing in the calm shallow water alongside a lake. It's a great game for very young children to begin playing ball. Anouk stood knee-deep in water near the beach and I stood about 36 inches (91 cm) away. We pushed a plastic-covered ball, about the size of a basketball, back and forth in an effortless manner. The ball slowly slid across the surface of the water as she flicked it gently with her fingers. The game

Pot Hat Exchange

Ball Passing

enabled her to pass the ball accurately and to receive it successfully in return. For the first time she had a sense of control of the ball within a ball-sharing game.

Before long we discovered many different ways to slide the ball back and forth—for instance, standing in ankle-deep water and using the foot to propel the ball back and forth. To ensure success when you start the game, stand very close to your child, about 18 inches (46 cm) apart. You can also sit with your legs spread in about 3 to 4 inches (9 cm) of water and pass the ball back and forth along the surface. This can be done in pairs or in small groups sitting in a circle.

As children become more skilled, they can start to throw the ball to you, and often will spontaneously. You can return it by sliding it back along the water's surface for easy access and retrieval. A child can throw a ball long before she is able to catch a ball thrown through the air, and so your sliding of the ball on the return makes a "catch" a realistic goal for a young child. Other objects, such as plastic containers of various shapes and sizes, can also be slid along the surface of the water to the child's delight. You can use branches or sticks, too, to propel the container back and forth.

- *Ball Passing.* Little tots enjoy playing all kinds of passing games, not only in the water but also on land. Let them begin by passing a teddy bear or a large ball back and forth, around a circle, or under some legs (yours or a table's). Then they can begin to roll the ball back and forth by pushing it with their hands or feet. The next step is for the child to throw the ball in your direction. You retrieve it and hand it back for another throw. Another good option is to throw the ball onto the couch next to your child (where it will stop without a bounce) and then let her throw it back to you.

When my daughter and her cousin were twenty and twenty-two months old respectively, they started playing catch together. They rolled, pushed, handed, and lobbed a sponge ball back and forth, all on their own. The game did not continue for long periods of time, but the children were clearly capable of initiating and enjoying a game of catch.

- *Cup Roll.* Put a small rubber ball in a metal or plastic cup held by the child. Let him roll the ball out of the cup (in your direction, if possible), and then put the ball back in his cup. It doesn't sound like much but turns out to be good fun. After the child gets the feel of it, see if you can switch roles so that he retrieves the ball as you roll it. Passing a ball back and forth between two cups can be fun for a toddler and parent. Using two balls and three cups provides even more interesting options.

- *Pat-a-Cake.* Cooperative hand-clapping games go over very well with young children, especially when accompanied by a song or other music. As an introductory game, take your child's hands in yours and clap them together. Then you can put her hands on the outside of yours and let her help you clap your hands together. That should get a big smile, and it gives her a nice sense of control. A simple game of Pat-a-Cake can be played by first guiding her through the motions, then by getting her to hold her hands out with palms facing you, and finally by letting her participate in the clapping action. For the hand action, partners face one another and repeat the following sequence, clapping their own hands together before each step:

Clap your partner's right hand.
Clap your partner's left hand.
Clap both your partner's hands at the same time.

This song can accompany the clapping action:

Pat-a-cake, pat-a-cake, baker man,
Bake me a cake as fast as you can.
Pat it and prick it and mark it with *B*;
Put it in the oven for baby and me.

For older children, more complex hand actions can be incorporated, but for young children the simpler the actions the better. For example, playing Pat-a-Cake in water by simply patting the surface can be a good way to start. Don't worry if your song can't keep pace with the child's sense of rhythm.

- *The Smallest Caterpillar.* This is an especially good game for crawlers. Begin by crawling after your young child, making enough noise so that he knows you are right behind him. Touch the bottom of his feet from time to time, either with your hands or by gently biting his feet. That should get a healthy squeal. Then try placing your hands around his ankles so that you crawl in unison with him. (My daughter thought this was great stuff even after she had been walking for some time.) To reverse roles, crawl in front of him, look back now and then, and let him catch you. He may crawl up on your legs; then you can place his hands on your ankles and begin to crawl forward slowly on your hands and knees. You can also let him crawl up onto your back for a ride.

Shortly after I began playing this game with my daughter, she came up behind me, put her hands on my back, pushed me down and took hold of my ankles. She was ready to crawl.

- *Tandem Walking.* This is a game that can be played with both prewalkers and toddlers. With your child in front of you, facing forward, lift her so that her feet are on top of your feet. While maintaining contact with hands and feet, slowly walk forward or dance around to slow music.

- *Block Building.* Building blocks let you do a lot of giving and receiving. You can hand your child one block at a time with which to build, or you can hold out your hand to receive blocks from her for building a tower. In either case, both people contribute to the final construction. I found that I could help a block tower grow higher by letting my daughter build it in my hand. I handed her a block with one hand and held out my other hand palm up. She placed the block in my open hand, and I immediately gave her another, which she placed atop the first. I was able to help balance her creation in my hand, thereby allowing her tower to grow to greater heights than one perched on the floor.

- *Follow the Leader.* Between the ages of twenty months and two years, my daughter loved chasing (jogging) back and forth with me from the kitchen to the bathroom. We used to do it almost every night after her bath; one of us would start jogging and the other followed closely behind. When we reached the end of the kitchen, we both turned around so that the other was leading on the way back to the bathroom. She usually hummed or purred along the way, squealing now and then when we made contact in the kitchen or bathroom. She loved it.

Playing Follow the Leader with natural shifts back and forth in leadership between yourself and your child works beautifully for all kinds of things—making faces or funny sounds, running, turning, dancing, and so on. When you let the lead change spontaneously, who's leading and who's following doesn't matter.

- *Pulling Strings.* Find a thin piece of wood, an old ping-pong paddle, or a wooden ruler. Drill a hole through the center of it, and thread a piece of sturdy string 12 to 18 inches (30 to 46 cm) long through the hole. Attach a small, thick piece of wood such as a wooden building block to each end of the string; this will serve as a "handle" and will also "click" against the object threaded on the string. To start the game, hold the paddle upright. Let your child take hold of the handle on one end of the string, and guide him through a pulling action until your end clicks against the wooden paddle. Then pull your end until his block clicks against the paddle. You can string each other along, back and forth, back and forth, until he decides it's time to stop. A tight-fitting piece of string or yarn can make an interesting sound when pulled back and forth.

Consider playing Pulling Strings with your little one when he's between twenty-one and twenty-four months old. He will enjoy it and learn something about give-and-take at the same time.

- *Partner Pull-ups.* You can do a very simple version of this with one- and two-year-olds. Both of you start in a squatting position, facing each other and holding hands. On "up," you both stand up. On "down," you both squat back down together. We eventually turned this into a jumping game by jumping up at the signal instead of slowly pulling up.

• *Flying Hugs.* When a toddler first starts to walk, parents often kneel down on the floor facing each other while the child "walks" back and forth between them. The child usually ends up falling into one or the other's arms at the end of a few shaky steps, but it's a joyful time for everyone. Flying Hugs is an extension of this game that children can play with their parents once they have mastered partially controlled running (usually when they are between eighteen months and two years). Parents (or older children) spread out on opposite sides of the room and encourage the child to run toward their outstretched arms. The child runs and "flies" into a big warm hug with Mom before turning to run toward Dad for another flying hug. Once she gets flying she will squeal with delight.

• *Head Tilt.* In order to slow things down after jogging or before sleeping, we sometimes played head tilt. Sit facing your child. Catch his attention, and then slowly tilt your own head from side to side. Let him begin by following; then follow his lead. With older children, one partner can lead for four movements before the lead shifts automatically to the other partner for four movements.

• *Scotch Stick.* A moment before I began to write these words, Anouk came into my office to see what could be so important as to keep me stuck at my desk. She quickly scanned my desk and pointed to something that she found interesting, the scotch tape. I gave her a piece, and seconds later she gave me back half of it before waddling off to more interesting terrain. She had ripped the tape in half lengthwise, keeping one piece for herself and giving one to me.

That was her newest version of Scotch Stick. I began the game by taking a little piece of scotch tape and sticking it on the back of her hand. I let her pull it off and then held out the back of my hand. From that point on I let the game unfold, from her hand to my hand and back to hers again. Sticking and unsticking occurred in a variety of forms and sequences. Various body parts also came into play. We even made scotch tape jewelry for fingers, wrists, and toes by decorating little circles of the tape.

Sometimes simultaneous exchanges will surface naturally if you have more than one piece of tape; as you stick a piece on the child's hand she does the same to yours. With larger pieces of tape, older kids can be scotch-stuck together and then try to complete various maneuvers without becoming unstuck. Masking tape works just as well.

• *Candle Blow.* Why limit candles just to birthdays, when children between one and a half and two years old seem to be fascinated by them? With adult supervision, two or three children can try together to blow out a candle placed in front of them. The flame may simply flicker at first, but they will persist. Of course, if they succeed in blowing it out, you will have to light the candle again, and again, but they'll have lots of fun putting their lungs together to work for a common end.

- *Collective Coloring.*   For this activity you need one coloring book and a bunch of crayons. Join the children with everyone coloring the same picture at the same time. Encourage crayon exchanges and "good" comments. To promote more creative collective coloring, supply a large pad of blank paper and let the children make their own designs together.

- *Cooperative Musical Hoops.*   Children aged eighteen months to two years can support a regulation-size hula hoop by working together. In fact, the only way they can get the hoop off the ground is with the help of a friend. They can even get inside the hoop together and dance around to music.
    If the hoops are reduced in size, slightly older children can roll them back and forth or down the street. Start with a wheel from a child's wagon, then move up in size to a wheel from a baby carriage or a hoop from a small barrel.

- *Beach Ball Balance.*   On the cover of the first *Cooperative Sports & Games Book* there is a picture of two five-year-olds balancing a beach ball, forehead to forehead, without using their hands. This activity also works with children approaching two years of age—or for parent and child—especially with a squishy sponge ball. Remember, you have to get down low enough to be eye to eye with your son or daughter. Be prepared for giggles along with an occasional bite out of the ball.

- *Juggling Games.*   Simple juggling games can be fun for parents and absorb young children's interest. Inuit mothers juggle small stones or bones, while Papua New Guinea mothers juggle nuts and seeds to their babies' delight. I practiced one of their simplest juggling games called Singu in front of my six-month-old daughter. She became absorbed in the motion. When I sat on the floor to play beside her, she crawled onto my lap for a closer view. When she was ready for more active involvement herself, she could touch the seeds, bang them, and roll them around. Don't discourage your child from participating, even if her doing so disrupts the game a bit.

- *Dancing to Music.*   Most two-year-olds I know love to dance, and my daughter is no exception. She loves to spin herself around or be spun in the arms of others. When relatives come over she will often take them by the hand, one at a time, and lead them to the middle of the living room floor, until a whole circle of people are dancing hand in hand. She also enjoys being held in one of my arms and clapping her hand against my free hand in pat-a-cake fashion. Try letting your own child show you her latest steps next time the radio's on.

Beach Ball Balance

• *Bed Bouncing.*   Almost every kid likes to jump on beds. Here's a way you can do it safely together with a child that weighs up to about twenty pounds. He stands on the bed facing you while you stand on the floor facing him. You hold hands and you both jump up and down at the same time. After ten or fifteen jumps you fall onto the bed together. The most difficult part of this game is figuring out how to stop. At twenty-two months Anouk had endless energy for this game.

• *Sharing Time.*   How much time did you spend actively playing with your child today (running, rolling, tickling, exchanging interesting things, or nibbling on her belly button)? How much exclusive attention did you give her (reading, hugging, bathing)?

   Those of us who did not share enough time can try to be more fully devoted in the time that we do give. That means time free from interruptions. If I have an appointment to meet a student, client, or stranger in my office, I do not accept phone calls, watch television, read the newspaper, or listen to the news, since such inconsideration makes the person feel like a second-class citizen. Why, then, would I consider interrupting precious time with my daughter with similar distractions? Time lost with her is never returned, and spending time with her pays much greater dividends.

COOPERATIVE GAMES FOR THE TINIEST TOTS

games for children
three through seven

Kindergarten Cooperative

Every once in a while you run across a great teacher who really frees children to learn. Roberta Haley is such a person. She has been conducting a cooperative program with five-year-olds since the early 1970s. She is a master at nurturing cooperative values and is a delight to watch when she is introducing cooperative games.

The last time I visited Roberta's classroom was just before Valentine's Day. Naturally her cooperative games tied into the Valentine Day's theme (as is the case for Christmas, Easter, St. Patrick's Day, and so on).

She doesn't name the games or give lengthy instructions. She simply begins playing and the children follow her example. If she wants to get their attention, she sings,

"Children, children, listen to me" ("follow me," "find a friend," "swing your arms," "find a heart," and so on). She uses songs or music with virtually all cooperative games, and she plays most of them right in the kindergarten classroom. Her children absolutely love playing cooperative games, partly because of their nonthreatening structure and partly because of Roberta's creative and sensitive approach. Some of the games she so skillfully presented on my last visit are outlined below.

- *Half-a-Heart.* Cut a bunch of homemade cardboard or paper valentine hearts into halves. On one half of each heart write a number (for example, 3), and on the other half draw that number of small shapes (for example, ○ ○ ○). Distribute half a heart to each child and have them skip around the room to music. When the music stops each child tries to match up his half with the other. After everyone has connected, all the children trade their halves for a heart with a different number, skip around again, and connect with a new friend.

- *See How We're Jumping.* Roberta begins this game by joining both hands with one of her five-year-olds and starts to sing:

> See how we're jumping, jumping, jumping, [jump three times].
> See how we're jumping with our friends.
> You didn't know we could go so high [jump really high].
> You didn't know we could go so low [squat down and jump really low].

As soon as Roberta starts singing and doing the accompanying actions with her friend, everyone quickly finds a partner and joins the game in a natural and flowing way. They don't want to miss out on the fun. At the end of each verse the children are asked, "What should we do next?" They suggest skipping, walking, swinging, spinning, and so on. Each time, the new action is tied into the next verse of the song, so the children themselves get to make up the rules:

> See how we're spinning, spinning, spinning [link elbows and spin together].
> See how we're spinning with our friends.
> You didn't know we could go so high [spin on tiptoes].
> You didn't know we could go so low [spin in a squat position].

- *Heart Islands.* You'll need four large red cardboard hearts and some music. Place the hearts around the floor, start the music, and have the children skip around the room. When the music stops, each child tries to place a toe on one of the heart islands. Each time the music restarts, another heart is removed until, in Roberta's class, twenty-three children were trying to get their toe on the same heart.

Naturally, they had a little difficulty all touching the island at once. When Roberta asked, "What can we do about it?" a little boy suggested lying down with everyone's feet in the center. It worked! A little girl said, "Why don't we put our foot down wherever we think there is a heart?" Roberta, respecting the child's input and attempting to promote creativity replied, "OK, let's try it." The music played, the children skipped, and I wondered how this new game of Imaginary Hearts would unfold. The music stopped and the children huddled together, all placing a foot on a centrally located imaginary heart. One kid responded, "Hey, it's better that way!" It was better, probably because the size of the imaginary heart could be instantly adapted for all the children's feet to fit. Variations include playing with newspapers, mats, pillows, towels, hats, desks, and so on.

Halfway through the games session, Roberta took a break to allow one child to distribute some marshmallows he had brought in for everyone. He went around the circle distributing one to each wide-eyed child. When he sat down, Roberta said to him, "How about one for you?" He replied, "I don't even like them." But the other kids did, and he enjoyed the sharing.

Roberta's concentrated experience with hundreds upon hundreds of preschool children, as well as with her own children, has taught her that young children are extremely empathetic little beings. A sad story can bring tears to their eyes; another child in distress can bring forth pangs of concern; a lost mitten or kitten can bring a host of fellow searchers.

I asked Roberta to write down a few of her reflections on how she attempts to promote positive social development with her children. This was her response:

Seven years ago I looked forward to introducing cooperative games into my kindergarten program. Initially they had a time allotment unto themselves—twenty minutes twice weekly—enough, I thought, to produce cooperative children. Little did I know that this involvement was to become a change in attitude and teaching style.

The approach is a total one. Cooperation is an integral part of every aspect of the kindergarten, from helping each other find lost articles to playing games to beginning reading skills. Children learn the rudiments of sharing quickly when there is a shortage of materials. One bottle of glue at a table provides ample opportunity to practice this skill.

Many of our "academic" activities use the cooperative approach, and musical sharing games have become a way of life for my five-year-olds. Matching cutouts placed on the floor by number or shape, or even finding a partner by making similar sounds, creates a challenge for both intellectual and social development. Cooperation is a must in problem solving.

Discussing a new game

The method of making a group mural in art is well known; many work together to create a single product. This method also works well in other areas. For example, the children can all contribute to one large class book in a combined effort, rather than all having individual books. When learning the letter *B*, they can cut out one big paper *B* and then each can draw something on it that starts with that letter. A lot of cooperative and communicative skills are practiced in doing this task.

The spirit of cooperation is reflected in the quality of creative thinking used to solve a group dilemma. We wanted to set up a grocery store in our classroom. Together the children came up with excellent solutions as to the structure and operation of the store, and they were very capable of working together to achieve these ends.

The positive feeling that cooperation engenders about oneself is obvious in my class many times each day. Our tidy-up routine is expedient, the goal being to help one another clean up the entire group's mess in four or five minutes. Lost items, once announced, are found within seconds by several children spontaneously helping. Genuine concern for others is also prominent in my classroom. I watch bigger children help the smallest one in the class to get dressed. They sit close to Jamie, who is feeling sad, and there comes a suggestion that we sing him a happy song. When Cathy has a note to bring to her brother's teacher, her friend Michael goes with her because "It takes two to open the heavy door." Jermaine prints his name with all the letters there for the first time, and everyone cheers.

Co-op games bring rewards of their own. The children know how to work together in groups better than most adults I know. And I think that the games build self-esteem and a sense of belonging. They give children something to believe in—themselves.

Getting Little People Together

Roberta came up with some delightful games to group her kindergarten children in nonthreatening ways. Begin by making paper cutouts in the shape of circles, squares, rectangles, and triangles. (Later on the children can make their own.) Altogether you need two of each shape in four different colors (say, red, yellow, blue, and green) for a total of thirty-two shapes. Use fewer for a smaller class. Once the shapes are all made, place them on the floor and play some music, to which all the children skip around. When the music stops, each child picks up a shape and tries to get together with another child in one of the following ways:

1. Find a friend with the same shape.
2. Find a friend with the same color.
3. Find everyone who has the same shape.
4. Find everyone who has the same color.
5. Find a friend with the same shape that is also the same color (this is a little tougher).

For things to run smoothly, Roberta usually gives instructions for getting together at the beginning of the game, before the music starts.

Other possibilities for getting little people together include grouping by sounds or by a variety of simple puzzles. In the sound department, objects that make distinct sounds, such as cans or plastic jars partially filled with pebbles or dried peas, little bells, shakers, or tambourines, can be distributed. Each child plays her sound and tries to find a matching sound (or sounds) to form partnerships or small groups.

Musical Hoops

Playing barnyard is another way to group by sounds. After being given their animal noise to make, children close their eyes and group by sound.

For simple puzzle connections, we cut interesting pieces of paper into easily reconstructible pieces (usually two or three pieces). So far we have used Christmas cards, calendar pictures, magazine pictures, numbers, letters, and various shapes. The puzzle pieces are distributed at random, and each child tries to find his other half.

• *Puzzled Partners.* This musical partner-game—a reverse of the usual—was suggested by Margaret Mulac. Once partners have been formed, music is played and the children walk or skip *away* from their partners. As soon as the music stops, both partners rush toward each other, join hands, and squat down. The moment the music starts again, they are both up and away. Margaret felt, "The most fun of the game is when the intervals between getting up and coming back are made very short. Start the music and then stop it almost before the children have had a chance to get on their feet and move away. The children bounce up and down like rubber balls on the short stops, screaming their heads off."

• *Comment Ça Va?* This is a good "warmer upper." A record is played or the children sing a song as they skip and dance around the playing area. How they move is totally up to them—they can run, leap, crawl, or roll. Everytime the main verse of the song is sung, children exchange greetings by shaking hands, nodding heads, embracing, and so on . If you are looking for musical accompaniment, consider the song "Comment ça va?" ("How Are You?") by Edith Butler on an album entitled *Asteur qu'on est là (Now That We Are There),* or you can choose any other appropriate song and teach it to the class.

• *Circle Ball Pass.*   Little children begin by sitting in a circle close enough to be touching their friends on either side. They pass a ball around the circle by handing it to the person next to them. They can also stretch their legs out straight and use their hands to roll the ball around the circle on top of one another's thighs. Older groups can try this seated lap roll without using their hands, or they can extend their arms out straight and try to roll the ball around the circle on top of their arms—first slowly then as rapidly as possible.

• *Cooperative Chair Exchange.*   This game is an outgrowth of our original Cooperative Musical Chairs. Start with one chair for every three or four players (of course, the number is adaptable; two per chair is enough for younger children). The chairs are spread out around the room in some kind of circle, and everyone proceeds to find a chair to share. Once everyone is delicately perched on his shared chair, a series of exchanges are called out. "Everyone who has a dog move one chair"; "Everyone who has long hair move two chairs"; "Move the same number of chairs as there are children in your family." The calls for exchange are infinite, and the enjoyment can be enhanced by asking children on various chairs to make up their own exchange signal. This game can be a fun way to learn something about others. When playing with combined groups of children and grown-ups, some of the adults can get down on their hands and knees to serve as chairs.

• *Silly Bones.*   This is a fun game to play with four-, five-, or six-year-olds and it's super when each child is paired with an adult. Simple instructions are given to the players: Touch another person's elbows with your elbows, touch knees, touch ankles, touch ears, touch necks, touch belly buttons. The peewees usually touch the first part mentioned and let go of that connection to do the next touch, either body to body or hand to body. Slightly older children can maintain two or three connections at once. For example, they may touch toes, stay connected with the toes, and touch shoulders. They may then maintain the previous connections and touch another (for example, the sides of their heads), or they may be asked to let go of the first connection and maintain the second while adding the third. You can get into lots of interesting tangles in pairs or groups, and trying to move while connected can add a new dimension.

- *Toesie Roll with Control.* Partners lie stretched out on the floor feet to feet with soles touching. Once you decide in which direction you would like to roll, hook your foot on your rolling side over your partner's foot. The top of your toes on that foot will be hooked over the top of your partner's toes. Roll in one direction and then try reversing the direction of your roll, but first unhook your toes on one side and hook them on the other side.

- *More Sticky Popcorn* This is an extension of a game from the first *Cooperative Sports & Games Book,* in which children become kernels of popping corn. We usually start this game off by pretending that the floor is the hot part of a range. All the children crouch on the floor, and the stove is turned on. The "floor" becomes hotter and hotter, and the children begin to "pop" all over the place. They can pop as many times as they like. Once the children have popped into fluffy kernels, an imaginary syrup is poured all over them so that they become very sticky. When the children brush (or pop) against one another, they stick together. The stuck-together ones then pop around to find other people to stick to, until everyone is in one giant popping popcorn ball.
  We heard of a case in which one little boy remained immovably crouched on the floor. When asked why he wasn't popping, he replied that he was "burned to the bottom of the pan." In a situation like this, pour a little syrup over him and send over a few sticky helpers to pop (or scrape) him free.

- *Raindrops.* The children begin lined up behind one another; the line then joins up to make a circle, with each child gently resting her hands on the person in front of her. As the rain begins to come down "softly," the fingers begin to patter very gently on the shoulders of the person in front while the children tiptoe around in a circle. As the rain comes down "harder," the finger-pattering intensifies. If the children remain silent and listen carefully, they will hear the rhythm of the falling raindrops. Various actions can be added to the game—thunderclaps, for example—until the rain begins to subside and stops falling from the sky, at which point all fingers (and feet) rest.

- *Penny Bucket (Cover Up).* Jim Deacove tells me this one will keep young children amused for half an hour or so. A bucket is filled with about 8 inches (20 cm) of water, and a quarter is placed on the bottom of the bucket. Fifteen or twenty pennies are divided among the children. Each child takes a turn dropping one coin into the bucket, the object being to cover the larger coin on the bottom. The children continue dropping and retrieving pennies until they feel like stopping. Children who feel they are ready for more of a challenge can be informed that if they cover the quarter before they run out of pennies (no fishing any out!), they win the game. If not, the water (or bucket) wins, and they try again.

Blanket Options in Finland

- *Blanket Options.* A group of eight to ten young children can do all kinds of interesting things with a blanket. They can get under it and pretend they are a moving turtle, giraffe, buffalo, or whatever they decide. They can turn it into merry-go-round by having one child (or two) sit in the center while all others take hold of the edge of the blanket with one hand and walk around in the same direction (the center person is not lifted off the ground). It can become a slide (or a ride) by pulling someone around the room, a cradle by gently swinging a doll or little person back and forth, or a fort by draping it over a large box or several chairs. It can also be used for tossing balls and teddy bears or simply as a meeting place where children regroup after an activity. There is no limit to the creative options that become available when a group of children cooperate with a blanket.

- *Inner Tubes and Cardboard Boxes.* Large inner tubes from truck tires and cardboard boxes large and small, both of which are thrown out by the thousands, can be the basis of many exciting cooperative games. Children can roll inflated inner tubes back and forth or around the edge of a circle, like a big ball. In pairs or small groups, children can stand on them, float on them, jump on them, slide on them, throw things through them, toss them, or lie on them for a rest. They can link arms and bounce themselves around in a circle while staying on top of the tube in a sitting, kneeling, or standing position. Inner tubes also make good sleds for sliding down hills with friends. Older kids can even roll the tube on end like a hula hoop, with a willing friend perched inside.

  Cardboard boxes offer just as many possibilities. Children can transform them into boxcars, trucks, sleds, hats, caves, houses, hideaways, and animals of every sort. Let's say you want to play a game of Dragons, in which children link together to form a large dragon. One simple way of making the skin for your dragon is to use large cardboard boxes. The children can work together to cut out the bottom of the box for easy walking and to cut a hole in front and sides for viewing. They can decorate the sides and front of the dragon in any way they please. The kids can hardly wait to get under those boxes to get the dragons (or hippos) moving. Several big boxes can be linked together with string, rope, tape, or by holding hands to form giant dragons or elephant trains; or children can move around in pairs under one box to make a small two-headed dragon.

- *Three-Legged Ventures.* This traditional racing activity can be adapted to co-op games very easily—cooperation is at its heart! Partners stand side by side as their inside legs are tied together above the ankle with a thick soft rope, a winter scarf, a wide loose band from an inner tube, or some toweling material. Then the children run, hop, skip, or skate around in any direction, being careful not to run into anyone else. Make sure they know it's not a race but a friendly outing. If you want to increase the

Three-legged Stilts

challenge, try it on ice skates or small stilts, or restrict the use of the inside legs so that partners hop around using only their two outside legs. Another possibility is to play the game by hopping around a circle. As in the New Guinea game Ihihna Pohophna (page 135), the objective would be for all partners to get back to their original starting point on the circle without losing their balance (or without moving outside a certain area). Three-legged ventures can also be turned into four-legged ventures by connecting three people together.

Three- or four-legged hops can also be done in a large circle formation with everyone facing the center of the circle. The object is to get to the other side of the circle without hopping into other people. All the pairs can go at the same time, or pairs can count off by twos so that only half the children go at once.

Using this idea of a group moving across a circle, groups of two, three, or four kids can get inside a little people's big sack (see the first *Cooperative Sports & Games Book*) and try to make their way across a circle to the other side. How they decide to do it is up to their group. They may hop, crawl, or drag their sacked friends.

• *Can You Be Things Together?*   This game has as much room for variations as you have imagination. The common thread running through the activities is to create the response or act out the request together. Can you be a string of beads? A forest, a big canoe, a giant tent, good friends?

People of the mountain

• *Wagon Wheel Reshaped.* The first wagon wheel we created was formed by a group of seven children joining hands and moving their wheel in a circular motion around the walls of a gym or building. Since that time several new versions of the wheel have been developed.

A kindergarten teacher in western Canada adapted the wheel so that it could be done in a sitting position, rather than in the original standing position. The children sit on the floor in a circle with their legs straight out and their feet touching in the middle of the circle. The palms of their hands are placed on the floor beside their hips. To get the wheel moving, they all lift their behinds and move one step to the left (or right), keeping their feet in the center of the circle. This continues step by step until the wheel makes a full circle.

When the class first tried this, they periodically got bogged down with too many kids (spokes) jammed into one area. Their immediate response was "flat tire," which they very much enjoyed. At the end of one game a little boy said, "Next time let's not try to have a flat tire."

Since the idea of a sitting wheel was introduced to me, I have come up with two additional variations that are slightly more challenging and thus more appropriate for older groups. In one version, the group forms a seated circle with legs extended into the center. While maintaining this basic *L* position, each person rotates his body (like a seated log roll) to turn the wheel. The rotation is accomplished by looking over your left shoulder, putting both hands on the floor beside your left hip, lifting your behind off the floor so that you are in a front support (or push-up) position, and then continuing to rotate in the same direction until you lower your hips back into a seated position.

In another version the children lie down with their feet in the center of the circle. They get the wheel moving by all rolling in the same direction at the same time, like a log roll. You will get a few more "flat tires" on this one but no one seems to mind. It is actually quite a good co-ed game for older groups.

Our original standing version of Wagon Wheel was adapted very successfully for use with blind children by Dennis Peck in South Australia. In addition to having the backs of two or three children (the bottom of the wheel) touching the wall momentarily as the wheel spun along the wall, another point of contact was added to help guide the wheel. The instructor gently pushed a large cage ball against the backs of the children who momentarily formed the top of the wheel (the part of the wheel opposite the wall). From all reports this worked great and seemed a natural for these kids.

Another variation of Wagon Wheel can be played by forming the wheel around a parachute or a circular blanket. The children hold onto the material and spin the wheel along an uncluttered wall, the outside of a building, or a flat-surfaced fence or around a large tree.

• *Devine.* This game was introduced to me by a divine friend of mine; it's a good party game for all ages. Actually, "devine" means "guess" in French. The game goes like this: The players sit in a circle, and a sheet is spread out in the center of the circle so that it covers everyone's hands and lower arms. A bizarre object, such as a piece of liver, a peeled grape, or several toothpicks stuck in a piece of cheese, is passed around the circle under the sheet. Each player tries to guess what it is. If one guesses correctly he has the privilege of giving someone else a present or choosing the next exciting thing to be passed around the circle. With young children it is often best to pass the object all the way around the circle so that everyone can touch it before anyone begins to guess out loud. If there is any concern about guessing wrong, the children can all make a silent guess and then all be shown the object.

• *Tangerine.* This is a guessing game that ends by sharing a healthy treat. Kindergarten children can be asked, "How many tangerines do we need in order to give everyone one section (or two)?" Each child "thinks" her own guess, and when the paring and sharing of the tangerines begins, she sees for herself how accurate she was. Tangerines are great for young children to share because they peel and divide so easily. A two- or three-year-old can separate them into sections and even help peel. You can use only a few tangerines, and make sure they're shared around (if the sections don't divide evenly among the total number in the group, ask for ways to make each portion even for everybody), or you can have one tangerine per child, but ask them to split and pass the sections around all the same.

- *Collective Jacks.* Jacks is a game played with a small rubber ball and a series of metal counters (jacks), each of which has three tiny aluminum rods that intersect at the center. They have a starlike appearance and can be bought in almost any department store or toy shop in North America.

The original game of Jackstones consisted of throwing a stone up in the air and doing various maneuvers with other stones (such as picking up a certain number or moving them to a certain spot) before the tossed stone was caught. When using a ball in place of the tossing stone, it is usually allowed one bounce before catching.

Collective Jacks allows several people to play the game at the same time. The ball is tossed and several players try to accomplish a common goal before the ball is caught—for instance, picking up a certain number of stones among them or tossing a stone to a partner. The players can decide among themselves before they throw the ball what they will try to accomplish while the ball is still in the air. With the collective version, it is often necessary to add additional jacks or stones for maneuvering.

An interesting variation of Collective Jacks involves spinning the jacks without throwing anything in the air. The last time I played was on my living room floor with a six-year-old girl and a seven-year-old boy. We had a total of ten or twelve jacks. Each of us picked up a few and began to spin them (they spin very well on a hard surface). Our collective goal was to get as many spinning as possible all at the same time. If any jack stopped spinning, someone would quickly start it spinning again. This is an excellent cooperative game for mixed age groups, playable with anything that spins, from jacks to spinning tops to metal plates spun on edge.

- *Bandaids and Belly Buttons.* You don't always need to be playing a game to communicate feelings of sharing and concern. Lee Allsbrook is one of those delightful schoolteachers who is loved by his children. Among his special secrets are bandaids for comforting his pupils' pains. He uses them for all kinds of things, even stomachaches. "Let me have a look at that stomach. . . . OK, we'll fix it up." Out comes the bandaid, and it is plastered across the belly button. The pain subsides almost immediately; self-healing has taken over. The child has been acknowledged, the adult has been responsive.

Susan Buck has tried using bandaids to heal little people's hurt feelings. Let's say the group is forced to leave an area before one child has had a turn. He is feeling bad. "Where does it hurt?" she asks. "Right here," he says, pointing to his forehead. The bandaid is gently placed on the exact spot. It helps! The only problem is reassuring worried parents who wonder what great injury lies beneath the cherished bandaid. Susan assures me that bandaids are also very exciting playthings for three-year-olds. Take out a box and see.

Making a three-people three

• *Little Beavers.* In Canada the youngest group in the scouting organization is called "Beavers." They are a group of five- to seven-year-olds who earn their name for being such eager beavers. Their motto, "Sharing, Sharing, Sharing," fits in beautifully with the concept of cooperative games. They have adapted our original game of Numbers, Shapes, and Letters Together from the first *Cooperative Sports & Games Book* to help Little Beavers learn to spell their motto. First each Beaver is asked to find two or three friends. In these groups of three or four, they are asked to make the letters of "sharing" with their bodies. Each group works together to make an *S*; then after a suitable time for the leaders to view the *S* and praise their efforts, they make an *H*, and so on. At the end of the game they all jump up and shout "S-H-A-R-I-N-G, sharing!" In one group all the children in attendance joined hands and made the letters as a group. Twenty-five people linked together to make a giant *S*, then an *H*, *A*, *R*, and so on. When they got to the letter *I*, six boys spontaneously broke away from the group and ran to the top of the line. What were they up to? They were making the dot on the top of the *I*, "of course."

• *Chopsticks and Doughnuts.* Children can play this game either sitting or standing in a circle. Each child has a chopstick or other small stick. Every other child is given a doughnut or similarly shaped object with a hole in the middle (a bagel, a roll of tape, a plastic ring). The doughnuts are passed from person to person via the chopstick, which can be held either in the hand or mouth. Once every doughnut gets back to its original position, each player with a doughnut (if that's what you're using) shares it with the person on his left.. If you have no chopsticks, then toothbrushes, spoons, unsharpened pencils, or even an extended index finger will do fine as passers.

Another alternative is to pass some Lifesavers around the circle using only a lollipop stick, a matchstick, or a thin straw. Younger children can hold the stick in their hands; older kids or young adults can hold it in their mouths.

- *Rubber Band Toss.* This game can be played by two or more children. Each child begins with a wristful of rubber bands. One child tosses or shoots a rubber band onto the ground, and the children then take turns throwing one rubber band at a time, trying to make it hit any other rubber band on the ground. If a child is successful, he immediately picks up all the rubber bands on the ground and redistributes them among all the players. They then begin tossing again, with the winner each time being given the privilege of redistributing the rubber bands for the next game. The play goes on until the children tire and take their rubber bands home for use on another occasion. This game can also be played with marbles, stones, sticks, paper clips, pennies, or unopened bandaids, but it works best with rubber bands.

- *Paper Pat-a-Cake.* To add an interesting variation and challenge to Pat-a-Cake, two players can attempt to support a sheet of paper between their two hands as they go through the clapping actions. Each person extends one hand and the sheet of paper is slipped between them; they then try to separate their hands and connect them again without dropping the sheet of paper. If successful, they can switch hands or go through a variety of other Pat-a-Cake hand sequences.

- *Log Roll Revisited.* In our original game of Log Roll, about six children, acting as logs, lie side by side on their stomachs while a rider lies at right angles across their backs. All the logs begin rolling in the same direction, carrying the rider all the way across the top of the logs. As soon as the rider rolls off the last log, she becomes a log herself, and the first log becomes the new rider.

When adults are playing this game with young children, it is best if the adults do all the log rolling and the children do the riding. The children can form a line and go one after the other. In order to avoid log jams the adults must roll slowly and keep a little space—about 12 inches (30 cm) between them and the next log. Another possibility for groups of kids and adults is to have the adults remain stationary on the ground and let the kids roll over the adults. To do this the adults lie side by side as above, but without any space between them. The children lie on top of the adults in the same direction—not crosswise. The children then roll themselves like logs across

Bring down the mountain

the adults' backs. A simpler Log Roll can be done by having two children stretch out head to head on the ground, join hands, and roll along on their own.

• *Creative Dance.* Certain forms of creative dance—folk dance, square dance, along with contact dance—have much in common with cooperative games in that they promote cooperation, choice, and total involvement. You can incorporate collective— and highly creative—challenges into the free and exciting medium of dance. For example, ask a group of four to six children to create a dance in which, together, they illustrate the concepts of high, medium, and low. Both the creation and the execution of the dance are cooperative. Can you think of some other concepts that can be transformed into motion through dance?

• *Circle Lap Tap—Singsong.* This is a nice way to slow things down in order to bring an entire group together before ending a session. To play the game, the participants first form a sitting circle. It helps if people cross their legs and sit close enough so that their knees touch the knees of the players on either side. Players share in the singing of a simple song (such as "Row, Row, Row your Boat"), adding simple hand actions to the song. Below is an example of one song with accompanying actions.

GAMES FOR CHILDREN THREE THROUGH SEVEN

A dot above the words indicates the beat on which each action takes place—twice for each phrase:

WORDS	ACTION
1.–Row, row	Tap your own thighs twice.
2.–Row your boat	Tap your left thigh with your right hand and the right thigh of the neighbor on your left with your left hand.
3.–Gently down	Tap your own thighs twice.
4.–The stream-mm	Tap your own right thigh with your left hand and the left thigh of the neighbor on your right with your right hand.
5.–Merrily, merrily	Tap your own thighs.
6.–Merrily, merrily	Cross your hands and slap the nearest thigh of each of your neighbors.
7.–Life is but	Tap your own thighs.
8.–A dream-mm	Cross your hands and tap the nearest thigh of each of your neighbors.

The entire song can be repeated a few times with the same hand actions or with a variety of different ones. For example, players can clap their own hands twice and then cross their hands to clap one hand of each of their neighbors twice, or tap different body parts (shoulders, elbows, knees, and so on). Hand actions can be very simple or quite intricate, and almost any song with an appropriate rhythm can be sung. Ask the children for suggestions for songs and accompanying actions.

To add an interesting and not so simple twist, try the following. To the beat of the music, grasp your own nose with your left hand and your left ear with your right hand. Then switch, grasping your nose with your right hand and your right ear with your left hand. Try it right now. How did you do?

When presenting this or other new actions to a group, have them try it a few times without music; then add the song. If they're successful they're ready for step two, holding their own nose and their neighbor's ear.

• *Three-Part People.* This is a fun drawing activity that will hold the interest of children aged five to nine for some time. Take a piece of paper and fold it in three. On the top third of the paper (the first fold), one child draws a head; on the middle third (second fold), another child draws a body; and on the bottom third of the paper (third fold), a third child draws some legs and feet. Fold and pass the paper so that

Playground cooperation

no one can see the earlier work. Once the third person has added her touch, the paper is unfolded and a complete (often funny) person emerges. The trio can sign their creation and pin it up on the wall. They will definitely want to do another, once the first is viewed. Consider also three-part animals and friendly monsters, as well as three-part stories for older children.

There is one little trick that helps the connection flow smoothly. After drawing the head, the first artist should flip the paper over and extend the neck lines about a quarter of an inch onto the next fold. The second artist then picks up the drawing from this point and extends the body lines over onto the third fold, for the last artist to add legs and feet.

After the children have completed their creations, ask them to meet at some central point to share their three-part people (or animals). Each group of three artists literally stands behind its creation so that others can have a look. It's fun to try to guess which of the three people drew each section.

To add a special effect to the game, have each group of three divide their sheet of paper into three pieces (by tearing or cutting the paper along the folds) so that each child can hold onto his own section. The children then mingle, looking for new connections either in silence or by calling out what they need (for example, "head," "body," "feet"). New connections can be done several times in succession. The kids (as well as adults) will enjoy it.

games for children
eight through twelve

There is nothing sacred about the age categories suggested for the games in this book. The games in this chapter are generally well received by children aged eight to twelve; however, many of the games are also enjoyable for younger children and teen-age and adult groups.

Getting Bigger Little People Together

There are a variety of successful and nonthreatening ways of getting children this age into partners or groups. You can connect them with visual cues (for example, color of eyes, hair, or shoes or type of clothing). "Find a partner whose eyes are the same color as yours" (or "a different color from yours"). "All people wearing jeans by the tree; everyone else by the post."

Connecting according to personal preference is another possibility. You can ask kids to find a partner who likes the same kinds of food (or cars, sports, TV programs, movies, friends, desserts, or weather). Once connected, partners can find out two interesting or fun things about each other on the way to the play area or while sitting where they are. This information exchange can be simply a way to get to know each other better, or you can then have partners introduce their new friends to the group.

To divide the group into approximately equal sides, consider letting the children choose between, for example, apples and oranges, pizza and hot dogs, or *Star Trek* and *Star Wars*. You might say "All the apples on my right and all the oranges on my left," and let *them* figure it out! People choose which team they would like to be on and go to stand on that side. This does not always produce exactly equal sides, but most of our games do not require that sides be equal. If perhaps the oranges have a larger number, you could ask all those oranges who have no seeds to join the apples. There are usually a few willing souls who will change sides, particularly if you point out that a few more apples are needed to fill the basket.

For a more action-oriented connection, children can be asked to skip or run around the play space with either one hand in the air, both hands in the air, or both hands at their sides. They then connect with someone else holding her hands the same way. Once children connect they can engage in partner activities, mutual interviews, or group games.

An additional option is to divide according to the alphabet. The first group could be those whose first names start with *A* to *F*, the second group would be *G* to *K*, and so on. If one section is too small, people whose family names start with those letters could join the smaller group. We have also done the same thing with birthdays, grouping several months together.

If you and the children with whom you play begin to think about getting together, you will discover lots of gentle ways to connect. The methods mentioned above offer variety and let the players share information about themselves. The important point is that any way of getting children together should take the focus off choices based on performance standards and place it on criteria that are nonjudgmental and worry free. Once children have learned to be considerate of other players' feelings, they can find partners on their own without anyone fearing rejection.

Warming Up

The most important and well-known word in the child's entire vocabulary is probably her own name. When someone remembers your name it makes you feel good, and when you remember someone else's name it makes him feel better about you. There are games that can make learning about people easier and more fun. Some of these games involve the use of names; others involve finding or interviewing unknown partners; and still others involve completing simple tasks together.

Some good activities for warming up people's emotions and responsiveness to one another are presented in the following section.

• *Beach Ball Name Game.* I often use this game as an introductory activity at workshops and playdays or when classes first come together. A group of six to ten people form a circle and pass a beach ball or similar size sponge ball back and forth at random. Each time a person passes the ball she calls out her own name. This continues for a few minutes, until everyone has made some connection between names and faces. Then the challenge begins. Now each time a person passes the ball she must call out the name of the person to whom she is passing. If she forgets, she simply asks, "What's your name?" Start with one ball, then add another and another, and perhaps even another. Additional balls increase the action, the fun, and the good-natured name calling. An imaginary ball also works well; it's easier to catch and doesn't hurt if it lands too hard. Players can change its shape from throw to throw: beach ball, medicine ball, grape, pumpkin, cat (see Imaginary Ball Toss, below).

The only time I have run into problems with Beach Ball Name Game is when people are wearing name tags or when everyone already knows everybody else. In the first instance, people can remove their name tags or widen the circle so that they cannot read the names. In the second case, players can give themselves new exotic names or choose sounds, favorite things, or gestures to represent themselves. These steps increase the challenge of the game and counter any boredom that might otherwise arise. Another way to keep people's interest high is to have lots of balls flying at once.

You can follow up Beach Ball Name Game with other games involving the use of names (for example, a name-calling version of Hide-and-Seek or All Touch). The rule of All Touch can be added to almost any game and ensures that all players on a team receive a pass before one takes a shot at the net. In the "naming friends" version of All Touch, a player must call out the correct name of the person to whom she is passing before she passes the ball. If someone forgets a name, teammates help her remember.

For a variation that results in additional physical movement, place one person in the center of the circle. She passes the ball to someone in the outer circle and calls his name. She then runs to his spot while he runs to the center of the circle. He then passes to someone else, calling out her name and then switching positions. To increase the action and fun, add more balls and another person(s) in the middle. Passes in the air or bounce passes are fine.

• *Imaginary Ball Toss.* This is a game similar to our Beach Ball Name Game but played in a circle with an imaginary ball. The first person describes the kind of ball she is holding, calls out someone's name, and throws the ball to him. If she does not know his name, she asks. The original imaginary ball goes all the way around the circle so that everyone's name has been called and everyone has caught the ball once. On the subsequent rounds, after calling out the receiver's name, each thrower is free to change the imaginary object or keep it the same. For example: "Jim, it's a basketball"; "Marty, now it's a beanbag"; "Jody, it's a watermelon"; "Carol Ann, it's a live chicken"; "Bruce, it's still a live chicken."

When playing with young children or with people who do not know one another's names, the game works best in small groups (four to five people). With larger numbers the children can become confused trying to remember the names of the people and the changing object.

In addition, with larger numbers the game can become too slow (there's too much waiting around) unless more than one imaginary object is in play.

Games with imaginary equipment can work very well in a variety of activities. We've used this approach with our Inuit Skipping, Three-Way Tug of Peace, some parachute activities, and even softball, playing with imaginary bats and balls. Whenever you don't have supplies, try using imaginary equipment. Children's imaginations are often more colorful than reality.

• *Beach Ball Boogie.* This is an outgrowth of our earlier game of Beach Ball Balance. Everyone finds someone with whom to dance. About three-quarters of the people are connected to their partners by beach balls or sponge balls, which can link any part of the body: stomach to stomach, side to side, head to head, behind to behind, forehead to chest, and so on. When the music begins, all the partners who are connected by beach balls shuffle around to the beat and then pass their balls—without using their hands—to the nearest partners without balls whenever they can. Those connected only by the sound of the music dance to the beat while waiting to receive a ball. Beach Ball Boogie usually lasts the length of one (or perhaps two) upbeat songs.

This game can also be used as an introduction game wherein you find out a few interesting things about your partner as you boogie around and then introduce her as you pass the ball. Mutual introductions, perhaps with new information, can take place with each exchange of balls. If one person feels like changing partners, he simply communicates his intentions, and on the next exchange, one person goes along with the ball. That's more challenging than you think! It's also possible for two sets of partners to exchange balls or to boogie in fours with two balls. To keep things moving you have to have enough balls for continuous exchanges but not so many that there is no one around to pass to. Start with a ratio of about five pairs with balls to one pair without and adapt as you see fit.

- *Beach Ball Boogie Train.* For some added challenge and fun, keep the music going, give everyone a beach ball, and ask them to form a train. People's spirit and the beach balls are the only things that link the cars together. Once the children are connected, their arms can go out to the side so that only the gentle pressure of one person's stomach on another's back holds the ball in place. Start trains of two, with the front person holding his ball in his hands and the back person pressing her ball on the back of the front person. While moving to the beat of the music, the small units gradually link up until there is one long train, which they can then connect (with some skill) into a large circle train. This can be a good way to get a large group into a circle formation.

- *Touch Blue.* The game begins with six to eight children standing in a circle. A leader calls out instructions: First, all players must use their right hand to touch something that is blue on *someone else*, and *hold on*. It could be a bit of blue trim on a shoe or blue jeans or a blue shirt. Next, the left hand has to touch something yellow and hold on. Have the left foot touch something black and the right foot something brown. The head can touch something red, and if the group hasn't fallen into a crumpled mass, the shoulder can touch something green.

  The colors should vary from season to season. Playing the game in summer would probably call for more whites and yellows, but opening with "touch blue" is usually safe for all seasons in our blue-jeaned society. The final color chosen should be a color that is very scarce in the group, so that people have to stretch. The participants become tangled and twisted around one another and sometimes great contortions are required, but laughter always accompanies this game.

- *Circle of Friends Revisited.* This game, in which you literally fall into the hands of your friends, appeared in my previous games book, but we have since discovered a more joyful way of playing. About ten people face inward in a tight circle, shoulder to shoulder. One person in the middle stiffens her body and falls back into the gentle grasp of her friends, who use their hands to catch her. The middle person should keep her feet "glued" to the floor (no stepping) and her arms at her sides. The added enjoyment for the middle person comes from closing her eyes and being gently moved around the circle *in very slow motion*, the slower the better. It is a really peaceful and uplifting sensation. Wherever possible, at least two supporters should be in contact with the middle person.

  A more difficult version of the game grew out of one of my workshops. This variation is probably best attempted with older children, teen-agers, or adults. I was in the middle, and the teachers who formed the circle around me decided to try passing me while lying on their backs. They all lay down with their feet toward the center of the circle, keeping their knees bent up with feet on the floor. While they stretched their arms forward, I was slowly lowered, back first, to the outstretched hands of one supporter. He then passed me to the next person, and away I went around the circle. I ended up lying in the lap of a young woman, amid healthy laughter. It was a great way to fall, and happily the drop wasn't very far.

• *Reversing the Gauntlet.*   Do you remember the old game Running the Gauntlet? As originally conceived it was a terrible game, consisting of a double file of men facing one another, who beat or struck the helpless individual who was made to run between them. I remember "playing" it as a kid; sometimes people crawled through your legs as you paddled them on the behind.

In our version of this game, the new objective is to make the person running the gauntlet feel good. Two lines are formed and one person walks or skips between them. She stops at will and looks someone in the eye. That person must say or do something to make her feel good: Say "I like you," "You look beautiful," "What I like about you is . . . ," "You did . . . well," or simply give her a warm smile and a gentle hug. She can stop anywhere or anytime she wants for an uplifting remark. By the time she gets out of the gauntlet, she should be feeling even better than when she went in.

• *Hugger.*   This self-paced game, an outgrowth of Hug Tag, offers plenty of action for those who want it and ample opportunities to hug and rest for those who need it. About one out of every six players is given a glove, a piece of material, or a hat and is designated a "huggit." Huggits chase all the other players (the "huggers") and try to tag them before they reach the safety of their fellow huggers. The only time a player is safe from being tagged is when he is hugging another player or group of players. If caught not hugging he takes the glove, becomes a huggit, and chases the others.

Begin the game by selecting the huggits and asking all the huggers to link together in groups of two or three and spread out around the playing area. Once the hugging groups are well spread out and the huggits are ready, give a signal to switch groups. At that moment all the huggers must switch partners by finding someone else to hug. Any number in a hugging group is safe. If one person is stranded, a yell of "Hugger!" should bring a friend flying to the rescue. If huggers are caught in transit they miss out on the hugging and become huggits, but usually not for long; another switch is just around the corner. Calling out "Switch groups!" is a good idea to get the game rolling, but once players have the feel of the game they can switch at will. They run when they feel like running and hug when they feel like hugging. As the game unfolds be prepared to give out more gloves or to take a few away so that the game maintains a balance.

Hugger

It is interesting to note that kids and adults who normally reject hugging games will get totally absorbed in this one. I think this happens largely because the action and focus is not on the hugging itself. The hugging is a part of a bigger game and is the only acceptable means of being safe. An alternative to Hugger that will also get your heart pumping is Hooker, in which the players hook elbows instead of hugging to be safe.

• *Hug and Hum.* A beautiful variation of Hugger, good for any age group, was suggested to me during a cooperative-games workshop in Atlanta, Georgia. You are allowed to hug only for as long as you can continue to hum on one breath. Once you run out of breath, you must switch and find another person or group of people with whom to hug and hum. Some great harmony can be developed while in the safe embrace of your friends.

Partner Activities

- *Taketak Tie.* The idea for this game came from a combination of several aboriginal games. It can be played with two or more people. Players each spin the same readily available object—a top, a football, a plate, a coin, a bottle, or a hard-boiled egg, for example. They begin spinning at the same moment; the objective is simply to have both objects stop at the same time. Players can try as many times as they like by adjusting their spins so that they match. To play in groups, select large objects that require the help of all team members to spin.

- *Rump Bump.* Partners stand back to back, bend down, and place their hands on the floor in front of them (with or without bending their knees). They then place a balloon (or a ball) between their behinds and try to move around without dropping it. As they move around they can look through their legs to admire their partners. To end the game with a bang, the partners can press their behinds together until the balloon pops.

- *Partner Pull-ups.* For the normal version, partners sit on the ground facing each other with knees bent and toes touching, keeping the soles of their feet flat on the ground. They reach forward, grasp hands, and pull each other up to a stand before lowering themselves back to a sitting position.

  The easiest way to get up is to begin with both legs and arms bent. For added challenge, try Partner Pull-ups with straight arms/bent legs, straight legs/bent arms, or straight legs/straight arms, or try pulling each other up by hooking only index fingers rather than grasping each other's hands. If that works, try hooking index fingers on one hand only. A broomstick version is also a possibility. Partners sit facing each other with legs straight and the soles of their feet touching. They reach forward, keeping their knees straight, and grasp a broomstick lying across their legs. By pulling together both come up as high as possible and then try to return to a sitting position. Or they may pull each other up by grasping *opposite ends* of a small stick or by both pulling on a ball placed between them.

- *Partner Stand-up.* Two partners sit, one directly behind the other, both facing in the same direction, with legs straddled and knees bent. The front partner helps the one behind to a stand by placing her hands above her head with elbows bent and the palms of her hands tilted backward. If the back partner grasps her hands he will probably be able to get up as a result of her support (she stays on the ground). Partners should try going up and then down slowly a couple of times in a row before switching positions. This can be a good abdominal exercise for the person standing up

Jiggle and Swiggle

and a good upper-arm exercise for the person who remains seated. Partners can think of other possible ways of coming to a stand. Both could try coming to a stand at the same time (from this same starting position), but doing so is a tough challenge.

• *Jiggle and Swiggle.* A stick about 24 inches (60 cm) long and 1 inch (2½ cm) thick is held parallel to the ground, supported between the waists of two partners. A string about 24 inches (60 cm) long hangs down from the center of the stick, with a small rubber ball at the loose end. Adjust the length of the string so that the ball hangs free a few inches above the ground. The two players work in unison to wind the string (and ball) around the stick and then to unwind it. For older children and adults, this is done without placing their hands on the stick.

In order to keep the stick tight against each partner's waist, two cords, each 54 inches (135 cm) long, are attached to each end of the stick. They are then tied around each partner's waist to serve as makeshift belts. This belt keeps the end of the stick tight against the stomach, so that the players are then free to place their hands on their own heads as they swiggle and jiggle. Advanced partners can try to hold the stick between them without using a belt.

When Sally Olsen tried this game with her youngest son Jon, she found that the unwinding went best when he jumped up and down in quick little jumps while she continued to swiggle in a circular motion.

For young children, the game can be modified to let each partner hold the end of a broomstick in his hands and try to work with the other to wind and unwind the ball. It is also possible to tie a jump rope around two people's waists and swiggle a ball around the center of the rope, but doing that presents a greater challenge than using the stick.

If you are wondering how to get the ball onto the end of the string, here's what Margaret Mulac suggests. Find a small ball that is either spongelike or made of thin rubber with a hollow center. Push a crochet hook through the ball until the hook is visible on the other side. Hook a piece of string onto the crochet hook and then withdraw it, pulling the string through the ball. Tie a button onto the end of the string to prevent the string from coming out through the ball.

• *Rowboat Walk.*   Two partners sit facing each other with knees bent up and the bottoms of their feet on the floor. Each one slips the front of her feet under the other's thighs so that her toes are touching the cheeks of his behind—not all the way under, though, or the toes will likely get squished. Then they join hands and inch forward in unison by moving one cheek forward followed by the other. As one partner moves forward, the other moves backwards. Later reverse directions. For an interesting challenge upon which to end, try to come up to a standing position together from your seated row-boat position.

• *Shaping Twin Statues.*   This is a quiet game which allows for touching and mental imagery. Three people are needed to play the game; one is the statue shaper, another is a statue and a third is the statue's twin. The statue shaper closes her eyes (or is blindfolded) while the statue strikes a pose. She feels the statue and then attempts to shape the twin into the same image keeping her eyes closed. She can go back and forth between the statue and his twin until she is satisfied with her new sculpture. She then opens her eyes. The children can take turns being statues, shapers, and twins, and many groups of three can shape their statues at the same time. Help the children find the similarities between the twin statues and remind them that twins are never exactly the same; each has her unique qualities.

• *Hug and Roll.*   After reading about Cooperative Musical Hugs in the first *Cooperative Sports & Games Book*, Shiro Tanaka, an accomplished Japanese gymnastics teacher, created a new co-ed gymnastic activity called Hug and Roll. People leap around the room to the music of the delightful beat Shiro sings out. When he bellows, "Hug and roll!" everyone grabs a partner and hugs him, and then they do some kind of roll together while still maintaining contact. Shiro tells me his co-ed classes "love it," especially at the university level. Children enjoy it just as much.

With people who are not gymnasts, partners might first work their way through some slow-motion rolls together before getting into the full swing of the game. You might even consider having partners leap around the room together discussing how they intend to roll before the "hug and roll" signal is given. Those who like lots of company can try rolling in threes or fours. Once people have figured out ways of rolling, the activity can be fun for a variety of age groups. During one demonstration, a player told me that she didn't roll on the first date, but other than that the game has always been a success.

• *Put Your Trust in My Hand.*   In the first version of this game, the children move around the area in pairs, hand in hand and with their eyes open. They begin by walking very slowly and then go faster and faster until they are running; the objective is to avoid bumping into anyone. In more responsible and trustworthy groups, one partner then shuts her eyes, and they repeat the sequence, still trying not to bump any other pair. Only hand communication—no talking—is allowed for guidance. The signals to be used are worked out between the partners themselves. The kids say it's "fun, but scary running." The eyes-shut version is particularly appropriate when young children are paired with older children or adults.

• *Car and Driver.*   This is a game in which trust between partners can power a human vehicle. Players first form pairs; one partner (the driver) stands directly behind the other (the car) with his hands placed on his partner's shoulders. After trying with eyes open, the "cars" close their eyes and the drivers direct or vice versa, stopping, turning, and starting the cars with only their hands through touch signals. Cars can begin slowly (for example, walking with arms out in front of them), building up to the point where they can maneuver through obstacles and crisscross one another's paths. For more cooperation consider making buses, which are longer than cars and thus require more people. The signals could be passed from the last person to the first for changes in action or direction. Eyes can be open or closed.

• *Co-op Golf.*   This is a game I adapted from an idea presented to me by Jack Coberly. Pairs or small groups of players work together to draw a nine-hole golf course on a large piece of paper, indicating greens and holes. Then, one at a time, each "golfer" closes his eyes and tries to draw a line from one hole to the next. Partners help by directing the route of the golfer's pencil (ball). Each player can use a different-colored pencil to keep track of his ball. Younger children can open their eyes after each hole to line up for the next; older kids can try to go through the whole course. For variety, a player can close his eyes and try the course alone, and then try again with the help of his friends. Which works better?

• *Paper Airplanes.*   About halfway through the school year, I walked into one of my classes, asked the students to take out a sheet of paper, and had them write down their suggestions for improving the class—for example, what they liked best, what they liked least, how to make the remaining classes better. After they had finished, I asked them to make a paper airplane out of the sheet of paper and "air mail" it to the front of the room. First there were some uncertain looks, followed by careful folding of paper; then the planes started flying. This introduced a whole new playful atmosphere into a sterile classroom setting. The students subsequently returned to discussion topics much more ready to learn.

People appreciate the opportunity to provide input into their activities, and children really enjoy making and flying paper airplanes, especially in classrooms. One fun way to do it is to let kids pair up and "fly" their airplanes (and messages, when appropriate) toward each other. Each retrieves the other's airplane and fires it back again.

• *Aura Encore.*   Since first learning Aura we have made a few refinements. Partners stand facing each other and stretch their right arms out in front until the palms are touching. Both partners then close their eyes, trying to feel the energy between the hands. They drop their hands, take two giant steps backward, and turn in place three times. Then, keeping their eyes closed, they try to reconnect the palms of their right hands. When trying to reconnect, they should keep the outstretched arm slightly bent so that it will "give" in case of collision.

Aura can also be played with a slightly bent arm by trying to aim at a specific body part (other than the palm), which partners agree upon before closing their eyes. Doing this tends to add to the reconnecting challenge.

Aura can also be played in groups. Players form a circle, connect the palms of both hands with those on either side of them in the circle, close all eyes, take three steps backward, spin three times, and then try to reconnect.

Part of the fun of this game is in watching others, so give players an opportunity to watch as well as play. It's a good way to break up the routine in a classroom or a stuffy meeting.

Group Activities

• *Humans Merrily-Go-Round.*   To play this fun-filled game it helps to have a gym scooter: a little wooden or plastic platform about 12 × 12 × ¾ inches (30 × 30 × 2 cm) to which four ball-bearing swivel casters have been firmly attached. It resembles a small mover's dolly and permits free movement in any direction. (To order scooters, see the list of equipment suppliers in the Resources section.)

Give each group of eight people one gym scooter with which to form some kind of "human merry-go-round"—don't tell them how, though! I first tried this activity with a group of very receptive elementary-school physical education teachers. Within a few minutes some great carousels were rolling, presenting a variety of creative formations. The simplest of these began with four people sitting on the floor facing inward, with their legs straight and their heels on the scooter board in front of them. The other four players stood in between the seated ones, who reached up to grasp the wrist of the standing person on either side. When the seated persons lifted their behinds off the ground, the standing players then walked around in a circle, supporting the seated ones between them. This formed the merry-go-round, and it worked "wheely" well. By lifting their behinds only slightly off the ground, the sitters avoided any hard bumps if the merry-go-round suddenly ground to a stop.

The configurations of human merry-go-rounds are endless. Some possibilities include having some or all of the sitting people rest their hands on the scooter board, with standing partners holding their feet; several people standing with one foot on the scooter board while a partner supports the other foot; or several people lying on top of each other on the scooter board with standing partners providing the propulsion. It is a very merry game for almost any age group.

Marianne Torbert suggested a variation of this game using a parachute or large circular blanket. Several children lie on the parachute with their bodies straight and their feet in the center. The people around the perimeter of the chute lift the edge high enough for the center people's backs to be raised off the floor; then they walk the chute around in a circular motion.

• *Group Pull-ups.* Group Pull-ups add fun to exercise and introduce an element of creative challenge. Players begin in a seated circle of four. Grasping hands or arms, they try pulling up to a stand as a unit. If successful, they can try a circle of six or eight people. The more people added, the more difficult the challenge becomes. Group members can experiment and discover workable ways to get up. Some possibilities include linking elbows with the people on either side or linking wrists with the people on the other side of one's immediate neighbors.

• *Love Handles.* This is another very active game that is enjoyed by all age groups. Players begin in pairs, with one person holding on to her partner's "love handles" from behind. (In this game, "love handles" refers to the fleshy material located on either side of the waist.) Interspersed around these connected pairs are several single "love-its," or taggers, who run around trying to catch the back partner's love handles. If they are successful, the front partner takes off and automatically becomes a love-it in search of some juicy love handles. It helps if the back partner gives the front partner a departure signal (for example, a gentle squeeze and the word "flow") to indicate that a love-it has made contact.

As with the game Hugger, the number of taggers must be adapted to the number of players to keep the action at an appropriate level. Cathi Foley, a co-worker who introduced me to this game, seems to have a distinct advantage over the rest of us: great speed and small love handles. We all enjoy playing with her anyway.

A variation is for love-its also to move in pairs.

• *Tingling Fingers (Circle Massage).* I picked this one up in a Mothercraft Course, which prepares expectant parents to work as a team for the delivery of their child. It was often used to get the group warmed up at the start of the session or cooled down at the end. Everyone stands in a circle, faces in the same direction (right or left), and places his hands on the shoulders of the person in front of him. The circle slowly shuffles around while each person receives and gives a gentle shoulder massage. After a few minutes everyone makes an about-face so that he is now massaging the shoulders of the person who just massaged him.

This activity felt very good to me (I always was a sucker for a back massage) and relaxed the whole group. Tingling fingers can be combined with relaxing thoughts, such as silently repeating "re-lax" with every exhale or with every other step.

• *Runaway Train.* This is an action-packed game that introduces an element of challenge and ends in a common goal. Groups of four or five people form a train and chug around the play space. Players maintain contact by wrapping their arms around the waist of the person immediately in front of them. The front of each train attempts to link up to the back end (caboose) of any other train while trying itself to avoid being linked onto from behind by another train. If one train does hitch up with another, the two parts continue as one unit, trying to join up with other smaller pieces. Before long all the small trains will be linked into one large one. The front engine can then try to catch and link up to the last car. As long as the engines don't get too revved up, Runaway Train is a good way to end up in a circle formation for a quieter game.

• *Frozen Shoes.* This is a variation of Frozen Beanbag, presented in the first *Cooperative Sports & Games Book.* In this version, each person walks, hops, spins, runs, or dances around while balancing an upside-down shoe on her head. If the shoe falls off, the child is frozen and a friend must pick up the shoe and replace it on the frozen child's head—upside-down—to unfreeze her. Hugs can also unfreeze people, as long as the hugger doesn't lose his own shoe in the process.

To increase the challenge for older children, this game can be played in pairs or small groups. Two or three people link together and move around as a unit, each with a shoe on his head. If anyone drops a shoe his whole group is frozen, and another group must unfreeze them as a unit. To do this rescuing, the group must all squat down together, pick up the dropped shoe(s), and replace them on the frozen group's heads, without losing their own shoes in the process. If one of the helpers' shoes drops to the floor, both groups are frozen. Adding music that makes you feel like moving gives a little spice to the game.

• *Frozen Tag.* A nonstop version of Frozen Tag (presented in the first *Cooperative Sports & Games Book*) can be played by "freezing" only the body parts that are tagged rather than the whole person. If a person is tagged she can keep on running while holding on to the part that was touched. A "warm" touch from a fellow runner unfreezes the part so that she can run again normally.

• *Kings of the Mountain.* Marc Blais, one of my former graduate students, tried the People of the Mountain concept after a fresh snowfall. His objective was to make a snowball large enough for everyone to get on it (though not necessarily standing on it). The group began with a small ball of snow and rolled it bigger and bigger until their collective effort could no longer move it. Then they tried to perch as many people as possible on top of the giant ball of snow. They ended their playful venture by making a huge snowman.

• *Tug of Peace Revisited.* This is a variation of our original game of Tug of Peace. A large group of people (ten or more) sit in a circle holding on to a thick rope placed inside the circle in front of their feet. The ends of the rope are tied together to make a huge loop. If everyone pulls at the same time, the entire group should be able to come up to a standing position.

Tug of Peace can also be played by stretching the rope out straight and having people sit on either side of it, facing each other in two lines. If both sides pull on the rope evenly, they can help each other up. It's a good cooperative alternative to Tug of War.

• *Magic Number 11.* A group of three people stand or sit in a small circle facing one another. Each holds one clenched hand in front of him, which he shakes up and down three times as all three chant, "One, two, three." On the count of three, each puts out any number of fingers, from none to five. The object is for the three players to extend a total of exactly eleven fingers, without ever talking to one another. When they are successful, each person shows his appreciation to his partner openly by shaking hands and telling each one what a good job they did. You can change the magic number as well as the number of people in the group and the number of hands, feet, or other objects that are brought into play to add variety and fun.

- *Leaning Ring.* Players stand in a circle, join hands, and count off by twos all around the circle. Keeping their bodies as straight as possible, all the ones lean forward toward the center of the circle and all the twos lean backward away from the center. Each group is kept in balance by the counterbalancing action of the others. Once the leaning ring has been formed, the ones can alternate with the twos by slowly reversing the direction of their lean, the in-leaners becoming out-leaners and vice versa. The game is easier to play with an even number of people in the circle, though that's not absolutely necessary. Groups of eight or ten are more manageable than larger groups. Normally everyone's feet are kept stationary on the floor throughout the activity, but for added fun and challenge the entire leaning ring can try to move in a circle—like Humans Merrily-Go-Round, but without scooters.

- *Cooperative Musical Desks.* Bernie Swords, a graduate student in one of my classes, came up with a version of Cooperative Musical Chairs that worked well in his seventh-grade classroom. Cooperative Musical Desks follows the same format as Cooperative Musical Chairs, except that desks (instead of chairs) are removed one at a time as the game progresses. The object of the game is to see how few desks the students need for the whole class to be off the floor for a period of ten seconds. The desk must be sturdy, of course.

  Bernie reports, "At first the children responded to the game as they would have to Competitive Musical Chairs. Gradually though, they came to realize that they could be successful only if they worked together as a class. The results were thirty students on three small desks for ten seconds, plus a better understanding of what cooperation truly means. . . . What better place than a classroom, which is often the nursery for competitiveness, to sow the seeds of cooperation." As one student said, "Cooperation gets things done faster. You have to help each other to make things work."

- *Water Slide.* Aboriginal children have some beautiful mud slides down which they delight in sliding. City kids often miss out on this opportunity. The same effect can be created by stretching out a sheet of heavy-duty plastic about 42 feet (13 meters) long and 12 feet (3½ meters) wide and securing it at the corners; players can stand or sit on it to do this. A smooth grassy surface provides a nice base. The plastic is kept wet and slippery by a garden hose or a water bucket brigade. For better sliding, some people recommend soaping the plastic with biodegradable soap and water and hosing down the sliders before they slide. The children run toward the plastic and slide across it in a variety of ways—alone, in pairs, as a train. It's a big hit.

  A variation of this slide that has been successful in North America is the sloping version. A big sheet of plastic is laid out on a sloping lawn, with about five large inflated inner tubes placed underneath the bottom end of the slide. The plastic is wet down with a hose, and water collects in the little dam made by the inner tubes. A few

Cooperative Musical Desks

people sit on the upper part of the plastic sheet while the others take a little run and slide right into the dam. Players take turns sitting at the top of the plastic sheet to hold it steady, filling the dam, and sliding. This is a great cooler on a hot day; all the kids in the neighborhood will want a turn.

• *Incorporations.* This is a fast-paced version of Can You Do Things Together? (see the first *Cooperative Sports & Games Book*). The game involves forming and reforming groups as quickly as possible. The leader bangs a cowbell and calls out a variety of groups to get into in quick succession; for example, "Bong—get into a group of three"; "Bong—three plus one"; "Bong—form a group of five with everyone in the group wearing something the same color"; "Bong—make the letter *H* with your bodies"; "Bong—find four people born in the same season as you and link pinkies in a circle with them." The game goes on in this manner at a rapid-fire pace. Players should not worry if the first group is not yet formed when the second group is called; they just head right to the second group. The only cautionary note I have when young children are playing is to make sure all the calls allow all children to take part, so no one feels left out.

• *Balloons Over and Under.* A single line is formed with one person behind another. Four or five balloons filled with water are placed in front of the first person. One by one, the first person takes each balloon and passes it over her head to the person behind her. He passes it under his legs to the next person, she passes over her head to the next, and so on. When the balloon gets to the last person he runs to the front of the line and passes it over his head. Adventurous groups can choose to toss the balloon over their heads and hike it (or toss it) up from between their legs. For some variations of this game that can be done with water balloons see Over and Over in the first *Cooperative Sports & Games Book*.

One note of advice: When playing water balloon games in hot places, such as southern Australia, balloons will burst all by themselves if left out in the sun. Put them in a bucket of water so that they will still be in good shape when you start the game.

• *Tire Toss*.   You've heard of tossing horseshoes, but how about tossing tires? Japanese children play a cooperative game that involves tossing old tires over upright poles. The poles must be sturdy; they're also scaled to different heights for children of various ages. Younger children swing the tires together—"one, two, three, throw!"—and are delighted to ring a pole. Older children can sometimes ring the lower poles alone, but in order to ring the higher poles, some of which extend about 20 feet (6 meters) into the air, they need the help of their friends. For the older kids the collective objective is to toss all the tires over the pole with the least number of throws. The children can easily remove the tires ringing the pole by pushing on the bottom of the pole. This action slips the pole out of a socket, and the pole can then be lowered to the ground to slide the tires off. Inflated inner tubes and hula hoops can also be used for throwing purposes; they are probably more practical for those who simply want to bang a few poles into the ground to use as targets. Removing the "ringed" inner tubes over the pole can also become a cooperative venture.

• *Dragon Dodge Ball*.   This is good for a big group—fifteen or so. Everyone joins hands in a large circle. Groups of two people form dragons, several inside the circle with one player holding onto his partner's waist from behind. Two or three beach balls, other soft foam or sponge balls, or bathroom sponges are put into play by the people forming the circle. Their objective is to hit the behind of a person forming the tail of a dragon. This usually requires some fast passing to players on the other side of the circle. If the tail of a dragon is hit, the head of the dragon becomes part of the circle, the tail becomes the new head, and the person who made the set-up pass (the assist that resulted in the hit) becomes the new tail. To decrease the speed of the ball and increase the challenge, allow only bounce passes and bounce hits onto the dragon's tail.

• *Lap Sit Step, Step, Step*.   At least three or four of the books listed in the Resources section of this book describe a cooperative game called Lap Sit. I'm not sure where the game originated, but it certainly is cooperative in structure. It requires at least eight or ten people to work properly. A group of people form a tight circle by standing shoulder to shoulder, and then all turn to their right (or left). Each person grasps the waist of the one directly in front of him and takes one side step toward the center of the circle to tighten it. The players then attempt to sit on the knees (not the thighs) of the person behind them, creating a sitting circle. We have found that the real fun of the game begins after the sitting circle has been formed, through a variety of collective actions suggested and attempted by the players: having arms out to the side, clapping three times, touching the floor outside the circle, taking three steps forward, all together—left, right, left, taking three steps backwards. This last maneuver usually leaves the entire group in a cheerful heap on the floor.

As a natural lead-in to this activity we often play some sort of train game that allows groups to link together into one large circular train. It is possible to get entire schools in a single circle, but the stepping challenge becomes much more difficult. Regardless of who wins, the people or gravity, it's a great way to bring a group together to end a session.

Team Games

Most of these games require at least a dozen people and can be adapted to much larger groups, depending on your playing area and needs.

• *Blanketball Revisited.* Our original game of Blanketball continues to be enjoyed by groups of all ages. Something special seems to happen to people when they get around a blanket and toss a ball into the air. The Inuit discovered this magic centuries ago when they tossed people high into the air with walrus hides. Judging by the number of blankets we have shredded over the past few years, the walrus hides were a good choice. Rugs of various sizes serve well too, and we have never ripped one yet. Other possibilities for tossing balls include heavy plastic of the kind found on construction sites, durable nylon, thick towels, army blankets, and even sturdy plastic garbage bags.

One of my former students and co-workers, Pierre Provost, suggested tossing balls with a quarter-inch-thick (½ cm.) plywood disk instead of a blanket. This adds an interesting new dimension in that the ball bounces. Let everyone help move and direct the board, and try it with different kinds of balls and different objectives, such as continuous tosses, exchanges across a net, or tossing with one bounce. A tennis ball provides a real challenge.

Some of my students suggested a version of Blanketball that does not require a

Cooperative Rope-skipping

blanket. A small group of people form a circle and link their hands together in the center as if their arms were the spokes of a wheel. They bounce a large ball such as a beach ball off the tops of their arms, keeping their hands connected at the hub of the circle. Another possibility is for a small group to use belts or strips of material, which are crisscrossed in the center and held at the ends. Or two people can play together by rolling a ball back and forth between them, using two strips of material or lengths of rope as a track. The ball can also be tossed by "snapping" it off the strips, but this requires some skill.

• *Bump and Scoot Revisited.* Our original game of bumping a ball or a balloon over a net and scooting under the net has been integrated successfully into both children's programs and adult fitness classes. About six players start on each side of a volleyball net, badminton net, or rope stretched across the playing area. The six players then divide themselves into two teams each, making a total of four teams. Each team chooses a name. A beach ball (or volleyball for more skilled groups) is put into play; players usually hit it three times on one side of the net before they hit it over the net to the other side. The person who hits the ball over the net yells out her team's name and scoots under the net, together with her teammates, to the other side. When one person shouts her team's name, a little spice is added if all the other players repeat the team's name. When played with six people per side the game provides plenty of action, especially if two balls are put into play.

A variation was developed by a few of my students in a game creation project. Six people begin on each side of the net. On Side A, two players are "ones," two are "twos," and two are "threes." On Side B, two are "fours," two are "fives," and two are "sixes." The ball must be hit three times on one side before it goes over the net. Each time it is hit, the other person with the same number as the player hitting the ball runs under the net to the other side. For instance, if a "five" hits the ball, the other "five" runs under the net. The object is to get three people to the other side of the net on each volley and then to bump the ball over the net to keep the game going. Players can call out their numbers as they hit, to help out. It is a lively variation that requires a lot of mutual awareness.

• *Three-Sided Soccer.* While traveling through Scandanavia I was told about an interesting multigoal soccer game that was played by three teams at the same time and with three goals. As originally played in Denmark, the three goals were set up on the field in the form of a triangle. The rules were similar to those of regulation soccer, except that the teams rotated from goal to goal at specified intervals while the goalies remained at the same goal throughout the game. Each team started by defending one goal and being able to score on either of the other two goals. As the game progressed, the teams rotated so that they defended a different goal (and goalie).

In our version, we put several balls into play rather than just one, thus guaranteeing plenty of action for everybody. No official scoring system is necessary; the multiball, multigoal approach, along with team rotation, heightens the focus on play and diminishes concern about who wins.

I shared this game with a group of people attending a cooperative-games workshop in Saskatchewan, and together we set out to adapt it for more cooperation and fun. We tried playing one version for four or five minutes, regrouped, made some changes, tried them, regrouped for suggestions, and so on. At the end of about twenty-five minutes we had collectively created the game of Saskatch Soccer.

• *Saskatch Soccer.* Fifteen or twenty players link up into lines of four (threes are fine if the group is uneven). The linking is accomplished by the players' holding hands or putting their arms around one another. Several goals (usually three) are designated around the field with jackets or shoes or trees or whatever. Each goal is defended by a team of two players—gone are the days when the poor goalie had to be all alone with so much anxiety and no company. The goalie pair may, though it need not, hold hands.

The number of balls in play should be about two fewer than the number of playing units. Any member of each team of four can shoot any ball at any net. However, before doing so each member of that unit must touch the ball. Usually this is accomplished by kick-passing the ball from player to player as the team approaches the goal. If a member of another team makes contact with the ball, the team trying to score must start over, and each member must again touch the ball before a shot is taken. Goal teams are replaced regularly by members of the field units.

We found the game to be full of action, fun, laughter, challenge, and joy in accomplishment. Everything in the game is adaptable: the size and surface of the playing area, the size and number of balls and goals, the number and sex ratio of players per unit, and so on. See what your group can do with Saskatch Soccer.

• *Co-op Four Square.* This game is filled with fours. It is played by four players on four adjacent squares that are each 4 by 4 feet (slightly over 1 by 1 meter). The squares are outlined on the ground by drawing one large one 8 by 8 feet (2½ by 2½ meters) and dividing it into fours. One child stands inside (or just outside) each of the squares. One child bounces a ball to another at random or in a prearranged order. The ball must be hit or pushed into a new square with each bounce, therefore being handled by a different player each time. The objective is to see how long the group can keep the ball going. Less skilled groups can catch the ball before bouncing it into another square; more skilled children hit it on the bounce without holding it.

• *Team Juggle.* This is a good game for a small or large group; it can start in a circle. One person begins by throwing a sponge ball (or similar object) to another player. That person throws it to another and so on until everyone has caught the ball once and the last person has thrown it to the person who began. Throughout the game, each person always throws the ball to the same person who threw it to him in the first round. The leader throws the ball again and, after a few seconds, starts another ball and another. Players have fun seeing how many balls the team can get moving at once and must be ready to receive from their thrower as soon as they have made their pass.

Another version of Team Juggle that I find more fun than the original involves "connecting eyes." It works well when children (or adults) are gathered informally, for example, sitting around on the ground in a random pattern or sitting on couches or chairs. Start by tossing out balls—yarn balls, rolled-up socks, or any other soft object—to various people until there are as many balls in motion as there are players. As soon as the first person receives a ball the game starts. The only rule is that you must make eye contact with another person before throwing that person a ball. Before long, ball exchanges will be flowing in all directions. If you are concerned that someone might be left out of the action, after a couple of minutes of play, ask anyone who has

Parachutes on ice

not yet received a ball to raise a hand or foot. Then remind the group to try to "connect" with everyone.

• *Alaskan Baseball.* Any open area will do for this game; it's like baseball, but without the need for running bases! The group divides into two teams—four or more on a side is good. The members of the batting team line up one behind the other. The fielding team scatters around the "diamond," ready to receive the ball. The first batter moves out of the lineup and kicks a rubber ball (or bats a ball off a stationary tee or shoots a ball with a hockey stick). As soon as she makes the hit she begins to run, circling around the line of batters as many times as possible. Each time the batter passes the front of the line, one run is scored.

The first member of the fielding team who gets to the ball picks it up, and all the other fielders quickly line up behind this player. The ball is passed over their heads, one to another (or it can simply be thrown to each player on the field without lining up). When the last player receives the ball he yells, "Stop!" At this time the batter's turn is up.

The two teams can take turns at batting without changing positions on the field or court. A player from one team bats and runs, then a player from the other, without wasting time having the entire team move from a special batting area to a special fielding area. If playing indoors or in a restricted space, a sponge ball, beach ball, or yarn ball is recommended.

• *Semicircle Soccer.* I got the idea for this game from a game called Konta Wai in Papua New Guinea. In Konta Wai two semicircles of about five players each stand facing each other about 12 feet (3½ meters) apart. The fruit of a local tree is thrown, lifted like a hockey puck, or batted back and forth between semicircles with the use of sticks. The main object of the game is to try to prevent the fruit from passing through one's own semicircle of players. Semicircle Soccer, which is a semicooperative game, takes off from here and adds a few new wrinkles.

Two separate semicircles, of four or five players each, are formed by linking arms around the next person's waist. Semicircles begin by facing each other and kicking a sponge soccer ball back and forth. The objective of each team is to prevent the other team from kicking the ball through its semicircle. However, both semicircles are mobile. They can move at will and can kick the ball from anywhere on the play space. They can even attempt to get around behind the other semicircle in order to kick the ball through their unit in a rear attack. Additional semicircles and balls can be added for more action.

• *Strike-outless Baseball.* One of the most humiliating aspects of baseball for children (or adults) is striking out. Who said, "Three strikes and you're out," anyway? I don't think it was God. So why not just eliminate the possibility? For those who would prefer an alternative, solve the problem by giving children the option to bat the ball off the top of a stationary tee (such as a marker cone, an upright plastic pipe, or a plastic bat with its end cut off) or by increasing the size of the ball; then let them swing until they hit (or kick) a fair ball. With a motionless ball on top of a tee that lines up with a child's bat, the probability of hitting the ball more often and farther is greatly increased. Every child can at least hit the ball before her team retires to the field.

Another possibility is "Three strikes and you're in." If the pitcher from the opposite team is not able to deliver the ball in a manner that enables the batter to hit it within three throws, the hitter automatically goes to first base (or all the way home).

Other major criticisms that children levy against baseball relate to standing around waiting for a turn to hit the ball, standing around in the field waiting for one to come their way, and never scoring a run. To increase the activity element, as well as the sense of success, consider the following rule changes.

All Bases Count   Assign one point for each base. Each time a player progresses to a new base, she gets a point for her team, rather than only receiving a point for making it back to home plate. This version makes a lot more sense for young children, who sometimes get on base but often do not make it all the way around to score. For younger groups assign half a point for getting halfway to base.

All Batters Run   Let groups of players, or even the entire batting team, run when the ball is hit by the batter. Great big bases help with this "all run" process. The more players who get to a base, the more points scored. Remind the players that the next batter up must run back to the batting area or stay there when his teammates "all run."

In one Inuit version of baseball called Anauligak, the ball is pitched to the batter until it is hit, and the runner must be tagged with the ball to be put out. The runner is in no way restricted to running in a straight line to get to a base but is free to run anywhere to avoid being tagged out. Perhaps this concept could be tied into "all run."

All Fielders Touch   Consider making it necessary for every fielder to make contact with the ball after it is hit in order to stop the runner. You should probably move the bases farther apart in that case. Think about increasing the number of balls in play at one time to increase the overall action. Continuous-action games can be created by having batters hit sponge balls one after the other, either off a stationary tee or by throwing the ball in the air. As soon as one batter starts running, the next batter hits the next ball. The fear of being hit by the ball can be reduced by using a sponge ball, which doesn't hurt.

• *Basketball Adaptations.*   Basketball is a good and healthy way to get exercise and can be adapted in many ways to the co-op spirit. Some simple options to increase the success ratio in children's basketball include using lighter balls (they're easier to shoot), bigger baskets, lower baskets, or a smaller court, and moving the free throw line closer to the basket. Another interesting possibility is to have one or two children hold a peach basket or wastebasket at either end of the court instead of the usual stationary goals. Then helpers can move it to aid the scoring effort. These basket holders can rotate regularly with team members who are on the court, perhaps after each score. Consider also having three people join hands to create a large, mobile, circular target that serves as a modified basket.

• *Long Shot/Short Shot.*   This game can be played as a cooperative version of basketball, water polo, soccer, European handball, and a number of other games. The objective is for an entire group to score twenty-one points by shooting balls into a goal or a net. Long shots count two points and short shots count one point. The group can determine among themselves what counts as a long shot or a short shot by establishing a line of separation. Each player gets a ball and must alternate between long shots and short shots. Part of the fun is having balls collide in the air.

• *Multiball Games.* This modified form of ice hockey or ball hockey is semicooperative in that there are two teams going in opposite directions, but because of the extent of continuous action it's virtually impossible for anyone to keep score. It is played with the usual rules, except that two nets are set up at each end of the playing area, making four nets in total. Up to twenty players are assigned to each team and six to ten sponge balls or sponge pucks are put into play at one time. A noncontact rule keeps the players alert dodging each other. It may sound chaotic, but as Cal Botterill (the game's originator) will tell you, the kids love it because there is plenty of action and always a challenge not far away.

BEING "IT"

Games that are completely cooperative in structure do not normally have people who are "it"; however, semicooperative tag and guessing games do have such a person. The challenge in such games is to keep anyone from being frustrated, humiliated, or stuck as "it" for too long. How can these games be adapted to prevent bad feelings from surfacing?

In a game like Hugger or Hug and Hum, many taggers and many runners are usually playing in a relatively congested area. Having many taggers and lots of action reduces the spotlight on any one person. Because the huggers are constantly moving from group to group, tagging someone is not difficult. Even if a player happens to be overweight or not highly skilled, he can station himself in anticipation and catch someone on an exchange.

In the tag games I observed in the rivers of Papua New Guinea, if it appeared that the tagger was slowing down, the other players slowed down just enough to allow a tag and thus a change of taggers. Where this concern for the other person is not evident, some protective rules might be built in. For example, in Mush Mush or any other similar guessing game, after three incorrect guesses (or three taps on the behind, or fewer if desired), the guesser is free to choose whomever he pleases to be the next guesser. Similarly, in tag games, whenever a player is tired of being "it," she should be free to make the switch. The "it" player could be viewed as capable of extending her touch (perhaps through ESP) so that when she's ready to change, she simply points to a new "it" and calls out, "Switch" or "Zap."

To maintain a "delicious uncertainty" in games involving people with mixed skills, perhaps the most talented runners or taggers could hop on two feet while the young children and grandmothers run normally; or people can simply choose how to move for themselves to maintain an appropriate challenge.

Bill Michaelis recently presented some interesting ideas in this light (see the Resources section). Let's say we're playing the game Chief, with a young child trying to guess who is beginning the action that everyone else is following. She's obviously having trouble, since she missed the last three guesses in a row. What can we do? Bill suggests having her stand on the outside of the circle (on the periphery) rather than in the center, giving her hints (for example, "It's a boy," "She's wearing red," "The last guess was close") or having the leader change motions on the guesser's signal. You could also have the leader begin the change in slow motion, increase the number of guesses, or have a small group of young children work as a unit to identify the "chief." These are all approaches that may reintroduce an element of playfulness into the game.

One-family co-op can-walk

games for teen-agers
and young adults

You might think that teen-agers would be reluctant to try out cooperative sports, but we've found that when properly introduced to them, many have become enthusiastic players. It's important to keep the skill level and challenge factors in mind, though. Chapter 10, on presenting cooperative games and programs, will give you some more general suggestions for ways to encourage cooperative ventures; this chapter provides specific ideas and games to get you going and new ways to remake traditional games.

Many of the Inuit, German, and Chinese games presented in Chapters 7 and 9 will appeal to older groups, as will the team games in Chapter 5 and the cooperative innovations in Chapter 11. However, remember that players aren't likely to spend hours playing these games every day, nor are they likely to spend years training to perfect their skills for them. We play cooperative games for a different reason—to free us from the work of play, even if only for short periods of time. The activities and games that follow hold enough challenge to maintain the interest of a teen-age group, and offer an appealing alternative to the anxiety of competition. See Appendix A for some further thoughts on stress control.

Getting Teen-agers Together

One of the first things that occurs in preparing to play many games is that players must somehow group themselves into partners or teams. We want to accomplish this in the least threatening way possible for all age groups. We don't want anyone waiting to be chosen or, worse yet, not to be chosen.

Many aboriginal people had face-saving ways of forming teams. Often they spontaneously divided into groups, but in some instances they were more systematic. In one Inuit method of choosing sides, all those born in the summer played on one side, all those born in the winter played on the other side, and anyone born during "freeze-up" or "break-up" (of the waters) could choose to play on either side. This simple procedure eliminated the fear of being chosen last or not being chosen and the associated feelings of rejection.

Malaysians often divided themselves into groups by simple games of chance. For instance, all players extend one hand from behind their back with palm up or palm down. The people with palms up would make one team; palms down, the other. If the teams were unbalanced, the larger team repeated the process so as to send some people to the other side. Another method used was to have each person flip a seashell or half a coconut shell and then divide into teams based on whether the shell landed face up or face down.

Here are some other possibilities for getting teen-agers together with minimal anxiety and maximum pleasure. These can be used alone or as a prelude to more active sports.

• *Puzzled People.* This is good for groups of people who don't know each other well. Take a bunch of 3-by-5-inch (8 by 13 cm) index cards and cut them into two pieces each. Sheets of typing paper or note-pad paper work equally well. Cut each card (or sheet of paper) differently so that each piece only pairs with one other. Distribute half a card to each person in the group and have each one find his other half. Once two people have made the appropriate connection, they can spend five or ten minutes getting to know something about each other. If time is short, partners can take a few moments to find out two or three things about each other that each is willing to share. The "getting to know you" part of this exercise can be a casual conversation, or it can be more structured, taking the form of a reciprocal interview. The interchange can be extended to include introductions of one another to another pair or within a small group. We've used this equally successfully with both teen-age and adult cooperative-games groups.

• *Sports Collage.* The initial idea for this activity came from my friend Bob Wiele, an innovative adult educator from Toronto. A basket filled with old magazines is distributed to each group of six to eight people, along with scissors, glue, and a blank piece of poster board. The objective for the group is to create a sports collage poster (or any collage with a specific theme). When the poster is completed, all group members sign their names on their collective creation. This is a good icebreaking activity, particularly when a language or culture barrier exists between the players. It is also a good way to create a personal touch for one's work area or play space. For example, a group of teen-agers attending a recreation training camp made their posters and then hung them on the walls of their dining hall. Poster making has also worked well as an introductory activity in classrooms and at conferences.

- *Connecting Eyes.* One thing I admire about little kids is the way in which they can look you straight in the eye in a completely open and nonthreatening way. This game attempts to reconnect the eyes of those who have learned to avoid looking at each other. The game begins with a group of people standing in a circle, facing inward. Each person attempts to make eye contact with another person in the circle. It could be a person across the circle or one right next to you. Once mutual contact has been made, the two people exchange positions while maintaining eye contact. Many pairs can exchange at the same time, and players are encouraged to try to ensure that every person in the circle is included in the exchange. First try it in silence (walking), then exchange greetings at the center of the circle on your way to the other side ("Hello, I'm Terry"; "Hi, I'm Barbara"). Finally, for a different touch, add music so that players can skip or dance across the circle at a livelier pace. Connecting Eyes goes over really well with almost all age groups.

Another interesting way to connect is for players to clap out a beat representing the number of syllables in their own first name. Sam would "clap" (once), Jo-ann would "clap, clap" (twice), and Mar-i-lyn would "clap, clap, clap" (thrice). By clapping out different rhythms, people come together into similar sounding groups and share their names. Ah . . . I remember you, you're a two-clap person.

- *Good Vibes Circle.* This is an activity that should be done early in a game session to set the right current. A circle of about eight people is formed, and players gently connect hands with those on either side of them. Everyone then closes her eyes and tries to feel or imagine a current moving around and around the circle. Visualize (or feel) the current come in through your right hand and exit through your left hand. The current we pass should reflect our personal assets, our strengths, our humanness. The current should be viewed as all positive, drawing on all the good energy and vibrations that exist within the group. This is the spirit that every person should try to hold onto throughout the games. Good Vibes will work well with certain game groups and has even been used successfully as a pregame ritual with some sports teams. However, it's best to know your group first, as some groups will not respond well.

• *Kanga Ball.* This is a spin-off of Inuit Skipping (see page 107), adapted for widespread use by almost all age groups. It is a good active game that requires little space.

Players divide into groups of three. Two partners face each other and roll a ball back and forth. As the ball passes between them, the third partner jumps over it, making a half-turn as he goes so as to keep eye contact with the ball.

The partners rolling the ball start off slowly and gradually increase the speed of the ball so that the jumper can just meet the challenge. The ball can be "rolled" in a variety of ways; for example, players can kick it back and forth in a standing position or sit down with their legs spread and roll it back and forth.

The jumper can say, "Slower," "Faster," or "Perfect" to make sure the speed is right. Balls of different sizes can be used to vary the challenge. When one jumper gets tired, or after a certain number of jumps, the players can switch positions. Kanga Ball can be a very good conditioning activity if kept up for several minutes. It can even be done on one foot by strong kangaroos.

• *Chinois Shuttles.* The Chinese, who are currently the best badminton players in the world, have devised a series of fast-action multiple-shuttle badminton games. In one such game, the objective is to keep as many shuttles in play as possible between two teams. If, for example, there are four or five players on each side, each player begins the game with two or three shuttles in hand. Everyone serves the first shuttle at the same time and then launches the others while trying to keep the first ones in play. If a shuttle hits the ground, it is picked up and launched again immediately. The Chinese have reported keeping as many as twenty shuttles in continuous flight.

The Chinese use another multiple-shuttle game to help teammates learn to respond quickly to oncoming birds. Two receivers stand on one side of the net, facing a group of four or five players, who each have several birds in hand. The senders fire a rapid barrage of shuttles in the direction of the receivers, who scramble to keep the birds in flight. These games are quite demanding when played with shuttles but can be adapted for younger or less skilled players by using small balloons in place of shuttles.

• *Co-op Scooter Ball.* This game is similar to cross-court dribbleless basketball or European handball, except that once the two teams are formed (up to ten people per team), half the players on each side sit on little wooden scooters, and the other half maneuver their seated friends around. The action of the game resembles basketball, with these cooperative modifications: Only the players on the scooters can handle the ball; and all the seated players on one team must make contact with the ball (that is,

Co-op Scooter Ball

receive a pass) before the team can try to score. There should be at least three progressively difficult pieces of equipment for scoring arranged at either end of the court. For example, you can hang a hula hoop from the basketball hoop, or stretch a soccer net across the end of the court (the players then shoot the ball into the net). Each player can then select her own scoring challenge. All goals score the same number of points for the team. Partners should switch positions every four minutes or so, rotating players between teams as well if they wish. Regular rotations ensure that no one "pushes" or sits on the scooter too long. The rotation of pushers between teams helps keep "winning" in perspective by preventing team identity from becoming too entrenched.

A squashy sponge ball the size of a grapefruit is a good choice for this game. It can be caught in one hand and doesn't hurt if it hits a player, even in the face. Small beach balls have the same safety advantage and also work well. A harder ball which can be caught in one hand, such as a European handball or a water polo ball, can be used for more skilled groups. Use more than one ball for added action.

The swivel casters on the scooters used in this game allow free-flowing movement in any direction on a hard surface. You can find these scooters in some schools, order them through a sporting goods store, or make them yourself. Various things could be used instead of scooters: tricycles, wheelchairs, wagons, or cardboard boxes. This game is also fun to play on ice; the seated partner slides freely on a piece of plastic. Or it can be played in waist-deep water, with one partner propelling another who is perched on a floating board or air mattress. If the play space is the size of most gyms, it is possible to have three cross-court games going at once, involving a total of sixty players. More than five sets of partners on a team will make things crowded.

- *Matching Symbols.* This is a quiet game that can be played in pairs or small groups. The players huddle together with one hand behind their backs. By watching one another closely, and without talking, they try to extend that hand to the center of the huddle at the same moment. The object of the game is for all to extend the same hand symbol—palm down or palm up—without talking to one another. Players may take as many tries as necessary. Establish two or three different symbols from which players choose, including perhaps a fist (representing a rock), a flat palm down (the sea), or a palm up with fingers touching the thumb (a drinking glass). To make the game even more interesting, no preset symbols are given, and each player can extend her hand in any form she wishes.

• *Nose to Nose.* Bound to generate some laughter, this is a great game to play with a special companion. My daughter and I stumbled upon it in our play, but her mother likes it even better. Partners stand facing each other a couple of feet apart. One closes her eyes and moves slowly forward, trying to connect the tip of her nose gently to that of her partner, who remains still. After a few tries they can switch roles, or, if they have the nose for it, both can close their eyes and try moving together very slowly to end up nose to nose. To make it easier, heavy breathing, panting, or light whistling is allowed.

I bet you can't play Nose to Nose without laughing. Put this book down, find a prospect in your midst, and try it!

• *Wonderful Circle.* This is a game used by a group called Playfair to end their cooperative-play sessions on a positive note. It was the brainchild of Pamela Kekich, who seems to have a very special talent for creation within cooperative structures. The idea behind the game is to legitimize and encourage the expression of appreciation for one another. We have been taught to look for flaws and weaknesses and bad points, and consequently we are good at being negative. However, most of us are not so good at looking for and pointing out the good or expressing appreciation to others.

To play Wonderful Circle, players get into a big circle and put their arms around one another's waists. Each person finds out the names of the people on either side of him. The circle then begins to shuffle very slowly to the left and keeps going until someone says, "Stop!" That person then shares something that made her feel good while playing that day—something about how she played, interacted playfully, or appreciated how another player interacted with her.

When the first person is finished with her brief sharing, she says "Go!" and the circle begins shuffling in the other direction until someone else calls "Stop." He then shares some good feelings. This continues until the leader senses that everyone who wants to say something has had an opportunity to do so. If there are ten seconds of silence after asking, "Stop—are we done yet?" everyone knows the game is over. All rush into the center of the circle and give themselves a gigantic ovation.

Log Roll

Cooperative Rule Changes

There is nothing sacred about the games we play today. There is nothing that says that we cannot change the rules. Cooperative strategies can often be inserted into contemporary competitive games by simple rule changes, which ensure that all players are part of the action in a constructive way. Some examples include the following.

All Touch Every player on the court must touch the ball (for example, receive a pass) before anyone can take a shot at the net. After a point is made everyone must again touch the ball before the next shot is taken.

All Play Every player plays for an equal amount of time.

All Chosen Help players choose up teams in a humane way. For example, all players can throw their stick, glove, or shoe into a pile, and then the pile can be separated into two (or more) piles. Players simply find their shoe and play as a unit with the people who ended up in their pile.

All Positions Every player has an opportunity to play the most exciting or action-filled position in every game; for example, in games such as American football, each player has a chance to throw the ball, run with the ball, and catch the ball. In softball all players get a chance to pitch and catch even if they must move up close to the batter's box to pitch it to the batter. In other sports a simple position rotation—similar to what now occurs in volleyball—might be put into effect.

All Shoot   Every player must be given an opportunity to take a shot at the net before a team can win.

All Bat   In games like baseball or softball every player has an opportunity to bat the ball, either off a standing tee or as delivered by a pitcher.

Multiscore   A certain number of different players must contribute to the point total in order for a team to win.

Point to the Passer   In order to encourage teamwork and passing, Jack Donohue, Canada's national basketball coach, came up with this interesting and effective strategy. During scrimmages, whenever a basket is made, all the other players have to point to the person who made the last pass and not to the person who made the basket. This silent vigil helps drive home the importance of the passer.

No Hitting   Introduce nonhitting rules into all youth sports (for example, noncontact football and hockey). It is difficult, if not impossible, to encourage children to be concerned with the feelings of others and at the same time to encourage them to hit other people. Hitting facilitates dehumanization, and dehumanization facilitates hitting. It is a vicious cycle.

Remove the Armor   The further you get from the professional sport model, the more cooperative the game will likely be. For children and youths, consider doing exactly what the pros don't do. (For example, accept players as equally worthy people in victory and defeat; alternate team members to equalize teams; don't use special uniforms; get rid of heavy equipment; let kids from different teams share the ride to and from the game, locker and shower facilities, and food and drink feasts; encourage the participants to express their views; ask players for their suggestions and implement them; let the kids call their own plays and play their own game; don't use officials; help the players to learn to be more supportive of one another; help the players to let down worry barriers, which interfere with learning and fun; challenge irrational beliefs, which create anxiety; help the kids realize that losing does not mean you are an inadequate person; and if you have the courage, don't keep records, standings, or score.

Fun for All   No matter what the skill level, there is room for laughter, genuine smiles, new challenges, and fun. When you take the smile out of kids' games, you take the smile out of much of their lives. A goal for every practice and every game should be to keep the children smiling inside.

Collective Challenges

Some of our most well-received games among teen-age groups involve collective score or collective challenges (for example, Collective-Score Volleyball, Bump and Scoot

Partner Rope-skipping

Revisited, Blanketball). If you introduce collective games (such as Collective-Score Volleyball) and sense that someone might be worried about either missing a shot or somehow bringing down the team's performance, try one or more of the following.

Don't Keep Score When the Inuit batted inflated seal bladders back and forth centuries ago, the aim was to have fun trying to keep the ball up. No scores were considered and laughter accompanied off-balance hits *and misses*.

Continue Counting Count consecutive hits instead of goals or shots; if a ball is missed, players simply pick up the ball and continue the count from where they left off.

Introduce Collective Responsibility Use a group tossing game like Blanketball in place of one that requires an individual to deliver the ball alone. This increases the sense of collective responsibility for hits and misses, and the entire weight of a miss never rests on one individual's shoulders.

Make Everyone's Contribution Count Select activities in which everyone's contribution (no matter how small) increases the total group accomplishment (for example, calculating a total distance run or jumped by the whole group).

Make the Challenge Appropriate for the Group When a collective challenge is presented to a group, it should contain some "delicious uncertainty," but it should also be achievable. If young children function as a unit, they can make letters, shapes, or animals together; older children and teen-agers can make successful pyramids and surmount more difficult barriers by working together. With very young children, goal accomplishment should be a certainty if they engage in a cooperative effort. With older children and teen-agers, success should be highly likely with cooperative effort but not a certainty. The challenge component can be stretched with more mature groups.

Encourage Mutual Encouragement When groups of people are attempting to overcome difficult challenges, mutual support is essential. Take mountain climbing as an example. If people don't help one another, they simply will not make the ascent successfully. It is a group challenge and thus a group responsibility to help one another rise to the challenge. If a team fails to make the ascent successfully, all team members, rather than only one or two, are partially responsible. Perhaps if they had helped one another prepare more thoroughly, encouraged one another more during the ascent, and so on, the desired outcome would have been achieved. On the other hand, the challenge may have been too difficult for this collection of people. In either case, at the end there is no finger pointing (for example, "It's your fault"), as this serves no useful purpose, but there is learning from the experience.

Let's say a group is playing Collective-Score Volleyball, and they are attempting to set a new personal record of twenty consecutive hits over the net. At nineteen, someone misses. How does that person feel? If her teammates moan in dissatisfaction, it could be an anxious and unhealthy moment for her. However, if they support her, assume some responsibility themselves, or turn it into a learning experience, her feelings will likely differ. For example, teammates can do this by saying, "It's OK Joan, we almost got there"; "It was exciting to get so close and your earlier hits helped get us so close"; "We're only playing for fun so it doesn't matter"; "I would have missed it too; maybe we can try to set each other up better for the next hit over." Don't just make excuses, either—encouragement should be sincerely offered. The person who missed will be taken off the spot, even though a score is being kept. You can help kids to develop the skills of mutual encouragement by discussing its importance, by doing it yourself, and by encouraging players to do it within the real situation.

Collective-Score Activities

Jim Deacove, my colleague from Family Pastimes, has been busy thinking up collective-score games suitable for teen-agers and young adults. In this section I share some of his adaptations with you.

• *Cooperative Meets.*   In cooperative running events the emphasis is placed on a collective fastest time, and no one is eliminated. Each runner tries to run the race as fast as possible, to get a "best time," but the individual times are added up or averaged. In using this collective-timing approach, Deacove notes, intramurals become cooperative efforts in which one room of a school is sending out a runner to help another runner from another room. Both contribute something, both contribute their best. In intraschool meets, each school enters runners not to beat each other, but to help each other put together the very best time they all can for the event. Each runs an individual race down a lane or through a cross-country course and gets a pat on the back for full effort.

Sometimes names are drawn out of a hat and people are paired up so that partners run half the track (or half the distance) each, and the combined time at the end of the distance is contributed to the group average.

A similar collective approach can be followed for events involving walking, running for distances, cross-country skiing, jumping, throwing, lifting, hurdling, and so on. The total score is simply an expression of all the human energies and skills that come together at that particular time.

The attitude Jim promotes is one of "This is what *we* did," and no comparisons are invited with other records, individuals, or schools. "Who cares what Room 9B did? We are running for our own enjoyment." Everyone participates and adds a few points, and that is what is important.

Collective runs can also be done without recording times. As Jim states:

I use a whole class, usually about twenty-five or more participants of mixed sex, ability, and desire. Each runner runs once round the track and hands off the baton to the next waiting. Everyone gets one big run around the track. [Or, as mentioned above, two runners are paired up, giving each half the distance.] No times are kept, just a record of names and "incidents," if any. The school newspaper reports the relay with emphasis on the names and incidents. The names of each participant as they run around the track are announced. I encourage each student to run as fast as possible. If a runner is genuinely struggling he can signal the next runner who starts off and gets the baton from wherever along the track the previous one stopped. Quitting as such is permitted.

Active participation can be maximized by several people running at the same time.

• *Collective Marathons.*   The original Greek marathoners used a collective effort to deliver messages by passing them from runner to runner. Contemporary marathon relays consist of a chain of runners working together to complete the distance. The goal can be simply to complete the marathon distance, or a total time can be kept. The number of contributing runners and the distance each covers can be adapted to meet the running abilities of each participant. If the marathon takes place around a track,

Inflating the spirit

participants can stop whenever they feel like stopping and another runner can take over at that point. Similarly, marathon long jumps or triple jumps can be done on a field or a track, with each subsequent jumper taking off from where the last landed.

Ultramarathons—wherein all distances run are added to a total—are also a possibility. The sport can be running, hopping, skipping, walking, skiing, jumping, shot-putting, discus throwing, and so on. (See Running to the Olympics, page 179.) Each person adds something to the collective, no matter how far or short she runs or jumps. Every participant brings the group forward and cannot possibly detract from the collective objective. The same is true whenever the objective is to add time, distance, or number of times. For example, for how long can all of us keep actively running, walking, or jumping rope today? The more the merrier. How far or high can all of us jump—as high as the school? How many push-ups or partner pull-ups can all of us do together? As long as we select something that every participant is capable of doing, even at the most basic level, there is the possibility of that person's contributing to the group goal. Participants have an obvious reason to help one another by sharing encouragement, techniques, and strategies, since each good performance contributes to the overall goal.

- *Cooperative Archery and Darts.* Activities such as archery, darts, billiards, bowling, horseshoe pitching, curling, and so on can be easily changed into cooperative activities by introducing a collective-score concept. Instead of individuals or teams competing against another, they attempt together to score as many points as possible.

As Jim points out, "When a youngster realizes that a group is going out together and shooting toward a common objective with the others, there is a genuine release from competitive tension." One teen-age boy described the feeling to Jim. He said cooperative field archery, as well as the other co-op sports he played, reminded him of "when he and some pals used to go fishing together on Saturday morning." They went together, they compared notes about rods, bait, flies, or whatever. They helped one another in many small and big ways. There were good feelings all round. This kind of friendly relationship is immediately transformed when some enterprising adult comes along and turns the occasion into a fishing derby. Person against person. Prizes. Elimination. Tension.

- *Cooperative Handball, Squash, Paddleball, Ping-pong.* The idea behind these adaptations of their competitive counterparts is to keep the ball in play for as long as possible. This strategy is tied into the rules of the game. You begin with twenty-one points and deduct one point every time a ball is missed, a serve is broken, or the ball goes out of play. To maintain the challenge for paddleball players with higher skill levels, Jim suggests having them return the ball to a different wall from the one that the ball last hit. For skilled ping-pong (table tennis) players, he suggests putting up a blind or sheet that has an oval opening for the ball to pass through above the net. The players volley through that opening.

- *Cooperative Badminton.* In our original game of Cooperative Badminton, which we call Goodminton, two players stationed themselves on each side of a rope or a net and hit a balloon or small beach ball back and forth with a badminton (or paddleball) racket. Snowshoes also were used as rackets. The objective was to keep the "bird" in flight for as long as possible.

Jim has expanded this concept into the following game for use with teen-agers and adults. "Twenty serves make up a game, ten on each side of the court. The score is a running total of volleys and the team score is the total number of volleys made in the twenty serves." A fault on either side ends a serve. If a large number of players wish to play on a limited number of courts, each doubles team plays for a small number of serves. The collective score for each team of four is added to all other teams to get a final group score.

To add some challenge, follow the regulation service patterns for games and require two hits on one side of the net before the ball is volleyed over. The first hit is a pass to the other player; the second hit is the volley over. The same player may not hit the

A big caterpillar crawl over the earth ball

ball twice in a row. "A tournament for the entire school can be run or a field day can be conducted. A collective score representing a school will be a score to be remembered."

Nature a Natural

Nature is a natural for nurturing cooperation with almost all age groups. Many outdoor activities provide stimulating challenges that require cooperation for successful and enjoyable outcomes. Canoeing, camping, climbing, rafting, cross-country ski touring, and a host of other outdoor activities provide rich opportunities for learning about cooperation with self, others, and the natural environment. They can be self-paced, freeing us from the constraints of organized competition, constant external evaluation, and imposed human controls. The sense of freedom they offer is one of the major reasons for the rapid increase in involvement in these types of activities.

Outings provide ample opportunity for sharing skills, decision making, and the work load. For example, the group can come up with equitable (and usually pleasant) ways to make camp, cook food, break camp, carry equipment, or perform rescues. They can reach a consensus where each commits himself to carrying a realistic portion of the load. This kind of involvement helps prepare youngsters for taking on responsibility for themselves and for others. It's a beautiful setting within which to learn about the value of cooperation and the misery of conflict. See "Ecological Cooperation" (page 180) for more ideas in this area.

Will It Really Work with Teen-agers?

When I first encountered Harry Sawchuk, he told me that he liked the cooperative-games concept but wasn't sure how to use it with teen-age groups. He is currently doing some exciting things with his high-school students in the realm of games. His work is demonstrating that it is possible to rekindle a spirit of playfulness and cooperation in the games teen-agers play.

His overall plan actively involves the youngsters in pinpointing the problems of excessive competition and in searching for effective solutions. In grades nine, ten, and eleven, one full "teaching unit," or block of the phys. ed. curriculum, is devoted exclusively to the development of cooperative values and more cooperative games. His classes are co-educational and the rough breakdown of content in the cooperative curriculum at each grade level is as follows.

GRADE 9

The focus here is on creating games that fulfill the students' primary reasons for playing. Harry and his students discuss why they play games and what they want most from a game. This sets a values framework for the creation of their own games.

The students work in small groups guided by their own views of the ideal game (for example, fun, activity, participation, acceptance). Sometimes he will simply give them four odd pieces of equipment (such as a nylon stocking, a broomstick, a small ball, and a flat piece of wood) and ask, "What can we do with it?" The creation of games provides a good basis for exploring reasons for playing. It also helps students understand the need for and effect of rules, and teaches them how they can adapt rules to involve everyone in a satisfying way. In addition, it helps develop mutual communication skills.

A catalog of games is created by marking them down on a flip chart and then pinning them up on the gym wall. When the students begin to try their newly created (or adapted) games, "things start to happen." After playing, the students discuss which games they enjoyed most and why. This creative-games process is used to set the foundation for subsequent units on cooperative games.

GRADE 10

The questions of why we play and how we can play more joyfully are discussed further, with major points being stuck up on the wall. The concepts of cooperation and competition and what they mean to the students are also discussed. Generally cooperation is viewed as "doing something with somebody" and competition is viewed as "doing something against somebody."

The point is made by Harry that children "get enough competition so let's try doing some things with somebody." He starts by asking the students to "do a simple warm-up activity with a partner in a cooperative way." He then asks them to expand the partner exercise to include four people, eight people, and then the whole group. This introductory activity helps to communicate the concept of cooperation and provides an experience in helping one another for a common end.

He makes good use of cooperative parachute activities as well as cooperative pyramids, both of which are well received. When assigning group challenges, he points out the importance of *cooperation* and *communication* for a successful outcome. One way he promotes awareness of others and the improvement of nonverbal communication skills is to assign a silent group task (such as building a three-level pyramid with two people at the top, with no verbal communication allowed). You have to watch to communicate. Other group challenges include getting one group member to a high point on the wall, people passing, and Long, Long, Long Jump (see the first *Cooperative Sports & Games Book* for this last game).

GRADE 11

Harry starts this unit by coming into the gym and giving the following instructions: "Set up the volleyball equipment, split into two teams, and start playing volleyball." During this process he pretends he is busy but actually listens attentively and watches closely what happens. After the students have played for about five minutes, he stops the game and asks them to sit down. The scene unfolds something like this: "You've been playing for five minutes. If you have not yet touched the ball, please stand up." (Sixty percent stand up.) Why are some people left out of the action? Why were some people saying, "Get out of my way"? Why were some people arguing? Why are you playing? "For fun," the students say.

Is it fun to be left out, yelled at, or pushed out of the way? Is arguing fun? If 60 percent have not touched the ball, are they having fun? Those who are never given an opportunity to touch the ball, or who are rarely a part of the action, will never have an opportunity to develop their skills. Do you have a right to deny others the opportunity to learn and to have fun? Don't you have a responsibility to let others develop their skills and join in the action?

He reminds the students of what they discussed in grades nine and ten about fun and cooperation and playfulness. He helps them re-identify why they are playing and how they are preventing one another's enjoyment.

He asks them, "What can you do to equalize opportunities?" They give some suggestions and he adds a few of his own, which they try and adapt as necessary. He has them try Bump and Scoot Volleyball and jots down what he hears as they play. Again he stops the game after five minutes to ask about how many were actively involved in the game and shares the much more supportive comments he hears among players. Through this kind of process he gets the players tuned into playing more cooperatively. "Ask yourself, what do *you* have to do to make it work? Are you doing it?"

He introduces "regular" volleyball *with no score* and then asks, "Who's winning?" They tell him! He then introduces Rotational Volleyball, (see the first *Cooperative Sports & Games Book*), in which players rotate to the other team. Again he asks, "Who's winning?" First there is silence; then, "Hey, we're all winning."

He also introduces another rotational volleyball strategy that he calls "playing for people rather than points." If one team scores a "point," they take a person from the other team, rather than a point. The object is to play until one side has all the people. The students in grade eleven love it.

When students have really had fun playing, he initiates a discussion about what helped it happen and asks, "Can we apply this playfulness to other sports?" How about in basketball? How can we equalize opportunities and reduce pressure in this game too? Again they suggest and he suggests, and together they try such games as All Touch, Co-ed Pass, All Score (your team wins once everyone has scored one basket and you can't score twice in a row). He listens for within-game comments that indicate how the game is being received (for example, "Who hasn't had a shot yet?") and points out the improvements in team play.

Harry shared with me a high moment in his teaching career that made this all seem worthwhile. During a game of All Score Basketball, a grade-eleven girl came over to him with tears in her eyes and said, "That's the first time I *ever* scored a basket in a game."

The version of Frozen Tag Harry uses involves a piggyback rescue. If a person is

---

GAMES FOR TEEN-AGERS AND YOUNG ADULTS

101

tagged she is "frozen," and in order to be unfrozen she has to be carried piggyback across the freedom line. Rescuers have to take the chance of being frozen in the rescue process. Boys carry girls, girls carry boys, and some of the littlest people rescue some of the biggest people, to everyone's delight.

The students loved Blanketball but ripped a lot of blankets. They ended up using old carpet remnants around 9' × 9' (3 meters by 3 meters). They are extremely strong and were never shredded. For Blanket Toss they used carpeting materials which measured about 12' × 12' (4 meters by 4 meters).

For Scooter Hockey, one partner is a "pusher" and the other a stick handler. The stick handler must remain seated on a little scooter. The "pusher" cannot make contact with the ball or puck. Everyone must score for a team to win, and there is no goalie, which makes scoring quite a bit easier.

Two colors of hockey sticks (red and blue) are used. The reds form one team, and the blues the other. However, the "pushers" and stick handlers switch positions on a regular basis, and the pushers must switch with someone with the other colored stick. This serves to integrate the teams and thus reduce the pressure on winning. This game is a big hit with the grade-eleven co-ed classes.

Playing Competitive Games Cooperatively

If you choose to play within competitive structures (and virtually all games heavily promoted in our culture fit into this category), then the only way to make the experience beneficial for children and youth is to teach self-control skills and to promote positive human values. This includes teaching responsibility for self and for the welfare of others, along with fair play, respect for others, alternate ways of winning, learning from losing, appropriate goal setting, strategies for anxiety control, and basic relaxation techniques. Most important of all is helping people to see themselves and others as equally worthy human beings in victory and in loss.

The key is helping children to take the right kind of values into the game and to control the competition rather than letting it control them. There are countless opportunities for values education within competitive games. What better place is there to discuss the true meaning of values that are important to children and adults alike, such as winning, losing, success, failure, anxiety, rejection, fair play, acceptance, friendship, cooperation, and healthy competition? What better place to help children become aware of their own feelings and the feelings of others? What better place to encourage children to help one another learn how to cope constructively with some of these problems and concerns? Time-out can be called to take advantage of a meaningful learning opportunity. The value (or devaluing) can be discussed quickly, the action can be reinforced or another more appropriate way of behaving can be presented, and then play can be resumed. If a subsequent positive value (for example, helping) or troublesome value (for instance, hurting) surfaces, take another quick time-out for a few constructive comments and go back to the action. With a little direction, the players can decide for themselves what they want to get out of the game, how they think they should treat one another, and how to help one another follow the guidelines they feel are important. When in doubt, ask the kids—that's where I usually go with my difficult dilemmas.

There are numerous personal goals that can be set and achieved that have nothing to do with winning: for example, completed skills; new moves, plays, sequences, routines, formations; improvements in self-control, mood control, relaxation, coming back from a mistake; and improvements in interpersonal relations with teammates, coach, referees, and so on. When multiple goals are set, it is extremely rare that something good cannot be pointed out.

If you place children or youths in competitive win-lose structures, you also have a responsibility to help them learn from and grow through "lost" games and unmet goals. This is not something that happens automatically. As a leader or a parent, you can help point out the positive victories within the loss as well as the positive lessons that can come from losing. Even loss isn't all bad when you begin to look for the good.

lessons from the Arctic: Inuit games

Some of the warmest children with whom I have ever played lived in two of the smallest and most remote Arctic settlements in the Canadian Northwest Territories. Both of these settlements are nestled into beautiful Arctic coast settings and have excellent fishing and hunting. They're virtually cut off from the mainstream of North American society, with no television, no roads for hundreds and hundreds of miles, and no way in or out except for an occasional flight.

The children's play is spontaneous, creative, and filled with laughter. The children are continuously smiling, giggling, and laughing. In the winter they slide down a snow-covered hill on their backs, fronts, and behinds, one after another, side by side, in pairs and in small groups. They also slide down the hill on an old chair from which the legs have been removed and on anything else they can find lying around. For example, they make little sleds by attaching wooden boxes to old skis, wooden slats, or broken snowmobile runners. A wooden box or chair perched on a single ski seems to provide the most excitement.

Inuit free play under the midnight sun

When the wind blows the snow from a nearby lake, crystal-clear blue ice emerges. It is seven feet thick. The children run on the ice and slide across it on their bellies. One boy stood on a small sled while his dog pulled him to and fro. Another child skied behind his dog on homemade skiis. Both seemed to be having a delightful time. As we walked and slid across the lake, there was a great deal of linking of arms and affectionate contact among the children. Someone always waited for the little ones who straggled behind.

The children's indoor play also reflects a touch of harmony. For example, two or three children normally color together at the same time, using one coloring book and sharing several crayons. There is never any trouble. The fact that they have a limited supply of crayons and coloring books probably enhances cooperation.

In communities such as this, there is still lots of visiting, among both adults and children—something we lost with the advent of TV. During my summer visits groups of children often came to see me in my tent. They shared the beauty of their land, their knowledge, and their play. They took me for walks to show me plants that I could eat and baby snowbirds. We did One-Foot-High Kicks on the tundra and played hide-and-seek in the rocks along the hillside. Somehow I was elected to be "it." I could still be searching for them if they hadn't helped me by popping their heads out and giggling.

At three in the morning I watched a small group of children playing flowingly behind the community hall. Twenty-four hours of sunlight is a wonderous gift of summer, and children are free to take advantage of it. Before my eyes, the children made a slide out of an old piece of metal siding. They perched one end on a rock and slid down with younger children in their laps. They leaped across the boulder-strewn hill and ended up attempting to help pull other children up on top of a big boulder (People of the Mountain). Older children often picked up, held, or otherwise helped slightly smaller children.

While the Inuit live in harsh climatic conditions, they remain playful people—and offer us hundreds of fun games and activities which you don't need to live in the Arctic to enjoy! Some were designed originally to develop coordination and survival skills; others were purely for enjoyment. In "olden times" playtime involved no predetermined time, place, or agenda—when people got together, they played! If games had losers, the losers selected the next game to play. Everyone was involved, from old men and young children to mothers with babies slung on their backs.

When a game was developed to promote survival skills, there was no such thing as specialization, and everyone was happy to see someone else, even "competitors," improve. People (men *and* women) needed strong arms and legs and hearts—being able to jump a distance across the ice didn't help when you needed to throw a harpoon. Being able to sew well didn't help when you needed to skin an animal. People needed a variety of coordinated skills to survive, plus a happy disposition to enjoy the simple pleasures in life.

The inside of a large igloo (snow house) provided adequate space for playing almost all their traditional games. Their old-time games required little or no equipment, and where equipment was needed, people could make use of what was lying around. Some of their activities were cooperative in makeup and required the assistance of one or more partners. Other activities were more individual in nature but were performed within social settings. An element of humor often spilled off onto those watching and left everyone laughing. The games that I have chosen to share with you are some of my favorites, since they have a special twist of cooperation, challenge, or humor.

- *Sealskin Skipping (Inuit Skipping).* This is one of the best games I've come across in a long time. It is challenging, exciting, and fun. The skipping rope used by the Inuit traditionally was made from either the hide of a seal or a caribou. A sealskin was stuffed with a lightweight material, such as dried grass or moss, and sewn together. The sealskin "bundle" provided an obstacle, which was at least one-foot thick, over which to jump. The bundle was threaded to the center of the rope through a hole left in the ends and then securely attached.

When using a caribou skin, the complete skin was wound around the center of the rope, like a sleeping bag is rolled up, and securely tied to the rope. You can use a

Inuit Skipping with caribou hide

store-bought rope (if you're out of caribou!) between 15 and 18 feet (5 and 6 meters). Wrap a blanket, a sleeping bag, an old coat or winter vest around the center of a rope and tie it securely with ribbon or rope to produce a very simple and effective Inuit-style skipping rope.

The object in the center of the rope poses an interesting obstacle for all involved to overcome. A jumper has to jump much higher and duck more often. A turner has to use a lot more energy to get the rope spinning smoothly. Interestingly enough, this game is played mostly by teen-age boys and young men, although females also enjoy it.

As a first step in learning the game, place one person on each end of the rope and try to get the rope spinning. Then have a jumper skip as in normal jump-rope skipping. Once you've got that down, you are ready for the Inuit version.

In the Inuit version the rope continually changes direction. The game may sound complicated but stay with it because it's worth it. The rope turner swings the rope to his right in a pendulum fashion (up to about shoulder height) and then back down under the jumper's feet to the left and all the way over the jumper's head. The rope continues under the jumper's feet again in a pendulum fashion to shoulder height on the turner's left and then comes back down and towards his right under the jumper's feet and all the way around the jumper's head. The rope continues to change directions in this fashion:

Up (to the right), down, and over
Up (to the left), down, and over
Up (to the right), down, and over
Up (to the left), down, and over

The jumper must not only skip over the rope but also continue to face the skin *at all times*. Assume you are the jumper. Stand near the center of the rope facing the skin. The rope is swung away from you in a pendulum fashion up to a level in line with your chest. As the rope comes back down, jump over it and do a half-turn in the air so that you are still facing the skin when you land. The rope continues up and over your head. As it reaches the top of your head, do a little jump and half-turn so that you are still facing the skin. The rope will continue down in front of you, and you jump over the rope doing a half-turn in the air so that you are still facing the rope. The rope continues up to chest level in a pendulum fashion. As it comes back down, jump over it doing a half-turn in the air so that you are still facing the rope when you land. The rope will continue up over your head. Repeat the same sequence so that you *always* face the skin. If it sounds too complicated, I've found that going through the actions in slow motion with two people moving an imaginary rope is a very effective way of learning the skills involved.

As you become more proficient at the game, the turners can speed up the pace or make unexpected changes in directions. Jumpers and rope turners rotate positions on a regular basis.

• *Mouth Pull.*   This one is sure to stretch your mouth out of shape temporarily; but it is just as sure to evoke lots of laughter. It used to be played during times of celebration. To begin the game, choose pairs and sit (or stand) side by side next to your "mouth mate," with arms slung over each other's shoulders. Lift your arm off your mate's shoulder and gently slip one of your fingers into her mouth. She will do the same to you. You are now in a "ready position." Each of you pulls on the other's mouth trying to get the other to turn her head in the direction of your pull. The strongest mouth wins: As soon as one person ceases to resist by freely turning her head, the game is over. It's time to sit and enjoy watching someone else. If you have just been cutting fish or seal meat, it is much appreciated if you wash your hands before beginning. It's important to play this game gently, of course, since the object isn't to enlarge someone's mouth permanently!

I came up with a cooperative adaptation of Mouth Pull that is guaranteed to get some laughs. After first thinking of the game, I walked out of my office into the living room and asked my wife if she would try something with me. She gave me that look of "What now?" We sat down next to each other side by side. I put my arm over her shoulder, slipped a finger into her mouth, and asked her to do the same to me. I told her our objective was to stand together without using our free hands. We could,

Mouth Pull

however, pull on the inside of each other's mouths to help get up. She suggested that both of us cross our legs and rock up. That one was a bit difficult, but we laughed a lot in our futile attempt. We then tried what I had imagined when I first thought of the game. Each of us extended one leg out straight and tucked the other leg in tight, with the heel of that foot touching the buttocks. We rocked back and forth, "one, two, three," and up we came on one foot, each using each other's mouth to maintain balance. The game brought us a few moments of pure fun that sparked up the entire day. I think it would be a great game for a birthday party, particularly if played directly after eating chocolate cake, when the fingers are still sticky with irresistible icing.

• *Butt Bump.* This is another good one! Two partners stand back to back with their own legs together, with their behinds about six inches apart. The official Inuit measure is taken by one partner's placing his thumb on his own behind and his stretched-out little finger on his partner's behind. Without moving feet or looking back, partners both try to nudge each other off balance using only their butt. Most often both people end up off balance and laughing. Try it a few times in a row, and be sure to take turns doing the butt measurement.

• *Mush Mush.* I first played Mush Mush with a group of young Inuit in the Northwest Territories in 1978, and everyone howled with laughter. Since then I have played the game with friends and colleagues in a variety of settings, even in hotel rooms at conference sites. The game is not totally cooperative, but what it lacks in cooperation, it makes up for in fun.

You need at least ten people to make this work—sixteen is ideal. The people sit in a circle with their knees bent and their feet flat on the floor. The heels of their feet should be about a foot and a half (46 cm.) from their buttocks. The inside of their knees should be together, and the outside of their knees should be touching the outside of their neighbor's knees. It's beginning to sound complicated but it really isn't—this arrangement just allows enough room for a person to stand in the center of the circle but still camouflage a glove that is passed around the circle under the legs.

Choose one player for the middle, and then begin passing a glove around the circle; when the center person first gets inside the circle, he shuts his eyes for a few seconds to give the seated people time to "hide" it beneath their bent knees. For diversion and musical accompaniment, all players sitting in the circle beat the palms of their hands on the floor as the glove is passed around. After a few moments, the center person opens his eyes and tries to locate the glove. The seated people work to get the glove into the hands of someone seated directly behind the center person. If they are successful in doing so, this person swats the center person on the rump with the glove (amid roars of laughter) and quickly puts the glove back under her legs and passes it on. She must be able to complete this whole maneuver without being seen and caught by the center person; otherwise she switches places with him. The center person usually shuffles around in a small circle while searching for the glove. He's generally a little bent over trying to get a better look, a position that makes his rump a protruding target. If at any point he sees the glove and points to the person in possession, a switch takes place.

A three-swat limit means no one remains in the center too long. If the center person has still not located the glove after the third swat, he simply chooses the next person to go in the center. He usually chooses the person who whacked him the hardest. It's a fun game and the Inuit play it in a very skilled manner. (Note: When played with less than ten people, the gaps between legs are too big and too little space is left for the center person.)

• *One-Foot-High Kick.* This is a classic traditional activity that was played during celebrations in days gone by. A small piece of sealskin, which could be raised or lowered, was suspended from the ceiling of a large igloo to serve as a target. The kicker took only two or three steps (due to the restricted space), jumped off of both feet at the same time, kicked the target with one foot, and then landed on the same foot with which he kicked the target. The jumper had to maintain his balance on the one-foot landing for the jump to be totally successful. The target was raised or lowered to meet people's jumping ability. The game usually ended with the target at a height that two or three people could reach. It was not carried on to a "highest jumper"

Toe Jump

conclusion. We don't know how high the Inuit jumped in the past, as they never kept records, but today some of the agile young men are reaching heights of over 8½ feet (259 cm) on the one-foot-high kick. We are told the hunters used to jump much higher.

I watched children on Holmon Island play this once; they seemed to break into groups of two or three spontaneously. One partner held her hand as a target while another kicked. I kept hearing "This high" echo from every corner of the tundra. "This high" was a request by the jumper accompanied by a hand held out at the height she wanted to jump. Her partner then held out his hand to serve as a target at the requested height. They constantly adjusted the original height of the target to ensure some success and maintain challenge. Children jumped, then held their hand as a target, and jumped again, taking turns, until the moment seemed right to run up the hill in search of snowbirds.

• *Toe Jump.* This is an example of one of those uniquely Inuit games that houses a twist of humor. You have to try it to see what I'm talking about. Take off your shoes, squat down, and grasp the toes on each foot with the hand on the same side. By extending your bent knees, try to jump forward as far as you can, landing in balance, without letting go of your toes. I'll bet you don't go more than three inches on your first attempt . . . but you will laugh and make others laugh—and you'll improve. It is quite a sight to see a group of people attempting to move across a room in this manner.

For added challenge and fun try the Tandem Toe Jump with a partner. Partners stand side by side (like in a three-legged run), squat down together, and jump at the same time. Here's the clincher. With his outside hand, one partner grasps the toes on his outside foot but his inside hand grasps the toes of his partner's inside foot. Partners may or may not have to cross their inside legs. A little coordination and trust are needed to get this one together. Do you think it's possible with each partner using only her outside leg?

• *Butt Hop.* This one's always good for a laugh no matter where you play it. Sit down with your knees fully bent. Spread them slightly, placing your arms on the inside of your legs. Grasp your toes, gently lift your feet off the ground, and try to balance on your butt. Once you've got that, try to hop on your behind by quickly extending your legs. The challenge is to stay balanced, maintain your toe grasp, and not let your heels touch the ground while you hop. Players can hop in any direction they want and can see how many times they can hop without losing their balance. Beginners should start on nice, soft ground!

If you think you're getting pretty good, consider trying the double-barreled Butt Hop with a partner sitting beside you. Everything is the same except you grasp the toes of your partner's inside leg and she grasps yours. You don't have to cross legs, but you do have to cross arms to get a hold of your partner's toes.

• *Knee Walk.* In this one you really do try to walk on your knees, but first you have to be able to balance on them. Kneel down on the grass or ground, keeping your back straight. Lift your heels toward your rump, and grasp each foot in front of the ankle. You should now be balanced on the top of your kneecaps. See if you can move forward a few knee steps. To start, make it a little easier by grabbing the back of your pants leg instead of the front of your ankle. You can try this one with your partner too. Just get side by side and grab your own ankle with one hand and your partner's ankle with the other. See if you can figure out a way to do the Knee Walk in a small group.

• *Iglagunerk (Laughing Contest).* This game was played during social get-togethers, for example, when a group of people gathered in one of the igloos. Each player faced a partner, generally holding each other's hands. At an agreed-upon signal everyone began to laugh. The partners who laughed the hardest and longest were declared the winners. Because laughter is so contagious, people sometimes ended up rolling on the ground.

• *Inuit Circle Pass.* For this game a ball was made out of sealskin or caribou hide and filled with sand. The ball was usually about 3 to 4 inches (9 cm) in diameter, but any size will do. To play the game, players kneel in a circle and pass the ball around from person to person with a flat, open hand (palm up). When first learning the game, use two flat hands side-by-side rather than one. It's a lot easier. The object is to move the ball around the circle as rapidly as possible without actually grasping it. It can also be attempted with more than one ball at a time.

An alternative version of this game is to choose partners, then scatter the pairs around the circle so that no two partners are next to each other. Partners continuously bat (or pass) a ball back and forth to each other only. The fact that other partners are doing the same thing at approximately the same time results in some humorous happenings.

- *Missittanguah (Window Jump).* This game used to be played on the inside surface of an ice window in an igloo. You can also play it on a frosted-glass window or clear blackboard. Three small dots were made on the window with a warm fingertip (use a wet fingertip for placing dots on a blackboard). Each dot was a couple of inches from the next, one above the other, each at least a few inches higher than the player's height. Players took turns jumping up to try and place their tongue as close to a dot as possible. The mark left by the tongue told the story of one's accuracy. Sometimes two bone or wooden handholds were stuck into the wall of the igloo just below the ice window so that players could pull themselves up. The height of the dots was determined and adjusted by the players themselves.

Inuit Gymnastic Activities

- *Inuit Blanket Toss.* In the first *Cooperative Sports & Games Book*, I introduced the Blanket Toss, which has been played among the Inuit for thousands of years. Here are some further ideas about introducing this activity into other cultures.

First you have to find (or make) a safe blanket for tossing. Regular bed blankets are not safe—they are too small, the grip is poor, they can tear easily, and they "give" too much in the middle when a person lands in them. In that you probably do not have access to traditional materials such as walrus or caribou hides, I would suggest you buy the strongest canvas material or rug you can find. (The walrus and caribou also prefer that you use something other than their skins.) Lightweight synthetic materials that are currently used to make trampoline beds would also be good. Gymnastic supply companies such as Nissen, American, and Speith Anderson could probably supply information on the availability of this material.

Inuit Blanket Toss

The blanket should be roughly circular and 10 to 12 feet (approximately 3½ to 4 meters) in diameter, that is, as wide around as a regular trampoline bed is long. Smaller blankets could be used for younger children, as long as they are tossed in a very gentle fashion on their seats (or feet) and not too high (from a few inches to a few feet). It is important that the people doing the tossing have a secure grip on the blanket. For this purpose, loops can be sewn around the outer edge of the material so that a sturdy rope can be threaded through them. This provides for a secure handhold for the twenty-five to thirty people who spread themselves around the blanket, shoulder to shoulder.

When first learning to toss, it is probably a good idea to toss an object rather than a person. Doing so will give the tossers a chance to learn how to work as a unit in tossing and catching. It is important that the tossers on all sides of the blanket exert approximately equal force and that they are capable of moving quickly in all directions, in case the tossed person takes off on an angle. Once people have learned to toss and move as a unit, the blanket toss is probably safer than a trampoline because there is no danger of landing on a metal frame and little danger of landing on the floor. While you are in the air the blanket can be moved under you, if the need should ever arise. Another safety advantage is that you stop after every toss; a trampoline's continuous rebounds can make you lose control.

The person being tossed should stand directly in the center of the blanket, with legs straight and slightly apart. Begin with a few gentle tosses that send her only a few inches off the surface to start. This will allow her to get the feel of the blanket at her own pace. If she takes off the blanket in a perpendicular position (that is, not leaning forward or backward), she will have the best chance of landing directly back in the center of the blanket. When she wants to go higher, she simply tells the tossers "A little higher, please." When landing on the blanket, the catchers should "give" with her weight to ease the landing. It is best to try to land either on both feet (legs slightly spread) or in a seat-drop position (that is, on your behind with both legs extended out in front).

For most groups, tossing a person a few feet in the air will provide all the thrill and excitement desired. For gym clubs and similarly skilled groups, virtually all stunts that can be done on a trampoline (from a two-foot takeoff) can be done. Inuit youth are now doing back somersaults and double-back somersaults above the blanket, but you have to have a lot of practice for this, and so it's probably not a good idea to try such stunts, unless you have a qualified instructor. For added safety, overhead spotting belts, which are currently used in gymnastics, can be attached to the person being tossed on the blanket. They virtually eliminate the possibility of injury.

It is interesting to note that at the last Northern Games Festival, which I attended in 1980, the blanket was used as a safety net. It was held under participants in rope gymnastics who performed stunts on a horizontal rope about 15 feet (5 meters) in the air.

- *Walrus Pull.* This is a game that helped develop the strength and skills necessary to pull a big walrus out of the water. It is also a clear demonstration that many people working together are capable of accomplishing feats that one cannot accomplish alone. To play the game you need a long, thick rope and some stationary object, which the "walrus" props himself behind. Traditionally one person (the walrus) stationed himself behind a large boulder on the tundra and wrapped a rope behind his back and under his arms. He propped his feet up against the boulder to try to prevent the people on the other end of the rope from pulling him out from behind his perch. An element of progression in the pulling let the walrus attain success in the beginning while the people working together would win in the end. First one hunter would grab the end of the rope and start pulling. One by one more hunters would join in the pulling, until finally the group would pull the walrus straight up and out from behind the boulder. It was likely that they would all fall backward laughing. The game is best played outside where large rocks lay on soft tundra. However, you can also play it by perching behind a tree or a large rolled-up wrestling mat.

- *Four-Man Carry.* It's hard to believe one person can carry four others—but I've seen it done! It is very important to have a solid base—level ground or a platform— so that you can balance and walk supporting the weight of others. So it is with Four-Man Carry. One person stands firm with feet slightly spread. Four others stand around him: one on each side, one in front, and one in back. The two "side" people

Four-Man Carry

wrap (or hook) their arms around the base man's shoulders (near where the arms connect) and by holding onto him ease their weight off the ground together. The front and back people then extend their arms over top of the inside part of the base man's *shoulder* (near the neck) and by holding onto each other ease their weight off the ground (see photo above). The base man walks as far as he can. If you try this, start with two light people, then move to four.

My father used to do a similar carry in our family acrobatic act, a little more dramatically but with the same idea. My mother stood on my father's shoulders while my two sisters, brother, and I perched ourselves on my mother and father. My father then walked around supporting the weight of the whole family in the air. "Now that's what I call holding up the family," the announcer used to say.

• *Inuit Pole Tilt.* You'll need a sturdy pole about 12 feet (4 meters) long to play this game. Place one end of the pole on the ground; the other end is held a few feet off the ground by two or three people (supporting it) at an angle of about 30°. One at a time the other players try to kick themselves over the pole. To do this you stand beside the leaning pole with your back to those supporting the pole. You bend over and grasp the low end of the pole with both hands (one in front of the other), just above where the pole rests on the ground. You then move your weight to your hands and kick your feet up and over to the other side of the pole, as if you were kicking your feet up to do a handstand or a mule kick. Your feet extend in the direction of the supporters. If all goes well you will land in balance on your feet on the other side of the pole with both hands still holding the bottom of the pole and your back still facing your supporters.

The angle of the pole is progressively increased (for example, from 30° to 60° to 90°), making the challenge more and more difficult. When the pole approaches a perpendicular position (almost straight up and down), the player, after grasping the bottom of the pole, must kick through an upright handstand position to get his body over to the other side.

I was pretty proud of myself for getting over in a perpendicular position. I was sure that must be the limit. The Inuit smiled and moved the pole beyond perpendicular to an angle of about 105°. I ended up on the floor, and we all had a good laugh.

• *Eskimo Stand-up.* This one starts in a double push-up position. The bottom person lies flat on the floor, face down, with his hands in a push-up position. The top person lies on top of him in the same position. He slips his hands under the bottom person's armpits and grasps his own hands at the back of the bottom person's neck. This is known as a "full Nelson" in wrestling circles. Once in this position the challenge for the bottom person is to stand up and for the top person to keep his body straight and rigid. Those who are unsuccessful can try with a lighter partner or backpack. Those who are successful can try standing up without using their hands to push— elbows and forearms are OK—a stunt known as Nikivittuq in the eastern Arctic.

• *Three-Partner Pull-over.* Two partners (supporters) stand about two feet apart, facing each other with legs slightly apart. Each clasps his own hands together securely with fingers (or thumbs) interlocking. The hands are held palms up against the body just above the belly button. A third partner sits on the floor in between the two supporters and grasps their clasped hands, in the same way he would grasp still rings used in gymnastics. He then chins himself up and pulls his legs over his head so that he ends up in a standing position on the floor. He can start with bent legs and later keep them straight, which is much more difficult.

The pull-over can also be done with the two supporters grasping the bottom person's arms just above the elbow. Each supporter wraps both his hands around the arm on his side, and the bottom person then attempts to pull his legs over. If a person needs help getting his legs up and over, an additional helper bends down, puts his hand (or arm) under the bottom person's legs, and lifts.

• *Eskimo Push-up.* One person (bottom person) lies down on his back with his feet stretched out straight on the ground. His elbows are bent and tucked into his sides so that the back of his hands are on the floor next to his shoulders. The palms of his hands face up so that his partner (top person) can step onto his open hands. The bottom person grasps each of the top person's feet securely and pushes up until his

Eskimo Stand-up

arms are straight. He then lowers his arms to the ground and pushes up again as many times as desired. The action is similar to doing a bench press except there is no bench and no barbells.

To help the top person stay in balance, a third person (helper) can straddle the waist of the bottom person, face the top person, and give him his hands for support. The helper can also stand in this same manner holding the two ends of a stick (for example, a broomstick) so that the top person can grab the stick in the center. The bottom person can also help by raising his legs so that the top person can grasp his feet for support. The top person can also help the bottom person by jumping gently to ease the lift-up. With a little practice the top person and the bottom person can learn to work together to stay in balance without assistance. For more resistance, get a heavier partner; for less, find a lighter one.

Stick Stunts

For the next three games you need a strong stick about the size of a broom handle. The stick is held by two people (carriers), each of whom supports one end by bending her arms at the elbows so that her hands are held slightly higher than her elbow. The stick rests across the top of her forearms just at the bend in the elbows. She grasps

Eskimo Push-up

the palms of her own hands for added stability. A third person then performs stunts on the stick.

Partner stunts that involve carrying a person for a distance can be done either in a straight line or a circle. In the case of a circle, everyone faces the same way and carries the partner around the perimeter of a large circle at the same time in an attempt to get everyone back to their own starting point in the circle.

• *Bent-Arm Stick Carry (Two Arms).* Two people support a stick, as described above. The third person sits on the ground, grasps the stick with both hands, and pulls himself off the ground by chinning up. He keeps his knees bent and is carried forward by the two people holding the stick.

• *Bent-Arm Stick Carry (One Arm).* This is similar to the two-arm carry except that the bottom person grasps the pole with one hand (thumb facing the body) and grasps his own wrist with his other hand. He then chins himself off the floor and is carried until he begins to tire and lowers himself to the ground.

There is also another method that I find easier. You slip the hand by which you intend to hang over the top of the pole and flex your wrist so that you are actually hanging from a wrist-hold. Your free hand then grasps your own wrist just below the pole, thus providing additional support.

• *Toe Carry.* In the Toe Carry, the person being carried lies on the ground on his back and extends his feet into the air so that he can hook his toes over the top of the stick. When he looks up from the ground he can see his toenails as well as the bottom part of the stick. He wraps his arms around the back of his own bent legs and sometimes grasps his own hands together. To lift himself off the ground, he begins to flex his angles by pulling his toes toward his shins and then pulls on the back of his legs with his arms. He is carried in this position until he drops—gently of course.

Northern Games Festivals

In an attempt to preserve and rejuvenate some of the traditional values of the Inuit (Eskimo) and Dene (Indian) people, Edward Lennie and Nellie Cournoyea spearheaded a movement in the Canadian Arctic that began in 1970 and continues today. It is known as the Northern Games.

Each year groups of Inuit and Dene people from across the Canadian Northwest Territories gather together to share traditional skills, crafts, games, stories, dances, legends, and goodwill.

In 1980 the residents of the remote settlement of Uluksaktok (Holmon Island) hosted the games. For Holmon it was the greatest onslaught of people in its history. The two hundred or so visitors more than doubled the population of the entire settlement.

Local men, women, and children worked together to set up a tent village that housed most of the visitors. They shared their fish, caribou meat, seals, and good company, much as was common in the past. The whole atmosphere permeating the games is part of the hidden curriculum of the Northern Games.

Traditional games were characterized by simplicity, spontaneity, acceptance of all participants, and total involvement. When you live the life of a participant—eating and sleeping in a tent village and taking part in the events—you find this is still very much the case.

A prearranged schedule of events is distributed but never closely followed. Real starting times spread by word of mouth through the tent village just as events are about to begin. You need time to clean and cook your fish or to cut your caribou, you need time for good company, you need time to play spontaneous, impromptu games in your tent, and you need sleep after being up until six in the morning.

Who in their right mind would let a schedule interfere with that?

The twenty-four hours of daylight that shine over the games also dramatically affect one's sense of time. Children, parents, and grandparents all stay up dancing and watching others dance through the light of night. There really is no night, only a tired time that you fight and to which you finally succumb, resting until you feel rejuvenated

Tea-Boiling Contest

enough to begin again. Moonlight was also considered a joyous playtime for all ages—not to be shut away by preset sleeping rituals.

The Good Woman Contest is a unique and popular part of the Northern Games that, if adapted, could have great potential for many other groups and cultures. It focuses on the many skills and talents that are necessary for the survival and well-being of the family and community. The Good Woman is able to perform skillfully a variety of traditional activities, such as building a fire, making tea and bannock (bread), cutting fish, plucking geese, skinning seals and muskrats, making clothing and crafts, and dancing. A Good Woman also demonstrates and lives important traditional qualities, such as hospitality, kindness, generosity, and humor, at home and over the duration of the Games. A woman with inner beauty who is well versed in the practical skills of living is a most valued woman. Superficial qualities sought out in "beauty contests" elsewhere are notably avoided.

In the Tea-Boiling Contest, groups of approximately eight middle-aged women of all shapes and sizes line up awaiting the signal to start. Over and above their talking, giggling, and laughing, the starter bellows "Go!" They run, leap, and waddle to a wood pile and begin clutching at the wood, amid roars of laughter. The fires are quickly ignited without the use of paper, and the pots of tea are soon simmering on the fire. When one woman has trouble getting her fire going, another contestant offers her some wood while uttering, "What's wrong with your fire?" The other woman responds, "I dunno!" Another woman, who has difficulty getting her water to the

Inuit children at the Northern Games

boiling point, laughs heartily while repeating, "Just about boiled!" The woman who finishes first starts to dance, while other contestants stop to joke with her. As each remaining woman lifts her simmering tea from the fire, she offers it to everyone around, sometimes emptying her pot before getting to the locally recruited "judges." The Bannock-Making Contest, which also takes place over an open fire, is similar to the Tea-Boiling Contest in terms of harmony, enjoyment, and sharing. It is more important to the women to share their tea and bannock and to have people enjoy them than it is to have them judged and declared the best.

The sharing of food, dance, and festivities among *all the people* was a common occurrence during gatherings in the old days. Games were a way of bringing people together, more for joy than for contest. This tradition continued on Holman Island when all the women in the village prepared a feast of geese and bannock on the final evening of festivities. Since acceptance as a worthy human being is in no way dependent on placing in an event, people were free to enjoy themselves and one another. Cooperative people can bring a special kind of orientation to a game that makes it constructive rather than destructive. Likewise, cooperative play and games can bring a special orientation to people, freeing them to be more human.

play among aboriginal children: games from Papua New Guinea

Naomi Martin, the daughter of a high tribal chief of the Hanahan society, returned to the village of her youth to study the traditional play of the children, known as Hakokopeits. It was informal and noncompetitive and served as the basis for learning about aspects of adult life (from gardening, to food sharing, to marriage, to the value of cooperating).

As part of their traditional play, children went out to the garden early in the morning and brought back food to the oldest people in the village. They also went out to fish or collect nuts and shared their "catch" with their families. Sometimes this was acted out in an imaginary way; other times it really took place. The process was said to help young children learn to respect and share with others.

Parents respected children's play as a valuable and necessary time for learning about life. It was viewed as essential for children, as was work for adults. They also respected children's premonitions acted out in play. For example, if a child "played" weeping for a dead person, they would often say that someone would die soon in that village or in a nearby village.

In Hakokopeits, the whole group was boss. Children (boys and girls) played together and wandered in groups on their own. No parents were physically present. Parents never worried about what time kids came home. They never had to worry about something bad (for example, serious conflicts among the kids) happening, since the children had been taught from an early age to take care of one another. Often the kids would be gone (off playing) all day long.

With the introduction of school (which had a Western format and curriculum), much of this natural learning and group harmony began to break down. With all the older children in school, the younger children in the village had no older children with whom they could play and roam. Often it was only grandparents and very young children who remained in the village.

There is no word for "winning" in the Hanahan language. In traditional Hanahan culture, winning and losing did not exist. If people did something well, it was simply said or acknowledged that they were able to do the skill. The important thing was to participate and to develop your skills. Participants simply tried to learn the skills of the game. "If they could not do something, others would help them learn to do it."

Traditional games in the North Solomon Islands are similar to those of other aboriginal cultures I have studied in that there are no officials, no boundary lines, no specialization, and no exclusion. As pointed out by one village elder, "A child was never excluded from the group."

Lots of spontaneous and creative free play takes place in the village square, in the water, and on the banks of the river. The kids played beautifully in the rivers, running along the banks, swimming, diving, laughing, jumping off cliffs, volleying nuts back and forth with an open hand, and chasing one another.

I noticed a big difference in how the children played on the school grounds and along the river. The kids were much freer and more open away from the teachers and the school environment. Their interactions were much more playful and creative. There were more smiles, no matter what game was being played or what they were doing. For example, the kids would not dance on the school grounds but did so willingly next to the river. Even the melodies of their songs were more joyous and louder in this context.

A great deal of affectionate physical contact took place among the children in almost all informal settings. Often a group of five or six children left the play area, walking along with arms draped over one another's shoulders. They also wanted to touch and handle babies and were allowed to do so. In any activity that might have been dangerous, the older children cared tenderly for the little ones, helping and protecting them.

Sinaki is a very small jungle village hidden away alongside a small river in the

Free play in the downpour

Konga area of the North Solomon Islands, where I have witnessed some of the most beautiful free play ever. During a tropical afternoon downpour, the children ran out into the rain with their hands outstretched to the sky, squealing with glee and then ran back under the protection of a corner of the thatched roof. They darted to and fro individually, then in pairs, then as a group with all village youngsters joining in.

The children became most excited when they played directly under the sloping corner of the roof where the water poured down like a waterfall. The falling water held them spellbound, and often they simply held one another and jumped up and down in total bliss. Their black skins glistened as they frolicked in mudholes, slid down small trenches, and fired sticks (canoes, I imagined) down small, fast-flowing water gullies.

The freedom to be allowed to go out into mud puddles, to run naked, unrestricted by clothing or adult warnings, surely heightens the spirit of play. The children can play when the moment is most receptive, whether in a storm or under a full moon. Preplanned, preorganized play in predesignated areas never seems to have quite the same quality. There is only the "now" in play and if the "now" is missed, the spirit is lost.

Children grow and play in constructive ways primarily because of the people around them. If we are considerate toward children, if we respect their rights to play, if we encourage their natural tendencies to share and cooperate, and if we are able to protect them from a regular diet of destructive models viewed in real life or by means of television, then their play and overall interaction can unfold in a joyful, cooperative, and considerate way in all cultures.

The play of these children is free from constant adult evaluation and threat. They do not have to worry about dirtying their clothes—they often don't wear them—or about breaking things or about marking up the walls—there's nothing irreplaceable to break and no beautiful walls to mark up. In addition, there is no need to worry about electrical outlets, onrushing cars or trains, or suspicious people lurking around, since they are nonexistent. This frees not only children but adults, too. There is practically no adult intervention in children's play and no structured organizations that require children to specialize or play by adult rules. The children make most decisions on their own and create many of their own play opportunities. In industrialized societies adults often plan children's days and lives, with children having very little to say.

If I take my daughter out to eat in North America, she is expected to sit quietly and wait (like an adult), even if there are all kinds of interesting objects and areas and people to explore. Strapped in a chair and outfitted with a bib, she isn't supposed to dump the sugar, stick her fingers in the honey, or bang her plate. She cannot play. Pretty boring for a one-year-old.

Now if I take her out to a village feast in Papua New Guinea, none of these restrictions are placed on her. The villagers don't expect children to sit quietly for an hour while orders are taken and adults chat. Children are free to do what is natural for them, thus eliminating potential hassle for everyone. My daughter can explore. She can sit on the ground, spill things, and eat with her fingers. She can play to her heart's delight, and she doesn't have to worry about getting dirty because we can just dip her in the river. Wherever she roams someone—whether a child or an adult—keeps a considerate eye on her. Everyone accepts some responsibility for helping children grow in constructive ways whether they are "yours" or not. It's an unwritten agreement of multiple parenting—and a relief for both parent and child.

The vast majority of traditional Siwai games are cooperative in nature; the few that are competitive in makeup always end with cooperative rituals. I have selected those traditional games that I found most interesting to share with you.

• *Makii (Spinning Top).* Two teams are formed. One team lines up any number of coconut shells, together with their own tops, as targets. One after another, players from the other team each attempt to hit those targets with their spinning tops; each time a target is hit, it is removed from the area of play and that player has another throw. If she misses, her turn for that round (or inning) is over. However, if a subsequent player on the same team hits the target, anyone who had previously

Unused fern scoreboard

Scoreboard after Team 1 has thrown and hit four targets

Scoreboard after Team 2 has thrown and hit five targets

missed has an extra throw. One whole team throws first, then all the targets are replaced and the other team begins throwing.

Score is kept with the help of a fern scoreboard. Each time a member of Team 1 hits one of the targets, three-fourths of one leaf extending from the fern is snipped off. Team 2 then takes its turn spinning at the targets. Each time a target is hit, the remaining one-fourth of one fern leaf is removed. If more points are scored than there are remaining quarters of leaf, then three-fourths of the next leaf is pinched off.

The main purpose of the fern scoreboard is to keep track of the difference in score, not the number of points scored or which team is leading. The teams try their best to score equal points, and a fern that is free from broken leaves (after all members of both teams have thrown their tops) designates a tie game. As one village elder expressed it, "If there is a difference in the number hit, the other team will try harder to be equal." What the players are after is to be equally good, without sacrificing their skills.

It requires considerable skill and some luck for both teams to end the round with an equal score. Doing so often means spinning a top into the midst of many targets without touching any. If the score is even and one player still hasn't thrown, she has to throw at the cluster of targets to miss. If the score is unequal at the day's end, the fern is put away somewhere, perhaps slipped between one of the interlocking bamboo slats in one of the village houses, until play is resumed another day. When players regroup to continue play, the team composition is often different, but the goal of equality remains the same.

Pao Poo'

• *Pao Poo' (Who Will Hide?)* Pao Poo' is a game of hide-and-seek played in the moonlight by boys and girls. All the children gather in the center of the village to play. One child is chosen to be a seeker. She gets down on her hands and knees on the ground and hides her eyes. Another child (the tapper) is chosen to direct the hiding chant. He gently taps the back of the seeker with an open hand. As he does so he chants:

> Tontoku pai pao pio
> Simolomo Tama Toki Tong
> Pao Poo'

When the tapper sings, "Pao poo' " ("Who will hide?"), the seeker sings out the name of one of the children. For example, she may say, "Anuku poo'," which means "Anuku hide." At that moment Anuku runs and hides. The tapper then repeats the entire chant and the seeker calls out another child's name. This process continues until all the children's names have been called out. If the seeker does not know all the names or does not remember who has not yet been called, the tapper simply says, "You haven't called so and so yet."

Once all the children have hidden, the tapper, who directed the hiding chant, walks around the seeker saying, "I'm still going around you" ("Ko koto no ko kai Ru Moinong"). He then runs and hides. Once he has hidden he makes a loud shrill sound like a possum ("Whoooo!"). All the other children make the same sound from their hiding places, signaling the seeker to come looking for them. The hiders remain silent from then on, unless the seeker has trouble finding them.

Anyone who is found then helps look for other children who are still hiding. If after looking for some time, they still cannot find someone, they simply shout, "We can't find you." At that point the remaining hiders come out. The game continues in this manner, with children rotating between the roles of hiders, seekers, and tapper.

When the children begin to get sleepy before going home to bed, they share the milk of fresh green coconuts, which have been collected by some older children during the day. It was not uncommon to see three young children drinking from a single coconut with the help of homemade straws (reeds), one of which was slipped into each of the three natural soft spots in the top of the coconut. Pao Poo' was often played several nights in a row, when the full moon shone bright. Following the final night of play, everyone took part in a feast, which both children and parents helped to prepare.

Several elements within Pao Poo' give it a cooperative orientation. First, there is the game component, which requires that every child playing be known by name to every other child playing. This is built into the game structure by the need to call out the name of the child who will hide next. Second, roles rotate between hiders, seekers, and tapper, who directs the chant. There is a role reversal within the game, wherein hiders, once caught, join together with the seeker. Lastly, there is a cooperative ritual (that is, sharing the coconut milk) among all players at the end of each game and a village feast at the conclusion of the last game each month.

• *Singu.* This is the most popular game played by the young girls in this region today. It is a juggling game played with a piece of coconut shell and two kukuinu nuts. The nuts are almost perfectly round and have a hard smooth outer shell. Wooden balls the size of golf balls work well as substitutes for those who do not have access to kukuinu trees. A small piece of coconut shell is cut so that it fits snugly into the palm of one hand when the fingers are bent. Seashells also work equally well and are often used. For city slickers, the bottom part of an appropriately sized spoon (stainless steel, wooden, or plastic) can be used as a substitute. The outer part of the shell faces up and is used as a hitting surface when juggling. The piece of coconut shell or the intact sea shell can be held in either hand, but for simplicity of description, assume that it is in the left hand.

To start the game, hold the shell in your left hand with your palm facing up, and place one nut (the left nut) on top of the shell. Hold another nut (the right nut) between the thumb and index finger of your right hand.

To begin the action gently throw the right nut into the air so that it will land on the shell in the left hand (making a "click" when it lands).

While the right nut is still in the air, quickly reach over with your right hand and grab the left nut out of the palm of the left hand. This brings you back to the starting position, except the nuts have changed hands.

Singu

Toss the left nut straight up in the air above the left hand. While the nut is still in the air quickly bring the right hand across to the left and tap the shell in the left hand with the right nut. This makes a "click."

Catch the nut that has been thrown straight up in the air on the shell in the left hand (making a "click") and move the right hand back to the starting position. You should have a nut in each hand. This completes one cycle. The same cycle (or more complex variations) are repeated many times in a row. You can make up your own patterns, too, with different clicking rhythms. For this simple version, the rhythm should sound like "click," "click click" ("one," "one two").

Once players can do this simple version of Singu, two lines with equal numbers of players are formed. Each player kneels down, facing a partner in the other line. A distance of about three feet (one meter) is left between partners. All players start the juggling action at the same time and repeat the cycle previously outlined three times in a row. In the middle of the third repetition of the juggling sequence, partners exchange nuts this way: Instead of throwing the left nut straight up in the air (as is done in the individual version), you throw it across to your partner. As this is done, bring the nut in your right hand across quickly to tap the shell in your left hand. Catch the nut that is thrown to you on the shell in your left hand as your right hand moves back to the starting position.

This sequence is repeated over and over with all players trying to maintain the same rhythm and attempting to exchange nuts at the same time. The players, especially beginners, sometimes count out loud as each cycle comes to an end (for example, one, two, three) to help them keep in time. The distance between the lines can be short for beginners and increased as the players improve. Singu can also be played while sitting, kneeling, or standing in a circle. In this case, when the nuts are exchanged, each player throws the nut to the person on the left and receives a new nut from the person on the right.

Singu is often played to reduce the boredom of waiting for turns in "modern" games. The nuts and shells are shared around, with many girls using the same ones over the course of the day.

There is an interesting story behind this game. In the Konga region it was originally played by women to give the men good luck when they left the village to settle tribal disputes. The fast and agile movements of the nuts was thought to be transmitted to the men, thereby giving them extra quickness to dodge any oncoming spears.

Apart from "protecting" the man, the game was effective in combating boredom while the men were away. It requires considerable skill and there are countless variations to hold one's interest and challenge for very long periods of time. The women often made up new versions as they played. The game also holds the attention of young babies extremely well because of the constant movement and clicking sounds of the nuts.

The Mandok people have still another version of Singu, which is called Takong Kong and is also played by females. The players sit in a circle and sing a song as they juggle in unison. In the song they go through the names of every family member of the participating players, starting with the eldest and ending with the last born. It's a good way to get to know all your friends' family members.

● *Eikai Pakai.* This game is named after an insect frequently found in young banana trees in this region, which moves up and down like a spider doing push-ups. To play the game a group of people huddle together closely and connect their hands in an attempt to imitate the actions of the insect. Each player grasps the back of someone else's hand by gently pinching the skin between the thumb and index finger. A vertical column (or chain) of hands is formed in this manner; it can go as high as people can reach and as low as people can go. It helps if the smallest people form the bottom part of the column. Once the giant eikai pakai is formed everyone moves their hands up and down in unison as they chant:

>Ei-kai   pa-kai
>Ko-ke-kai   pa-kai

This complete verse, accompanied by the continuous up-and-down hand action, is repeated four times. At the conclusion of the fourth repetition, the players shout "To-

Eikai Pakai

ma-to k-e-sau" ("The rope is broken") and shoot their hands toward the ground, releasing their grip. The game ends in laughter, and its sole purpose is to bring people together for enjoyment. In case you're wondering, "kokekai pakai" is another name for the same insect.

• *Komari Kong Kong (Possum Crawl).*   Kamari Kong Kong is another game played to make people laugh. It is played in pairs. One player holds one of his partner's hands and lets the fingers on his free hand walk slowly up his partner's arm. The finger-walking action represents a little possum slowly crawling up the arm. Then all at once the little possum jumps into the armpit and scurries around, giving a quick tickle.
    The following words accompany the action in the game:

Komari kong kong.	(The little possum is crawling.)
Hisuki kong kong.	(The little possum is crawling.)
Nappa nappa kong kong.	(The possum is crawling.)
Ongi tungoro kana!	(He goes up into there!)

    The first three lines are spoken slowly as the possum crawls up the arm. The last line is blurted out loudly and quickly as the possum suddenly jumps up into the armpit. Everyone, including anyone standing around watching, usually ends up laughing. After one partner has played the part of the little possum, partners switch roles. The game is particularly good for older children or adults to play with very young children.

- *Ihihna Pohophna (Hopping).*   This is another good game for the beach. First a few people make a large ring in the dirt or sand by turning their toes slightly inward and shuffling from foot to foot around the circle, plowing the dirt (or sand) out to the side with every step. The area of pressed-down earth should be about 6 to 8 inches (15 to 20 cm) wide. The players then stand on the ring of patted-down earth, face the same direction, and begin to hop around the circle on one foot. They can hold onto each other in a chain, if they like. The objective is to hop around the circle a certain number of times without landing outside the patted-down area and without putting the other foot down. The children themselves decide how many times around the circle will be set as a goal (one, two, or three). All the children who make it back around to where they started the specified number of times (without touching their foot down and without going out of bounds) are winners. In this game there are opportunities for multiple winners or even total group success. In addition, those who do touch their foot down still continue to hop.

   In an interesting extension of this game, the ring is widened and the children move around the circle in pairs. This can be accomplished by standing side by side and tying the ankles together on the inside with a very soft rope or with thick cloth. Young children can move around the circle in a three-legged fashion; older kids try to keep their inside feet off the ground.

- *Kuhai.*   This is an interesting unstructured activity wherein groups of children have fun clomping around on the halves of coconut shells. The two halves of a cleaned-out coconut shell are placed on the ground. The round part of the shell faces upward and serves as the top of the "coconut clomper." One-half of a shell is used for each foot. A homemade rope is put through a hole in the top of each half-shell and secured on the inside with a knot. Step onto the shells, and hold the other end in your hand—it serves as a rein to hold on to while walking and helps keep the coconut shell on the foot when lifting the leg to take a step. Large juice cans, soda cans, or sturdy pails also make good clompers. This is lots of fun when done in pairs, with two people sharing three clompers, or in trios, with three people sharing four clompers.

- *Huuring Huuring.*   This is a game of diversion that was designed to replace little children's tears with pleasure. It is also a story about the life cycle of plants. A column of hands represents a plant about to go to seed. As each seed falls off (a finger is removed from the top of the column), it is soaked in water (the finger is placed in the mouth), and then planted (finger is placed under the armpit). The bent arms moving up and down represent the growing cycle. Older children play this game with their smaller brothers and sisters, and parents sometimes play it with young children. The

Kuhai

Herekeepaitu

song that accompanies the action can be either a traditional song (see below) or one that the children make up themselves.

The game starts by each player pointing both of her index fingers into the air. Players grasp one another's index fingers by making a fist around them (keeping one finger pointed), so that a vertical chain of hands is formed. At the very top of the column, someone's index finger points into the air. Young crying children join in by simply being asked to "Put one finger up like this" and showing them. Babies can get absorbed in watching the action and listening to the chant that accompanies the game. An older child usually directs the action and chants the verse. He keeps one of his hands free. Once the chain of hands is formed, he begins a rhythmical chant and moves the index finger on his free hand back and forth to the beat, gently touching the finger sticking out at the top of the column of hands. When he does this, the small child who was crying often starts to laugh. Each time Phase 1 of the song comes to an end, the child directing the action points at the finger sticking out of the top of the column. The person who belongs to that finger takes her hand off the top of the pile, puts her finger in her mouth, "pops" it out, and then puts that hand under her nearest armpit.

Phase 1 of Huuring Huuring Song

VERSE	ACTION
Huuring Huuring peng peng to	The child directing the action moves his finger back/forth— back/forth back/forth—back/forth
Rikonapu kapukapu	back/forth back/forth
Pokonapu kapukapu	back/forth back/forth
Terei huma!	Remove that finger from the column of hands.
Kopuwai Kopu	Put finger in mouth. Pop it out; then place hand under armpit.

Phase 1 of the song is repeated in its entirety until everyone has removed both hands from the column and put them under their armpits (like chicken wings). The child directing the game also plays out all the actions. Since there is no one to brush the top of his finger on his free hand, he swings it back and forth, touching it on his own thigh before placing it in his mouth and under his armpit. He does this in rhythm with the chant and is last to do it. Once all hands are placed under the armpits, all the children sing Phase 2 of the song as they move their arms up and down (like chicken wings) in time to the music.

Phase 2 of Huuring Huuring Song

VERSE	ACTION
Makoko ma kao kao kao	Move arms up and down like chicken wings.
Huso koko ma kao kao kao	Move arms up and down like chicken wings.
Makoko ma kao kao kao	Move arms up and down like chicken wings.
Huso koko ma kao kao kao	Move arms up and down like chicken wings.

Humorous variations can be added, including checking under a neighbors armpit to see if the "fruit" is ripe or everyone's grasping the earlobes of people on either side while swaying back and forth. They end the game laughing. Extended versions of this game also include the "harvest" and even cooking and eating the "food."

Competitive Games with Cooperative Endings

• *Siikori.* This is a tag game played in and around the deep water channels of the river, where the children can jump off the cliffs into the water. What is special about this game is the way it is brought to a conclusion.

When everyone agrees to end the game, the group comes together and one child touches every other child. As she touches each one, she says, "Doko no peromo," which means, "I take it from you." She then touches a special tree, which has a sticky red sap under the bark. This is done to make sure no one leaves the game feeling bad. It is a way of sharing any bad feelings by taking "it" from everyone and putting "it" into the tree. Other similar rituals carried out to *end* tag games include all counting together, "One, two, three," and throwing "it" to the tree. If playing in water, some groups chant "One, two, three" all together and slap the water. The spirit, anxiety, animosity, or whatever else may ail a person is thereby collectively put to rest.

In the tag games themselves, the children run and chase and squeal but never so far away or so hard that one person is "it" for more than twenty or thirty seconds. Original tag games were played in groups, as was the case with many traditional versions of hide-and-seek. (Many individual versions introduced from the outside are played today.) The children used to split informally at some midpoint, and one player took it upon himself to start chasing the others. He had to try to touch (tag) someone on the other team. When he did, the newly tagged person had to try to touch someone on the other fellow's team. If a tagger got tired, he could pass on his tag to a fresher teammate, who willingly accepted "it."

The ritual involved in ending the game seems to indicate that some wise ancestors recognized that bad feelings could sometimes surface in competitively structured games. The ritual was an effective way of dealing with these feelings and preventing them from lingering on after the game. It was apparently more a preventive measure based on the concept of reciprocity than something that grew out of children's conflict within the game.

To use the Siikori concept in Western societies, we could begin by talking with children about the possibility of bad feeling arising in certain kinds of games. We could then have them act out the Siikori ritual at the end of competitive games to put all bad feelings to rest. When children go through the motions of physically removing anger or bad feelings, the chances of it really happening are increased.

• *Herekeepaitu.* This is an arrow-shooting game, which used to be played by all the unmarried boys and also by men. Today it is rarely played. Traditionally the players began by informally dividing themselves in two teams. To start the game, a player from Team 1 shot an arrow on a sharp angle into the ground to serve as a target. A player from Team 2 then shot his arrow at this target arrow, trying to break it. If his shot was successful, another target arrow from Team 1 was shot into the ground, and another member of Team 2 shot to break it. If his shot was unsuccessful, Team 1's target arrow was pulled out of the ground and a member of Team 1 shot at Team 2's arrow, which remained in the ground. The game continued in this manner, with players taking turns trying to shoot their arrows through the target arrow in the ground. The game was sometimes played for several days or even weeks in a row.

An interesting aspect of this game was the way in which it was brought to a conclusion. With bows and arrows in hand, both teams hunted possum together for a shared feast. On one day both teams hunted in honor of one team, and on another day all hunted for the other team. In both cases all players shared the hunt and the eating of the possum. The arrows that had been successfully broken in the game were used to burn the fur of the possum, a first stage for cooking it.

The final ritual involved cooperation and shared enjoyment among all players on both teams. As one village chief said, "It's just to make sure that people are friendly."

Village Games from Lahara Students

I played the following games with some summer-school students at the University of Papua New Guinea. All of them were teachers from various villages spread throughout the land. When we went outside to play and share our village games, two things struck me: First, we had absolutely no equipment; either none was required (except other human beings) or playthings were picked and/or adapted from what was in immediate reach (for example, small stones, sticks, trees, pieces of paper). Second, almost all the games involved singing and chanting. It doesn't take a gymfull of equipment to have a good time!

The concept of multiple winners and inconspicuous losers surfaced in many of the games played. In one such game, one player stood at the top of a hill and rolled (or in some cases threw) a coconut down the hill. Players lined up on the slope of the hill and threw spears (or rocks) at the coconut, trying to hit it as it went by. Many players hit the target (multiple winners). However, no one ever kept score, and in most cases the players were too busy throwing their own spears to notice or worry about who in particular hit or missed.

• *Spearing (With Little Sticks).* We had to improvise a bit to play this game, as most of us had left our spears at home. Someone crumpled a piece of paper into a ball and stuck it onto the end of a small tree branch about fifteen feet above the ground. The branch remains attached to the tree and a few friends help lift you high enough to place the ball of paper. We then picked up as many little sticks (spears) lying around on the ground as we wanted. Pencils, chopsticks, or broom handles would work equally as well. Each player could go as near or far away as he wanted from the paper-ball target to throw his spears. People threw at will, and often several people threw at the same time. We formed a very rough semicircle in front of the target so that no one was on the other side in the path of missed throws. Finally one little "spear" knocked the paper ball down and everyone cheered. Normally men played this game with a fruit target very high up a tree and used spears about three feet long.

• *Gemo (Peiai).* This is a very interesting, fast-flowing game of directional change, which requires good observational skills. Two trees about 150 feet (50 meters) apart were used as goals. They can be further apart or closer together, depending on how hot it is, how much shade there is, how many trees are around, and so on. Two teams of approximately even numbers are formed by simply splitting in half; about eight to ten people per team is good. One team defends a high tree (or post), and the other team defends a low tree (or another post).

The game starts with a player from the low trees calling out "Gemo," (which identifies the person carrying the spirit). She then tries to run to the high tree to touch it without being touched by members of the opposite team. If she is touched, the person who touches her now has the Gemo, runs in the opposite direction, and tries to touch the low tree. The Gemo is instantly transferred from one team to the other the moment a person is touched by a member of the opposite team. If a player is successful in touching the opposite tree, a point is scored. Each team has a "tree keeper" (or goalkeeper), who stands directly in front of the tree to prevent players on the other team from touching it with the Gemo. When a tree keeper touches an opponent to prevent him from scoring a point, he too gets the Gemo and runs toward the tree at the other end of the field.

Only one person carries the Gemo at any one time, and no one can interfere with or block another player's path, other than by touching him to transfer the spirit. Touching the tree is difficult, though not impossible. We tried our best to get to the tree, but score was not kept, nor was it important.

It's as if a spirit that automatically transfers upon touch is being carried. You touch a person, catch the spirit, and try to take it to your tree. You are touched, the spirit is transferred, and the person who touched you tries to take it to the other tree. Whether you view the Gemo as a spirit or an imaginary ball, the game results in a continuous free flow of action back and forth between the two teams.

- *Wok Tali Wok (Walk Round and Round).* This is a semicooperative game with elements of both cooperation and competition.

Outline two circles 9 feet (3 meters) in diameter about 75 feet (25 meters) apart. We used clothing to mark the circle roughly. One circle is designated a sitting circle (in our case, a shaded area under a tree) and the other a standing circle. One person is chosen to be the chaser. The other players (for example, seven to ten people) stand inside the standing circle while the chaser walks around this circle chanting, "Wok tali wok." At their own discretion, the players inside the circle try to run to the other circle and sit or squat down inside it, without being tagged by the chaser.

Once all the players have either gotten to the sitting circle or have been tagged while making their attempt, the second round begins. Those players tagged in transit join the chaser on the next round, and all walk around the sitting circle saying, "Wok tali wok." The players inside the sitting circle jump up at will and make a mad dash back to the standing circle. It's much more difficult to move untouched from the sitting circle because you start from a seated position *and* there are usually additional chasers (those caught on the first round). The play goes back and forth between the two circles until everyone has been touched, a process that usually doesn't take more than two or three rounds. It's a game full of energy and laughter among chasers,

---

those being chased, and even those being caught. It requires considerable strategy to enable some of your teammates to get to the other circle.

- *Finger Guess.* A small seed, chip of wood, or stone is used for this game. One player places the seed between her cupped hands and shakes them up and down. She then clenches both hands into separate fists, with the seed hidden and lodged under one finger. She extends her hands, knuckles upward. Everyone makes one guess as to which finger covers the seed by simply touching a finger. More than one person can choose the same finger, as guesses are totally free. Once all guesses have been cast, the player rotates her hands so that her knuckles face the ground and opens her hands, and we all see where the seed lies. Several people can win at the same time. Since everyone is involved in every round and no guesser is singled out or made to feel bad, choosing incorrectly is not an issue. No one worries about it because the game is played in a warm social setting for fun.

Village Games from Other Sites

The games presented in the following section represent a scattering of games played in several different cultural regions of Papua New Guinea. They were provided primarily through the work of Pensa Roleasmalik and Naomi Martin, both of whom have been studying their native peoples' games.

BEACH AND WATER GAMES

- *Tukapohowat.* Between ten and twenty children can play this game, either in the water or in the soft sand on the beach. First they form a "whale" by lining up behind one another in a standing position. They then bend at the waist, lean forward, and hold onto the hips of the person in front of them. The last player in line (tail of the whale) then crawls slowly over the back of the whale to the front of the line. The next tail of the whale then crawls over to the front and so on, until all players are back where they started.

- *Sopet.* This game is played by Ponam Island children in the shallow reefs near their village, usually in groups of four or five. Players try to imitate the traveling patterns of the dolphin. First they line up either behind one another in single file or shoulder to shoulder. Then, on a signal, they dive in and out of the water in unison, trying to keep in line and synchronize their movements like a school of fish.

• *Wali-Wali.* You can play this game in the water or on the beach, if you're careful. Two parallel lines are formed; players face a partner in the opposite line. Partners join together by grasping their own left forearm with their right hand and grasping their partner's right forearm with their left hand. One of the lighter people in the group lies on his back (head first) at the start of the column or platform of arms. He is gently tossed up and down so that he moves down the column to the end of the line. He is then tossed off of the column by the last few people in the line in a way that allows him to land on his feet. For children it's a fun game to play in shallow water, particularly the last part, where you are tossed off the end and must somehow get your feet under you. If playing on the beach or ground, it is best played with older people strong enough not to drop anyone. Having spotters at the end of the line to catch a person is also a good idea in the beginning to ensure that no one gets hurt when tossed off the end.

• *Wol Wol.* This is a spinning game that is played on the beach, in shallow water, or in the village square in many New Guinea cultures. About eight players spread out, stretch their arms to the side, and spin themselves around. A signal is given a few minutes later, at which time players must instantly stop spinning and try to remain in a standing position. This free-flowing game is a contest with gravity (the ground). Those who can remain standing are said to be in line with gravity; those who fall into the water (or to the ground) lose to the pull of the earth. Lots of people can win, and it's all done in good fun.

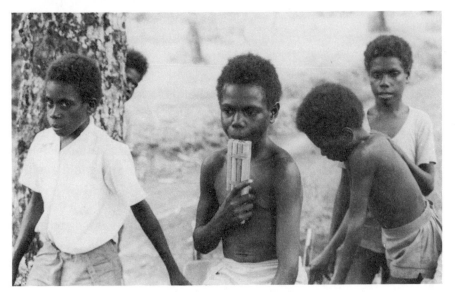

Playing on a homemade flute

LAND GAMES

- *Lam Selelele.* This is a very gentle "pretend" game of a Mahuake parent showing her infant the "moon floating in the sky." The game is played by the little girls and boys, but only during the night when the moon is bright. The children divide themselves into partners, one of whom acts as the parent and the other as the infant. The "babies" lie with their heads in the laps of their "parents," looking up at the moon. The parents raise one hand and point at the moon while everyone sings a song associated with the game. At the end of the song the "parents" lower their hand and gently rest it on the forehead of the "baby." It's a game that encourages young children to act out the caring for infants.

- *Salan Lalai.* This is a game of giving and sharing that was played by Buka women while the food was being cooked. The players sat in a circle with two coconut shells in front of each of them. In rhythm with a song, each woman picked up one shell in each hand and moved them one place to her left. Thus the coconut shell that started in front of the left hand was placed in front of the right hand of the person on the left, and the coconut shell that started in front of the right hand was placed in front of her own left hand. This continuous rhythmic picking up and clunking down of shells often continued until the food was cooked. The number of times the coconuts were passed around the complete circle was sometimes used to tell when certain foods were ready. You can use other, handier objects and pass time while waiting for anything.

- *Ver Ver Aras Lama (Taking Coconuts).* A large center circle is outlined on the ground, and four smaller circles are evenly located outside it. Five coconuts (or balls) are placed in the center circle, and one player stands in each of the four outside circles.

  When the game begins, each of the four players tries to get three coconuts into his circle. He can take the coconuts from the center circle or from another player's circle, but he can carry only one coconut at a time. Players are not allowed to guard their coconuts, and the coconuts must be placed (not thrown or rolled) in their circle. Although the structure of the game is competitive, the rules result in a continuous-action game that rarely has a winner. As soon as one player gets too many coconuts, the other players quickly remove them for a more equal distribution. By being aware of the other players, they can in fact work together to keep the game going until they get too tired and decide to stop.

- *Buka Game of Courage.* This game was played in the pitch dark of night. A group of children huddled together around a fire. One child took a burning ember to a special place (such as the burial grounds), placed it in a certain spot, and returned.

The group was told where the ember was placed. Another child then went out and moved the ember to another spot and returned to tell where. The game continued in this manner, with each child having a turn at retrieving and replacing the ember.

In order to accomplish the task, players had to overcome the fear of walking through the jungle alone in the dark of night. Fears were usually related to the belief in evil spirits. Games such as this were designed to develop children's courage. They were not intended to remove belief in evil spirits but rather to help children realize that they could deal with the spirits. If played with partners as well as alone, this would be a good game to demonstrate how sometimes doing something with a partner is much more pleasurable than doing it alone.

Papua New Guinea string games

more co-op games
from other cultures

Malay Games

In virtually all traditional Malay games, playthings were created or adapted by the players. Games ended when all players decided it was time: Predetermined playing times with preset breaks were unknown. There was a mixture of competitive and cooperative games. Penalties for "losing" competitive games were as mild as singing a song, doing a dance, pulling out a hair from an eyebrow, or being carried by the arms and legs and deposited anywhere the others decided, all of which usually produced laughter among winners and losers alike.

- *Sepak Raga (Kick Basket).* Sepak Raga is a traditional Malay game that in its original form was completely cooperative in structure. It is still a very popular game among Malay schoolchildren. A group of about six players form a circle and kick a ball in the air back and forth among themselves. The objective is simply to keep the ball from hitting the ground for as long as possible. Occasionally players count the total number of times the ball is kicked or hit. More often than not they just play the game (without counting), while creating different ways to kick the ball around the circle (for example, kicking it very high to a person across the circle, kicking it quickly to the person on the left or right using either the inside or outer edge of the foot, bouncing the ball twice on top of the foot and then making a looping pass, and so on). The ball can be hit or caught with the knees, feet, head, shoulders, or chest, but the arms and hands are not used.

The Malaysians use a very light ball about the size of a large grapefruit. It is made from rattan, which is the same material used to make wicker chairs and baskets. Traditionally the balls were made by the players themselves from the long tough stems that grow on climbing palms. Today the balls are still very inexpensive and can be bought in any Malay sporting goods store. If you are interested in getting one you can probably order it through the Ministry of Sport in Kuala Lumpur, Malaysia, or through your local sports shop. Another option is to use a similar sized, light, sturdy ball made of another material (for example, a sponge ball). One advantage of the wicker ball is that it does not bounce when it is caught on the foot before making a return kick. Yet when the ball is kicked hard it will soar high into the air.

Children and adults still play this game with creative and skillful maneuvers in the villages, streets, and courtyards of Malaysia. The number of players, the distance between them, and the manner in which they return the ball are all very flexible, and the variations add to the continued enjoyment of the game.

- *Main Sepak Bulu Ayam.* This is a game for at least two players; any number above that can play. Like the previous game, the object is to keep something up in the air by alternate kicks—but instead of a ball, a large feather shuttlecock is used. The feathers look like the large stiff quills with which people used to write. They generally come from the wing or tail of a cock. About four of these feathers are tied together and pressed through the center of a small wicker ring (or a coin that has a hole in the center). The points of all the feathers as well as the ring are then wrapped in cloth and tied securely, providing a soft surface for kicking. The quills are also sometimes fitted into the center of a thick wad of paper or rubber about 2 inches (5 cm) in diameter.

Before starting, the players agree on the maximum number of kicks each person can take before passing to another player. The first player tosses the feather shuttle into the air and starts to kick it, using the inside of his foot, the top of his foot, or his knee. Passes are made from the foot of one player to the foot of another. Although the Malaysians use feet only, the game could also be played with open hands. This game is also played in parts of China.

• *Sepak Takraw.*   An interesting adaptation of Sepak Raga has become Malaysia's national game, Sepak Takraw. It is played with a rattan ball on a badminton court, with three players on each side of the net. All contact with the ball is made by the feet and body, but many of the actions are similar to those used in volleyball. These include an overfoot serve (like an overhand serve in volleyball), foot spikes (like hand spikes in volleyball), and high foot blocks (similar to jumping arm blocks in volleyball). It's a fast moving and exciting game that requires a great amount of skill and agility. The game is generally played in a competitive fashion but can also be played for a cooperative outcome by using collective scoring, an "all-touch" rule, and so on.

• *Pana.*   This game is played by the Bidayuh youth of Sarawak during the clearing of the forest for farming. While clearing the land, the young men set aside some of the hardest wood to make sticks for the game. The sticks used for play are about 18 inches (45 cm) long and 5 inches (13 cm) in diameter. Each player needs one.

You need an open area about 44 by 20 feet (6.1 by 13.4 meters) (or about twice the size of a badminton court), with a hard and even surface for playing the game. A rectangular target area about 24 by 14 inches (60 x 35 cm) is scratched into the ground near one end of the playing area. A throwing line about 12 feet (4 meters) from the target area is scratched into the ground on the other end of the target area.

Pana can be played either competitively or cooperatively. For the cooperative version, several target sticks are laid down on the ground within the rectangular space. The number of target sticks is approximately equal to the number of players. Players throw other sticks, either one after another or several in unison, at the pile of target sticks to try to knock them out. Once everyone has thrown, players go and retrieve their sticks and begin throwing again. Target sticks are "retired" once they are hit out of the circle. If all target sticks are hit out, they are all replaced back in the circle. If a player's throwing stick remains within the rectangle, a teammate must hit it out (that is, rescue him) before the player can use it again. The object of the game is to knock all the sticks out of the target area in as few rounds as possible.

The competitive version is usually played by two teams, each with six or more players. One team lays all its sticks in the target area. The other team throws its sticks, one at a time, trying to knock the others out. All players on one team throw to complete a round, and the throwing occurs in random order. If a player's stick lands in the target area, it stays there until a teammate knocks it out. The throwing team is awarded a point if all the sticks inside the rectangle are knocked out in a single round, and it also earns another throwing round. It continues to throw until it fails to clear all the sticks in the target area in a single round. At this time the teams switch roles. The game continues until the players decide it is time to stop.

- *Memutar Pinggan (Plate Spinning).* The object of this group game is to keep a plate spinning. The players sit or kneel in a circle, leaving a large empty space in the center. One player spins a plate on edge in the center of the circle and calls out one of the other player's names. The player whose name is called attempts to catch the plate before it falls down. He then spins it again and calls out the name of another player. Depending on the player's skill level, she can stop the plate completely and then respin it, or respin the plate without bringing it to a stop. Don't use a china plate till you've had a lot of practice! This is a popular game among Melanau and Bidayuh children and young men in Sarawak.

- *The Penang Game.* In this popular board game, players use fruit seeds as markers and move them around the board. The object is to get a marker around to the finish line. I was most interested in the creative use of "dice"—four cowrie shells were used, but any empty seashell will work. The four shells are thrown in the air and assigned "moves" as follows. If all four shells fall with their openings upward, the player takes four moves plus an extra throw. If either one, two, or three shells land with their openings upward, the player takes one, two, or three moves, respectively. If all four shells fall with their openings downward, the player moves his marker eight times. To speed up the game, more shells can be used or more moves can be assigned to each of the shell-falling positions. This game is an example of how natural, readily available materials are turned into play implements and adapted by the players to meet their own needs.

PLAYDAY—MALAYSIAN STYLE

The People's Games were organized in conjunction with National Sports Week by the National Unity Board, a government organization charged with improving relationships among the three major cultural groups in Malaysia (the Malaysians, the Chinese, and the East Indians). They amounted to a big outdoor playday for factory workers from sixteen of the largest factories in Malaysia. The games that were played were low-key activities geared for fun. The guidelines to which they complied were that they be safe, require a low level of skill, be inexpensive, and allow for the greatest amount of participation. Most of the games played were semicooperative in nature in

Malay Balloon Bust

that each team worked as a unit but was judged against other teams. The games were played in good fun, and no one seemed concerned about scores or who was ahead.

A few examples of the games played are presented here.

• *Terompah Gergasi (Giant Sandal).*   Six leather straps (footholds) are screwed into long wooden planks 2 inches by 4 inches by 10 feet (5 cm by 10 cm by 3 meters). Six people slip their feet through these footholds, which look like giant sandals. With their right foot in one "sandal" and their left foot in another, the participants place their hands on the shoulders of the person in front of them and shuffle along as a unit. Moving forward, backward, sideways, or over an obstacle can provide plenty of cooperative challenge. For indoor sandals, two strips of carpet, cloth, cardboard, or towel, one for each foot, can be used. Small groups of players can stand on these makeshift sandals (with or without loops) and attempt to shuffle along the floor.

• *Mengisi Air Dalam Tong (Bucket Brigade).*   For this game a large container is placed at a central point on the field and filled with water. Groups of six people each form lines that extend out from around the container like spokes on a wheel. Each group is given a plastic bucket that is filled by the person in the center and passed down the line from person to person until it reaches the last (sixth) person. She dumps the water into an empty oil drum (or barrel) and passes the empty bucket back up the line. The bucket brigades continue in this manner for about five minutes, amidst a good amount of laughter and ample opportunity to be cooled off by splashing water and falling buckets. The amount of water in each oil drum is later measured with a stick. This can easily become a cooperative game if the amount of water all the groups move in the allowed time span is measured collectively.

• *Meniup Dan Memecah Belon (Balloon Bust).* This was probably the funniest game played during the entire day. Women line up in groups of six, facing a row of chairs about 80 feet (25 meters) away—one chair for each group. The first woman in each group runs to her chair, blows up a balloon, sits on the balloon to break it, and then runs back to the starting point. After she returns, the second woman runs to the chair and repeats the same process. I remember seeing one streamlined woman speed to the chair, quickly blow up her balloon, and then spend several minutes trying to bounce her balloon into submission. It just didn't want to break! An alternative way to play is for partners to run down in pairs, place the balloon between them and "squeeze" until it pops, and then run back.

Maori Games

"Rehia" is Maori for "pleasure." Traditionally all games and pastimes were known as "nga mahi a te rehia" ("the arts of pleasure").

Traditional Maori children (from New Zealand) engaged in a great deal of enjoyable group play, nearly all of which was accompanied by short songs, jingles, and chants. Many activities, including skipping rope, were done in groups. Even the name for the skipping games ("piu") reflected the importance of others. "Piu" refers to the swinging action of the rope (generated by the two children turning it) rather than to the actions of the jumper(s) in the middle.

Some of the more common Maori games and pastimes engaged in by various age groups are outlined here.

• *Tititorea (Maori Stick Games).* The Maori play a variety of games using sticks slightly thicker than a broomstick and about 18 inches (45 cm) long. In these games, two or more players tap their sticks on the ground and against other sticks and they toss the sticks through the air to make exchanges. Tititorea games were almost always played to the beat of music or accompanied by chants. They were often played in a circle (or in two lines), with players moving sticks up and down and tossing them across the circle in unison. The games were played by both males and females.

Maori Stick Games

To get you started, here is the simplest version shown to me by my Maori friends. Take two sticks and find a partner who also has two sticks. Kneel across from your partner so that you can look directly at her—you should be about 4 feet (1¼ meters) apart. Hold one stick vertically in each hand, so that you can tap the sticks together without crunching your fingers in between them. The sticks are usually held lightly with the thumb on one side and fingertips on the other. If the sticks are thrown in a lobbing motion they are easier to catch. Partners discuss and agree on a way of exchanging sticks to avoid mid-air collisions.

Part I: At an agreed-on signal (for example, "one, two, three—go!"), tap the bottom of both your sticks on the ground at the same time as your partner ("down"). Then tap your own sticks together in front of your chest twice in succession ("tap, tap"). Repeat this first sequence three times in a row (that is, "down—tap, tap"; "down—tap, tap"; "down—tap, tap").

Part II: Tap the bottom of both your sticks on the ground once ("down"); then tap your own sticks together once ("tap"). Following this tap, make a mutual "exchange" by each tossing the stick in the right hand to your partner—you'll catch the stick she's thrown in your right hand. Make sure the sticks are tossed at the same time and that they maintain a vertical position in the air. Repeat this second sequence eight times in a row alternating exchanges by tossing first with the right hand, then with the left, then with the right (that is, "down—tap—right exchange"; "down—tap—left exchange"; "down—tap—right exchange"; and so on up to eight).

Part III: Again, tap the bottom of both of your sticks "down" on the ground. Then "tap" your own sticks together once and follow up with a two-stick (double) exchange. In this exchange the sticks in both the right and the left hand are tossed vertically to your partner at the same time. One person tosses her sticks "narrow," on the inside, toward the center of her partner's chest. The other partner tosses his sticks "wide" on the outside, toward his partner's shoulders. Catch one stick in each hand. This third sequence can be repeated as many times as desired until the music stops (that is, "down—tap—two-stick exchange); "down—tap—two-stick exchange; ad infinitum).

This version of Tititorea (all three parts) is played to a three-beat rhythm (that is, "*one*, two, three"; "*one*, two three"). The rhythm gets faster and faster as you get better and better. This tends to hold the challenge and increase the excitement. As many players as you want can line up facing one another, all tapping and tossing in unison. There is no limit to what some creative input can do with respect to new stick sequences and exchanges. Have your groups make up some of their own versions.

- *Ti Ringa (Ti Mati-mati).* "Ti" is the name of a tree that was said to change its position in a magical way. "Ringa" means "hand." Ti Ringa is a fast-action hand game with a Follow the Leader format and many versions. In one, two players place themselves opposite each other and go through a very rapid series of finger or hand movements. Player 1 makes a specific movement of his choice and shouts, "Tahi (one) mati-mati." Player 2 tries to repeat the same movement and shout so quickly that the two players' actions seem to be simultaneous. Player 1 then rapidly makes a second movement of his choice to the shout "Rua (two) mati-mati," and Player 2 tries to follow, as before. This process continues until the numbers one to nine have been called out followed by the chant "Mati-mati." The shout that accompanies the tenth and last movement is "Piro mati-mati." Maori children become so skilled at this game that it is difficult for observers to know who is leading and who is following. It doesn't matter what kind of movements are used as long as one person tries to follow the other.

When playing this game, in addition to making quick finger and hand movements, players often swing their arms around, slap their thighs or chest, and jerk both hands up and down and from side to side.

One version of Ti Ringa involves a continuous change of leader. For example, Player 1 makes the initial movement that is instantly copied by Player 2, who then immediately does a second movement, and so on. In another version, Player 1 makes several movements in a row and Player 2 stands opposite him trying to anticipate his next movement so that they do it simultaneously. At that point Player 2 takes the lead, and the game goes back and forth in this manner. The new leader's action begins by slapping both thighs and shouting, "Ti" or "Mati-mati."

• *Poi Rakau.* Players stand in a circle with one player in the center. Each player has a light stick in her hand about 36 inches (90 cm) long. The players throw their sticks at the center person, who catches them one by one or two by two and throws them back to their owners. If the center person misses a catch, the thrower takes her place in the center. This practice helps ensure good throws. It was considered fair to throw only as many sticks as the center person could catch. The game is played to the beat of a song, which is sung by all the players. To simplify matters, throwers behind the center person's back can shout "Hi-ya" as they throw.

In another version of the game, players kneel in a circle. Some of the players begin without sticks, thus allowing passing of sticks around and across the circle between those who have sticks and those who do not.

In still another version, the game is played in a circle (or in two lines about ten feet—three meters—apart), with each player throwing her stick with the right hand and catching an incoming stick with the same hand.

• *Punipuni.* Perhaps this was the original source of the game Aura. One player (stationary person) holds out his hand with the fingers spread wide apart. A second player (seeking person) stands several feet away, closes his eyes, spreads his fingers, and tries to interlock his fingers with those of his partner. Maori children played this game with the stationary person keeping his eyes open and the seeking person keeping his closed. To make the game even more challenging, play it with all eyes shut. To make it easier for young children, the stationary partner can move his hand to help make the connection.

Australian Aboriginal Play

It was a physical beginning, without words. One of the first things the children did upon my arrival at one of the last remaining tribal aboriginal settlements in the Australian outback was to touch me. These people still follow tribal customs and have no form of permanent shelter. On our first desert outing, rabbits were skillfully caught and roasted and traditional dances were shared. One little boy in particular captured my attention as he wandered playfully, to and fro. He was one of the first to be given a chunk of freshly cooked rabbit. He waddled past my six-month-old daughter, stopped, glanced over at her, and then came back to hand her his meat. The boy was barely two years old. Later in the day he played catch with several other children and me. Whenever a new player wandered into the game, he was sure to roll the ball to that child the first chance he got.

Small groups of barefoot kids ran free in the desert brush. Golden behinds and stringy blond hair flashed in all directions. No mother called her child back from her playful explorations. A small aboriginal school was in operation in the region that I visited, and I was asked to teach there for "at least a week." I gladly accepted because of my belief that doing things with people is the quickest and best way to get to know them. I shared my games with the children, they shared their games with me, and we created some games together. Through a series of shared play experiences, the first touch grew into an intense feeling of rapport in a very short time. I was most impressed with the children's gentleness, creativeness, and willingness to share.

I discovered very quickly that these children love to throw things. They will throw anything at almost anything, but moving targets are especially motivating. They are

Sharing the playful spirit in Australia

very accurate in their throwing skill and use it as a means of hunting small game. I can vividly recall the time when a group of about twenty aboriginal youngsters formed a complete circle around one of the few water holes in the area. They stood ready, with arms cocked, waiting for a duck to surface for a breath. The moment its head broke the surface a volley of rocks peppered off the water. The duck dove again and the children struck their pose again, excitedly awaiting their next chance. If it had not been for the fact that the duck's life lay in the balance, this activity may have qualified as a great cooperative game. There was total involvement toward a collective goal; the activity was exciting; kids were free to throw anything in any way they chose; hits and misses were difficult for others to assess; and there was great anticipation in waiting and wondering where the duck would surface next. These children were perfecting skills that were traditionally linked to survival and were having fun doing it, but I was pondering how this activity could be adapted for other cultures so as not to snuff out the life of a duck. Perhaps an artificial duck that pops up in an unpredictable way or a large target that is fired into the air at a moderate speed (like slow-motion skeet shooting) could be used. I discussed some options with my Australian friend and expedition partner Ian Robertson, who is well versed in aboriginal play and games. We decided to use some readily available materials and try the following game.

- *Co-op Can Throw.*   Players form a semicircle or line. Each holds an empty soft-drink can cocked in a ready position in his throwing hand. Someone rolls a ball or a hoop on the ground a few feet in front of the line and, on a signal, everyone throws his can at the ball or hoop at the same time. The collective objective is for as many people as possible to hit the ball or to put their can through the rolling hoop. The cans make a lot of noise and are easy to retrieve because they do not roll very far. Everyone is in on the action. No one is singled out for missing, and there is a common goal.

Hitting a rolling target (for example, a soccer ball, a hula hoop, or a hoop from a wooden barrel) is usually quite a challenge in itself. The size of the target, the speed at which it is rolled, the precise moment it is released, and the distance between the ball and the throwers can be adjusted to maintain challenge and meet the skills of the players. The ball or hoop can also be thrown through the air at various speeds, instead of rolling it along the ground in front of the players. The game may not be quite as exciting as the duck in the pond version, but it does present an interesting challenge that involves everyone and the kids really enjoyed it.

- *Kotaut Mina Mieta.*   In this variation, tie a target to a long rope and pull it along in front of the throwers. In Papua New Guinea a local fruit is tied onto a fifteen-foot rope or vine and dragged along the ground at a normal walking pace. A group of

Aboriginal high jumping

youngsters simultaneously throw their spears (made from a local reed) at the moving target.

In one co-op games session, the moment children were asked to find a partner, two boys spontaneously linked arms and began hopping together using only their outside feet. Naturally this became our next game. I pointed at them and smiled, making a nonverbal effort to say, "Look, try that." They did, and also generated many new forms of "that."

For high-jumping activities (off of a springy board) one child held each end of a thin pole. They continually adjusted the height to suit each child's skill level—lowering it for the smallest kids and raising it for those bigger or more skillful.

When playing basketball on a small outdoor court after school, the children were totally free of concerns about winning the game. It was a Western game governed by aboriginal values, for children and adults alike. Keeping score was never even mentioned by anyone during the hour or so we played. The game was played virtually without interference. As a player prepared to shoot, the other players cleared the way to let him shoot. After the shot was taken, a few players attempted to retrieve the ball, but they never shoved, pushed, or elbowed. In addition, no player ever chastised another for missing a shot or for taking the ball away . . . no "oohs," "ahs," or "boos." A ten-year-old girl took the ball away from me on one occasion and there were some smiles for her, but no dejection for me. If someone else came along, he simply joined one side even if doing so resulted in that side's having more players on the court than the other. When it seemed like a good time to end, the game ended and people dispersed. It is interesting to note that the kids played "basketball" on this court at recess and after school with soft-drink cans, small rocks, big balls, small balls, and so on. There were often many objects in flight toward the net at the same time. The children did not let rules or scores get in the way of their creativity or fun.

One starlit night I watched a small group of children create a new game while adults busied themselves in dancing festivities. They began by filling up tab-top soft-drink cans with sand and then spun the cans in various ways. One child spun his can in the air (end to end) trying to make it land standing upright. This became "the game"—no rules, just play. Each time a child flipped her can, more sand came out, creating a continuously more difficult challenge in making it stand on end. If the game got too difficult, they simply refilled the can with sand.

I did not see one preschool child grabbing, pushing, or fighting during a full week of observations. Playthings were shared without incident. The preschool teacher said that the children sometimes do grab things from one another, but this was rare enough to escape my lengthy observations. There was a striking difference between the few white children in the preschool and the aboriginal children. The white children spoke much louder, as if needing attention, and they plowed their way through play, as if unconcerned or unconscious about others. The aboriginal kids were much more gentle and shared everything.

Older kids take care of younger children and younger children take care of those even younger. When children are left on their own, other kids are expected to take care of them and they do—just kids with kids; kids helping other kids. This basic philosophy was acted out during recess on several occasions. On one occasion I noticed that one boy had a handful of candies. Within a few seconds, he had distributed all his candies to all the other kids in the group. On another occasion I noticed one boy with a bag of chips (yes, junk food has come that far). Another lad came over to him and held out his hand. The boy with the chips turned the bag completely upside down, dumping a large pile of chips (at least half the bag) into the other boy's hand.

The sharing of responsibilities as well as food is still a way of life with these people, particularly when it comes to children. A child can wander a few hundred feet to the next camp and will automatically be fed, and this gesture will be reciprocated when the tables are turned. Similarly, someone always seems to be around to comfort a young child in need, most often before he ever reaches the point of tears. These people live outdoors, sleep under the stars, and might be considered "primitive," at least in terms of technology. However, they are highly socially advanced, as are many such groups. The warmth and humanism I felt flowing from within these people was something very special. Without this quality, people lose their most important asset . . . their essence of life.

- *Tjampita Yaaltji? (Where's the Shaker?).* Any number of players sit in a circle. Two children are in the center. One child is blindfolded, and the other is given a shaker or a tin filled with a few stones, which rattle when moved. The blindfolded child tries to find her stationary sighted partner by following the sound of the rattle. When the two children connect, two more children go to the center. The game can also be played with both partners blindfolded or with several sets of partners trying to connect at once, each with their distinct shaker signal.

  In a variation of this game called Papa Yaaltji? (Where's the Dog?), one of the center people wears the mask of a dog, and the other is blindfolded. Whenever the blindfolded person says, "Papa yaaltji," the dog barks, until the two are able to connect. In some cases several pairs of blindfolded children go to the center of the circle and try to find each other by voice alone. One partner asks, "Nyunta yaaltji?" ("Where are you?"). The other answers, "Hyangata" ("Here").

- *Yaaltjikutu? (Where Do I Go?).* A small group of children sit in a circle, and a blindfolded child stands in the center. A flat rock or a large piece of paper is placed on the ground inside the circle. The sitting children direct the blindfolded child to the object by saying, for example, "Tjampukutu" ("To the left"), "Ngalya pitja" ("Come toward me"), or "Wati pitja" ("Go across"). When the child steps on the object, another goes to the center of the circle. This game can also be played in pairs, with partners who are holding hands seeking the object together.

Games from the People's Republic of China

At the Beijing Institute for Physical Culture and Sport (in Beijing, People's Republic of China), a group of students and faculty members joined together to produce a very interesting collection of games, samples of which are outlined here.

- *Paired Skipping.* Three sets of partners (rope spinners) line up across from one another, each holding opposite ends of a skipping rope. Enough distance is left between sets of partners to ensure that their ropes do not hit. In unison they begin turning the skipping ropes. Pairs of children (skippers) line up facing the center of the spinning ropes, holding hands or linking arms around each other. They then begin to try to skip or run through the three sets of ropes staying together, one after another. When the first pair of skippers reaches the third rope, the next pair begins with the first rope. Turners and skippers trade places when a skipper completes a run. This activity was well received by North American children and adults. It provides a fun challenge, especially when groups of more than two children skip through together.

- *Ball Pass Skipping.* This game is played in two groups of three. Each group has two rope spinners and one skipper/ball passer (each of whom rotates positions throughout the course of the game). The ropes are spun parallel to each other, about 15 feet (5 meters) apart. The skippers face each other as they jump, and they pass a ball back and forth as they continue to skip. Really good jumpers could try exchanging two balls at once.

- *Group Obstacle Course.* This is similar to a normal obstacle course except that groups of about five people link hands to go through. Hand in hand they go over a box horse, under a side horse, through a tunnel, and so on. The objective is to get everyone through the course without letting go of the handholds. Other options include groups of two carrying or transporting each other through a course, or groups of three carrying one of their members through a course. The most efficient means of transport is a group decision. Try this one through your playground equipment and jungle gym!

- *Group Hop.* About five people line up one behind the other. Each person (except for the lead person) lifts and extends her left leg so that the person in front can grab her ankle or heel. She places her right hand on the right shoulder of the person in front of her for support. Supported in this position the group then hops around all on right legs.

- *Continuous Badminton Exchange.* Four players are needed for this version of badminton. One player begins in each corner of a court (or squared-off area). No net is used. Player 1 hits the shuttle across the court to Player 2 who hits it diagonally across the court to Player 3, who in turn hits it across the court to Player 4. Player 4 then hits the shuttle diagonally across the court back to where the action first started, and the process continues. What makes this collective game very active and interesting is the following position exchange, which is integrated into the action. After Player 1 and Player 2 have hit the shuttle, they run across the court to exchange position with each other. Similarly, each time Players 3 and 4 have completed hitting the shuttle they run across the court to exchange their position with each other. It's an interesting and fast-moving game with a good collective challenge.

- *Rotation Ping-pong (Table Tennis).* The Chinese have developed a whole series of interesting rotational ping-pong games that involve player rotation in the midst of the game. One example involves eight or ten people playing around three ping-pong tables, which are lined up parallel to one another, with several feet between each. One player begins at the end of each of the tables, (as is normally the case), and one (or two) players stand "ready" at the outer edge of each of the outer tables. Three balls are played at once—one on each table. After receiving and returning the ball, the entire group of players rotates one position to the right. Can you think of some other combinations of hitting and changing places?

In 1980 my good friend Michel Villeneuve visited the People's Republic of China. When he returned he passed on the following games, which were being played by children between five and eight years of age.

- *Chinese Circle.* A small group of children join hands and form a circle. They begin to walk in one direction and gradually increase their speed until they are going as fast as possible without breaking their handhold.

A variation of this game begins with several children inside the circle. Once the circle is moving around at a steady pace, the children inside the circle try to slip out by running through the slightly raised arms of the children making up the circle. The center children have to time their escape accurately, but the circle children do not try to prevent them from getting out. Wherever possible they help by slowing, dodging, or raising arms.

- *Train Dance.* This game was played by second-grade boys and girls in the Canton Children's Palace. To start the game the group forms a circle around one child. The center child walks over to a person of her choice, stops in front of her, bows, and then jumps up in the air doing a half-turn (saying "Ah!"). The selected person then leaves the circle and places her hands on the lead person's shoulders to form a two-person train. The train goes through a series of maneuvers as the entire group sings and goes through the following actions: Skip four times, putting left hand out, right leg out, left hand on head, right hand on head. The two-person train then stations itself in front of another person in the circle. The entire train bows to the newly selected person, lets go of their hands, jumps doing a half-turn, and in unison says, "Ah!" The slightly larger train reconnects and repeats the same sequence (skipping, bowing, turning) until all children in the circle have become part of the train.

Chinese co-op playground equipment

An interesting component of this game is that the train continuously changes its lead person. This results from doing the jumping half-turn immediately after each new person is selected to be added to the train. The newly selected person begins as the last car; however, as soon as another new person is selected, the previously chosen child becomes the lead person in the train. The turning process ensures that everyone has a turn leading the train.

If you play this game I would suggest that you start with two or three children (each a leader/engine) inside the circle. Each of these children can go to someone in the circle to bow and start a train, all at the same time. This will keep the game moving (there will be less standing around) and is a safeguard against one single child feeling like a leftover box car, last to be chosen. The three trains can join together once all children have become part of one of the minitrains.

● *Dragons.*   China has always been associated with dragons. In this game a dragon is formed by a group of children each of whom links his arms around the waist of the person in front of him. The head of the dragon (first person) attempts to catch the tail (last person). If the tail is caught, he does a little song and dance for the group before the children rotate positions and begin again. The game is usually played with about ten people in a dragon and sometimes within a restricted area, say, 30 by 30 feet (10 by 10 meters).

MORE CO-OP GAMES FROM OTHER CULTURES

Cooperative Gymnastic Activities from the GDR

Every year the German Democratic Republic holds massive sports festivals that include a variety of interesting group gymnastic activities. The cooperative activities require a certain amount of trust, strength, and skill, and they probably should be reserved for teen-agers and young adults. Some of the activities also require novel equipment that could be made by small groups of people working together in either schools or workshops.

- *People Pendulum.* Two parallel lines are formed, with ten people in each line. Each person in Line 1 faces a partner in Line 2. A space of about 18 inches (45 cm) is left between lines. The two people who make up the most central point in each line (persons five and six) form a base by placing one hand on the shoulder of the person directly opposite them and the other hand on a pole that lays across both partners' other shoulders. The pole should be sturdy enough to hold the weight of a standing person in the middle. A handle from a long-handled shovel works well as a pole, and a pad over the supporting shoulder is a good idea. For each of the two sets of partners forming the base, a pole is placed across the shoulder that is nearest to the outside end of the line of people.

Once the base is secure, one person is hoisted up onto each of the two poles. They become the "people pendulums." They start by facing each other in a standing position while holding hands to maintain balance. On signal they both lean back, let go of their handhold, and fall with straight bodies into the arms of eight of their friends (four people in each line). The eight people catch each falling pendulum by grasping wrists with their partner (interlocking wrists); they should "give" slightly as the pendulum makes contact. (A securely held mat, rug, or net could also be used for the catch.) They then work together as a unit to toss the pendulums back up to a stand. As the pendulums approach a standing position, each reaches out to regrasp the other's hands. This up-and-down process is repeated several times in a row. It is the responsibility of the fourth and seventh persons in each line (those closest to the four-man base) to help the top person maintain a proper position. This is done by grasping the ankle and the back of the calf, both to help him maintain balance and to ensure that the bottom of his foot is on the stick before he is tossed back up to a stand.

I tried becoming a pendulum for an evening and found it lots of fun. It does, however, require that the body catchers who await your descent be worthy of your trust.

This game as well as others that follow can be played in shallow water to reduce the element of risk. Another possibility for young children is to have someone stand on an orange crate or soft-drink box and fall back into the waiting arms of their friends or onto a suspended mat. Gradually increase the height of the box stand as trust builds.

- *High-Bar Pendulum.* A long narrow high bar is used for this activity. The crossbar is about 3 feet (1 meter) wide, and the uprights are about 12 feet (4 meters) high. To begin the activity, the bar is laid flat on the ground. One person (the rider) squats down and grasps the crossbar. Four people (the lifters) squat down and grasp the uprights (two on each side). On signal, the bar is lifted into the air, till the uprights are perpendicular, then lowered down on the other side. One or two additional people (catchers) stand next to each upright on the downside of the bar, waiting to catch and lower it to the ground. After one rider has had a turn, the bar is returned empty to the starting position, and a new rider squats down and grasps the crossbar. For added excitement, the lifters can increase the speed of pendulum, or the rider can do simple stunts along the way. One such stunt is to pull his feet over the bar on the ride up so that he ends up in a support position on top of the bar on the way down (that is, a pull-over).

- *Table Tilt.* This is a unique activity with an interesting tilt. It is done with a round tabletop about 3 feet (1 meter) in diameter. Three-quarter-inch (2 cm) plywood will serve adequately if you do not have any tabletops lying around. Two foot loops are securely attached to the center of the table. The loops are made of reinforced nylon strapping similar to the footholds one finds in a sailboat and are placed 18 inches (45 cm) apart. One person stands on the tabletop in a straddle position by slipping one foot through each of the loops. About ten other people form a circle around the table-top, squat down, and lift at the same time. If you attach four small pieces of 2 by 4 (blocks of wood) to the bottom of the table, there will be room to get your hands under the tabletop to lift. You can also place the center of the table on a mound in the ground or on a block of wood. If you want to get fancy, attach a slightly raised metal ring around the outer edge of the table for a very secure grip and better overall control. The center person can be lifted up and down at various speeds and can be tilted in various directions. The ride can be like one on a rocking ship in large waves, without the seasickness. Tilting to one side and then to the other side (rather than forward and backward) seems to work best and allows most control for the center person.

     This same tabletop can also be used for other activities without using the foot loops, like gently tossing the center person up in the air so that he lands on his feet on the ground, in a foam pit, or in water. Be sure to use spotters.

- *People Tossing.* Two people (tossers) squat down and grasp opposite ends of a sturdy stick. A third person puts a hand on each of their shoulders and steps onto the stick. The tossers then quickly stand, extending their legs and pulling up on their arms to send their friend into flight. There are several options for landing safely. One way is to toss people into large foam pits, deep water, or large soft snow banks. The East Germans toss their mates into suspended tumbling mats. Four people (catchers) stand on each side of the mat (eight catchers in total) and grasp the handholds along the sides. The flying person is tossed on an angle by leaning slightly forward and lands on the mat on his stomach. This is similar to doing a front drop on a trampoline, which one should have perfected before trying this. As the tossed person lands on the mat, the catchers "give" with his weight by bending their knees, thus making for a softer landing. This same catching procedure is followed for people who choose to land on their feet and then roll. For added spice, people are tossed over a crossbar from a high-jump standard.

One other method was used to propel people. The top part of a small trampoline that measured about 30 by 30 inches (75 by 75 cm), including frame, springs, and mat, was held by two people on each side (four in total). These people squatted down to allow someone to get on the trampoline and then tossed her into the air. In this case she was caught, stomach first, by twelve people who formed two lines and interlocked wrists with the person opposite them.

Chinese boys skipping rope

developing and presenting co-op games, programs, and playdays

Perhaps one of the hardest parts of playing co-op games is just getting going—convincing the suspicious and breaking down preconceived ideas about what cooperative sports mean. If you're with an informal group—say, in a playday, on a picnic, or at a weekend outing—you might be lucky enough to have with you someone who's familiar with the spirit of cooperative games who can help you out. Look everywhere for open-minded allies, and try to get people into the spirit as quickly as possible, usually by starting out with some simple but appealing activities.

When teaching or working with a group, it's extra important to choose activities that are suited to the players' special needs or abilities. Are there children as well as adults? What are the physical possibilities or limits of your play area?—Will you be outside or in? Playing on soft ground or in boulders? Is there room to throw a ball or work up a speed running and sliding? And find out what the group itself wants to do, too—Has anyone played cooperative games before, and can they suggest favorites for starters? Do you want to use traditional games remade into totally new experiences? Are your players good athletes (in the conventional sense) looking for a real challenge or less skilled people whom you can show how to find new talents they might not know they have? Are there physical or other limitations in the members of the group itself? Thinking about these kinds of considerations ahead of time will help make the experience more fun for everyone—including you.

If you have room—in, for example, a large area for an extended playday—you can launch several games at once if you set up a series of game "stations"; people can join different ones at will or rotate in a more structured way, as you prefer. Some should offer quieter, less strenuous activities, like Paper Pat-a-Cake or Mush Mush; at others, you can get some good steam worked up in games like Inuit Skipping or Bump and Team Scoot. People who have played a particular game can be responsible for each station and help out with the teaching. But don't forget to have them rotate, too, so that they don't get bored themselves. You can also put simple instructions or stick figures on bristol board and place them in different play areas. Wherever possible, spontaneity should also be encouraged: If there are several people who know various games, they can start a new one whenever they feel the time is right. Others around will naturally join in.

I've worked with groups of all varieties, from infants to adults to a mixture of everything in between. What follows are suggestions for presenting that come from my (and my colleagues') experiences in different kinds of programs; I hope our ideas will give you a hand in forming your own approaches.

Adult-to-Adult Approach

In more structured situations—at cooperative games workshops, in classes, and even at some parties—more often than not I find that people have a limited amount of time and they want to be guided through a sampling of cooperative games. So what do I do? With small groups, I present the games to the whole group at the same time and play along with them. Large groups are split into smaller groups for many activities, and group members are asked to watch a demonstration group in the middle in which

I participate and guide. Players are informed at the outset that I will raise my hand above my head when the time seems right to introduce a new game or make a comment. Players are asked to stop and raise their hand anytime they see a raised hand. This works beautifully for classes and workshops, and most often there is silence within a few seconds. It eliminates the need for whistles and also protects me from going hoarse in an hour!

Once I have people's attention I give a few simple instructions or comments and demonstrate another game. When possible I try to demonstrate three or four simple activities (for example, dual stunts) at once and then let people experiment with them. In some cases groups can stay spread out in various corners of the playing area while new activities are being presented. For example, if three parachutes are in use at the same time, the people around the outer chutes can glance at the middle chute (demonstration group) for new activities. Of course, it is advantageous to have in each group someone who is familiar with the games—even if she is briefed just before the session. Doing so will enable her to either follow your lead or go at a different pace. For games with complicated rules, for feedback sessions, for game leaders with soft voices, when there is difficulty hearing—and especially when presenting alone—it is often a good idea to signal all groups to the center so that they can sit in close proximity to you.

I prefer sharing the introduction of games, and usually ask anyone in the group who knows some of the games or has a good game of her own (and there often are) if she would mind presenting it to the group. If there are several people who know some games, we often set up a rotation (that is, you present this, I'll present that, and then you can present the other one). People appreciate being warned ahead if this is going to happen.

Here are some specific tips to keep in mind in presenting:

- Keep verbal instructions to a minimum—most people prefer and learn best by watching and then doing (for example, "See if you can do this"; "Watch this group"; "OK, give it a try").
- Start off with an activity that brings the whole group together (such as a parachute activity).
- With younger children or people who have been sitting for a long time, get them moving right away (using, for example, Hugger, Wagon Wheel, Parachute).
- Alternate between active and quiet activities.
- If people are tired or are just waking up (for instance, at an 8:30 AM session), start with quiet activities such as Mutual Interviews and Partner Introductions in small groups.
- Look for signs of "enough," and try to introduce a new game before interest begins to wane (because of boredom or fatigue).
- Have enough games in mind (or on paper) to last more than the entire session.

- Have some back-up games in mind in case you need them.
- Make sure all necessary equipment is on site before the start of the session.
- Encourage players to make creative adaptations within the games or to try different "homemade" versions of their own.
- Get some feedback during the session (for example, game adaptations) as well as toward the end (for instance, likes, dislikes, and suggestions).
- End with a quiet activity that allows everyone to regroup in a fun way (say, Lap Sit Stepping) and try to leave the group laughing.

Sample Co-op Games Workshop

I have used the following workshop agenda with groups ranging from thirty to one hundred people in a normal-size gym or similar-size outdoor area. It gives the participants a taste of the different kinds of cooperative games and can usually be completed in half a day—including a break for juice. Once people have experienced the activities, the chances of their using them is greatly increased. Listening to a talk about cooperative games may spark some interest, but actually playing the games leaves most people feeling, "Hey, that was fun—I can play those games with my kids tomorrow."

- A few parachute activities for the entire group (Position Exchange, Hug in Middle, Birds and Worm, Ball Roll Around Edge, and then into Hole in the Middle)
- Break into small groups (with, for example, eight members).
- Beachball Name Game (in small groups)
- Have each group make up a sound (which will later help them regroup)
- Hugger (tag game for the entire group), followed with Hug and Hum
- Barnyard (shut eyes; make sound to regroup)
- Circle of Friends Revisited or Humans Merrily Go Round in original groups
- Blanketball (in original groups or smaller groups depending on blanket size)
- Cooperative Musical Papers or Frozen Shoes for younger groups; Saskatch Soccer for older groups
- Sealskin (Inuit) Skipping or Inuit Partner Activities
- Mush Mush (in groups of about sixteen)
- Runaway Trains (start in trains of two or three; end in one large circle)
- Circle Lap Slap Singsong (entire group)
- Mutual relaxation (pairs share signs of stress, ways to relax, relax each other)
- Feedback session (small groups share a game, a like, a problem or concern, a solution; entire group hears highlights of small-group sharing)
- Lap Sit—Step, Step, Step (entire group)

An all-ages parachute playday

Feedback and Discussion Sessions

The combined experience of almost any group is extensive, and sharing collective knowledge results in everyone's gain. In small-group discussions, people can exchange ideas, feelings, good games, resources, problems, solutions, and so on. These discussions will often be the only opportunity they have to share with people of similar experience and interests, and in a nonthreatening atmosphere.

In a workshop setting the focus might be on the sharing of effective cooperative games and the way to implement a successful cooperative-games program. Smaller groups might meet first, with someone in each small group jotting down the major points discussed. Once the entire group reassembles, this input can be shared and pertinent questions can be posed (for example, "Where do we buy equipment and find resource materials?" or, "How do we overcome a certain sort of resistance?").

CHILD-TO-ADULT FEEDBACK

If you are looking for a quick and effective way of assessing all children's liking for a new game or a new adaptation, try this: Before the game give each child three colored cards—say, one green, one red, and one yellow. After each game, ask the children to pull the cards out of their pocket or shoe and flash one. The green means, "I really like it"; the yellow, "It's OK"; and the red, "I don't like it." If you are concerned that children may be influenced by their friends' cards, have the group form a circle with their backs facing the center. At a given time, they can all flip the card of their choice over their heads. This gives you a quick indication of how something is being received.

Leave some time as well for the participants to share *their* suggestions, adaptations, likes, dislikes, cooperative games, problems encountered with games, and solutions that have worked. You can do this through discussions in pairs, in small groups (four to six) or with the entire group. Small groups also work well when you're creating new cooperative games (see page 184).

If you are looking for more detailed individual feedback, you can use pictorial *evaluation questions* like these. Children answer by circling the appropriate face in a series of five that progresses from happy to glum or by writing in specific answers.

1. Which face were you when you were playing the game?
2. How did you feel about how the other players treated you in the game?
3. Is there something special about the game that you liked?
4. Is there something special that someone else did in the game that you liked? Can you share it with us?
5. Do you have any suggestions that might make the game (or players) more fun?

CHILD-TO-CHILD APPROACH

Young children often relate and respond to older children in a magical way. Child-to-child approaches to learning try to take advantage of this natural connection. Older children become the point of intervention, or the focal point, for positive change. This approach has worked well in helping to overcome health problems in third-world countries. For example, eight- and nine-year-old children were able to save many lives as a result of being taught how to recognize and treat diarrhea and related dehydration problems in their baby brothers and sisters.

This same process can be used for teaching any lessons, including positive orientations to play and games. The approach has several advantages. First, it draws on the great power of natural models. My one-year-old daughter got more absorbed in modeling the play of a three-year-old friend than in modeling my play. When she watched other relatively little people doing things (whether it was walking, climbing, or helping) she seemed to surmise that she could also do that. At the same time, older children are helped to feel important and responsible, for they are teaching valuable lessons. As they improve their own helping skills they are also improving the overall health and harmony within their group or community. Sometimes, though, when older children are first learning to share or transmit new games or skills to their younger counterparts, they have to be cautioned to do so in a considerate way.

One elementary-school teacher who had been involved in a child-to-child project asked the kids to observe how their parents showed love and affection to young children. She then asked them if they do the same. Essentially they were asked to look for "love and affection" and to come back to talk about it in the school. I immediately thought that the lesson could be extended another step, so that children would actually play a game of love and affection. The game would involve acting out the various ways to communicate love to little children. How many ways are there to show a child you love her? to make a baby happy? to hug a little kid? to help a younger friend? Can you show me one way? Children could play the game among themselves or, better yet, with a group of appropriately aged children (for example, kindergarteners, preschoolers, toddlers, or infants).

When can peer teaching (child-to-child) begin? When Anouk was one week shy of being a year and a half old, she and her cousin were playing with a little puzzle with eight different shaped vehicles, each of which fitted into a separate slot (Fisher Price's Vehicle #508). She had been playing with the puzzle for some time and knew exactly where each piece went. Her little cousin, as yet, had no idea where any of the pieces went and struggled in his attempt to make them fit. If they weren't aimed at the wrong spot, they were upside down or backward. One morning, when the two of them were playing with the puzzle together, Anouk handed him the sailboat piece, which I think is the easiest to fit in because it has fewer angles than any of the other pieces. He took the boat and glanced up at her with a blank stare. She immediately pointed directly at the slot for the sailboat. She held her finger about a half an inch above that slot and said, "Ci" (her version of "ici," which in French means "here"). He placed the sailboat in the slot, and a big grin spread over his face. Peer teaching can be extremely effective both within and outside the school setting, particularly when older children are matched with younger children.

THE SPECIAL ROLE OF WOMEN

The more I study other cultures and the more fully I begin to understand my own, the more convinced I become of the humanistic strength of women. The reasons most societies are hanging together at all are their women; I've seen this with the Inuit, the Australian aboriginals, and the Siwai of Papua New Guinea, and I think it is largely true in my own North American culture. Women in each of these societies are much more caring, considerate, dependable, and cooperative than their male counterparts. I have great respect for the pursuit of genuine equality for women but great fear that if women take on some of the negative traits of contemporary men, our humanistic values will be lost forever.

The nurturing of a sense of responsibility and sincere concern for the welfare of others begins at a very early age through play activities. One of the advantages women have with respect to developing a greater sense of humanity relates to the fact that a much greater percentage of females' childhood play and games is cooperative in nature. If parents, teachers, and community leaders make a special effort to preserve cooperatively oriented play and values for *both* boys and girls, more children will have a greater chance of hanging on to their humanity. If we can draw on the wisdom of our most humanistic people and focus our efforts in this direction, children will smile again and the future will shine much brighter for all of us.

Using Cooperative Ideas in Physical Education Programs

I am often asked by physical education teachers whether I feel that cooperative games should make up the entire gym program. I believe that all games should be played in a cooperative spirit but that they all need not necessarily be cooperative in structure. It is vitally important for children to get a solid foundation in cooperative skills, and so my program for preschoolers and children in the early school years would be *exclusively* cooperative, with the exception of some self-paced and creative individual activities. There would be *no* competitive games or pressured situations!

For upper elementary-school children and high-school students, you can begin to provide more options, trying to make sure that any competitive games introduced are played within a cooperative value system. Integrate semicooperative rules into competitive team games, and teach relaxation techniques along with a variety of adaptation strategies for stress, anger, and interpersonal conflict.

A large component of my overall program at the elementary-school level would revolve around creative games, creative dances, and enjoyable activities in the outdoors (for example, hiking, walking, jogging, cooperative orienteering, exploring, canoeing, cross-country skiing, surfing, and so on). You can play many cooperative games in a variety of places: in the water, in snow, on the beach, in the forest, or in almost any place kids enjoy being. Games like Cooperative Musical Hoops, Hugger, Lap Sit, or Circle of Friends have some special qualities for warming up people in waist-deep water, in snow, on the ice rink, or on the beach on a moonlit night.

Floating on clouds

At all levels, I urge teachers to be receptive to the students' input and to implement any suggestions, except for those that might hurt others physically or psychologically. Discuss why those ideas don't help individuals or the group.

Mollie Elie, a fitness instructor for the YMCA, decided her own four children needed a healthy alternative to after school TV watching, and she approached the principal of her son's school to see if he would be interested in letting her organize a fitness club for children. The club began meeting twice a week for forty-five minutes. Here's Mollie's report on the success of the first six week session:

Twenty children from the grade-six class attended and we tried to hold as many sessions as possible outdoors. During the program, twenty minutes were spent on skipping, jogging, and exercising, and twenty minutes on cooperative games. Three of the cooperative games we played were Three-Legged Soccer, Moving Basket Basketball, and Bump and Scoot Volleyball. In the beginning the children resisted playing some of the traditional games cooperatively. However, once we had started playing them the new way, they enjoyed them.

We also tried to choose sides in a more cooperative fashion. Instead of having the children choose their own teams, we would play blue jeans against all other kinds of pants or skirts, or those children born in January to July against those born in August to December. Another way to divide the children is according to who likes apple juice against those who like orange juice.

Combining the fitness activities with the cooperative games worked out very well. The children were able to learn that being fit can be fun and also that it can be fun playing cooperative games. Since the cooperative games we played are active, with everyone participating most or all of the time, they are ideal for a fitness club.

If you are interested in increasing levels of fitness, consider using Coopercizes, which directly combine exercise with cooperation. A few such activities that I recently developed are outlined below; you can add to them.

- *Tandem Cycling.*   This is a fun warm-up. Lie down on your back and connect the bottom of your feet with the bottom of your partner's feet. Get close enough to your partner (but not too close) so that you can do a simultaneous cycling action with your connected feet, first in one direction, then the other. It works well even when partners are different sizes, for example, with parents and children.

- *Tandem Sit-ups.*   This is for abdominal strengthening. Lie down on your back with your knees bent, holding a ball the size of a soccer ball (or a cushion) in your hands. Have your partner sit down facing you with his heels gently hooked behind your heels (to hold feet secure during sit-ups). Come up to a bent-knee sitting position, and pass the ball to your partner. He then lowers himself down to a lying position, comes back up, and passes the ball back to you, and thus the action continues. When doing this with very young children or with people who have very weak abdominal muscles, one partner can help pull the other up to a sitting position by grasping their hands (or the ball).

For a little variety try doing a partner stand-up (both holding onto the ball and pulling each other up to a stand) after every ten sit-ups or so.

For more continuous action, both partners, each with a ball, can spread apart on the floor (again facing each other). As they both come up to a seated position, they simultaneously exchange balls and then lower themselves down to a lying position. This works best if one partner throws his ball high and the other low. The distance between partners is optional.

- *Cooperative Skipping.*   This is for cardio-respiratory fitness. First place a skipping rope behind your back in a ready position, and try the following footwork alone a few times before adding the rope. Leap forward by extending your left foot forward and pushing off your right foot. Land on your left foot, take a very short step onto your right foot, and leap forward again, leading with your left foot.

The action feels like, "leap-step, leap-step, leap-step." Try adding the skipping rope to this foot action. Also try leading with your right foot (on the leap) without the rope and then with the skipping rope. Once you are familiar with the skipping action, alternate leaps by leading with the left foot for a few leaps and then leading with the right for a few leaps. You can change the lead foot without interrupting the skipping action.

Now for the fun part—Skipping on the Run—with two partners. One partner takes each end of the rope, and the third person does the skipping in the middle. Once the rope is spinning, everyone moves (jogs) forward at once while the jumper jumps and the rope spinners continue to spin. The foot action for the jumper is the same "leap-step" action mentioned earlier. The jumper sets the pace. If you are looking for additional challenge, try the same footwork while the rope is turned backward instead of forward. Make sure partners change places regularly. Once kids get the hang of this version of Skipping on the Run have them make up their own variations.

Susan Kalbfleisch, a teacher in Hamilton, Ontario, Canada, has been organizing cooperative playdays, collective-score track and field meets, cooperative carnivals, and the like for the past few years. Her efforts have met with resounding success: Her elementary-school students now organize the co-op playdays themselves. Susan has come up with something called "magic score," which provides another alternative way of winning. She writes down a score on a piece of paper before the game begins—this is the magic number. The teams play their games, and the group ending the game with the score closest to the magic score wins. Her kids have also played volleyball by using the whole length of the gym (stretching over several courts) in one huge game, with thirty beach balls in play at once.

As part of a running program she promoted Running to the Olympics. The object of the run is for the school (students and staff) to collectively run enough miles (or kilometers) to reach an agreed-upon destination. Either real or prorated miles or kilometers can be used (for example, one km run equals three km on the map). A large map with the route marked is posted in the hallway with pin-flag markers showing daily or weekly progress. Logging of individual mileage should be kept confidential so that pressure is not applied to children who choose not to participate, cannot participate (for medical reasons), or run only a minimal distance. Only collective mileage is recorded.

Rick McAllister sent in the following report from a hockey camp in Haliburton (sports camps are often tense with competitive energy):

Our theme [for campers and staff] for this summer is Winning Through Cooperation. Haliburton Hockey Haven 1979 has become a laboratory of sorts. We are using cooperative activities in a formal sense in swimming periods, field sports (altering rules of volleyball, soccer, and so on), and in the evening program. Cooperative games have proved much superior to the more competitive games that I formerly used as a swimming instructor. I see many more smiles, more active participants, and much less arguing about rules (which is the beauty of cooperative games—there's a minimum of rules). Games that have worked well with our youngest swimmers are Print (that is, make shapes, letters, or numbers while doing front or back floats, thus giving skills practice too) and Fish Gobbler. With the middle-age groups (nine to thirteen years of age), Whirlpool and Chain Tag have been popular. Cooperative Water Polo (that is, everyone must touch the ball before a goal is scored) has gone over well with our oldest campers (up to fifteen years). The staff in the Field Sports area are finding that cooperation is actually improving skills (especially *setting* in cooperative volleyball) while getting all kids participating more actively, with more fun.

Having been exposed to your thinking on children's physical activity has made me a much more questioning person. For example, I no longer get angry at kids who hesitate or outright refuse to go in the water for swim classes. Rather, I sit down with them (my assistants take the class over) and try to find out *why*. Generally speaking, their past experiences have been poor (for example, regimented lessons with little fun). I'm really making an attempt to find out what their needs are.

Most of the boys are competitive minor hockey players. Some seem unwilling to try new activities, although they usually like them once they do try them. Perhaps the overdose of hockey or its dominance in their lives is responsible. Also, most of the boys are not very self-reliant, and I (and our camp director) feel that minor hockey is in part to blame. Most coaches are quite autocratic, with very few decisions made by the kids playing. As a result, they may become very dependent. Anyway, by trying to understand their sometimes bizarre behavior this summer in an isolated boys camp has been much more enjoyable and rewarding for everybody.

Ecological Cooperation

Cooperation between people is only one step in reordering our world. A major factor affecting our future survival is our ability to work and play in harmony with our natural environment rather than destroy it. Creating or maintaining water, land, food, air, parks, city streets, and countrysides that are free from pollution is a realistic goal for people who are aware of the problems and concerned about solutions. This educational process can begin with children's play.

An Ecological Day Camp was started a few years ago in Pittsburgh, Pennsylvania, to develop greater awareness about the relationships of life. The kinds of activities used could be tied into a variety of settings, including the home, the school (units on ecology and gym classes), and recreational facilities. Katherine Linsley, a P.E. instructor at the camp, writes:

Every day the children are encouraged to save their lunch bags to use for the next day, to leave plants and animals undisturbed by writing and drawing what they see in small books rather than picking them up, and to observe the food chains around them. Some of the activities have included making useful paper products out of used scraps of paper, learning how to construct shelters with materials at hand (being careful not to disrupt the natural environments or the branches and vines they are using), growing a garden, making a compost pile out of the leftover garbage gathered from lunch, making baskets and clay pots out of natural materials, and firing the clay in a fire pit in order to learn correct methods of fire building and safety.

Here are some of the campers' specific activities. You might think about using them on your next hike or just in your own backyard.

- *Paper Kites.* The kids make their own kites out of paper bags, a project that introduces the concept of recycling paper in a playful way—just open the bags out flat and attach sticks and string as usual. Flying kites sets the stage for discussions on cloud formations, weather conditions, air pollution—and solutions.

- *Paper Balls.* Instead of buying factory-made balls, kids can make their own out of old newspapers and leftover scraps of paper. The balls are held together by masking tape or old string and are used in a variety of games in which you might use a sponge ball or another light, nonbouncing ball. Groups of children can collect litter on a site and make balls, thereby serving two useful purposes (that is, a cleaner environment and a ball with which to play—the bigger the ball the better!).

- *Musical Instruments.* Make "musical" instruments from objects found in the woods (for example, tin cans, rocks, sticks, rubber stretched across two knees, or rubber bands stretched between two fingers or two sticks). It gives a new meaning to the term "rock band"!

- *Leaf Passing.* This is a good game for autumn days, and can be played with one team or several. The players from each team stand in one line; the person at the front of the line(s) holds a broad leaf in her hand. At a given signal, the person in front passes the leaf overhead to the person behind, who passes it between her legs to the next, and so on, alternating over and under. The person at the back of the line runs the leaf to the front and passes it back again. This action is repeated until the one who started in front is again in front. If the leaf is torn or injured in any way, the team loses. If the leaf is uninjured, the game is won by as many teams as are successful in protecting the leaf. Try to avoid plucking healthy leaves still growing on branches.

- *Shadow Pictures.* This is a partner activity best played on a sunny day. First each pair makes a large piece of paper by flattening out used paper bags and pasting or taping them together. Then they hang the paper on a wall, the side of a building, or a tree, or place it flat on the ground. One partner assumes a position of his choice so that his shadow falls on the paper. His partner traces his shadow on the paper, and the two of them paint in the details. This project can lead to an awareness of sun and clouds as well as a discussion on the positions of the sun at various times. You can also try to guess whose shadow's whose!

- *Trails.* Two groups each mark a trail through a designated area without harming or defacing the environment (for example, by using small rocks in a certain formation, broken sticks found on the ground, small dots of flour, and so on). The two groups meet back at a starting point at an agreed-upon time and try to follow each other's trail. A scavenger hunt could be tied into this activity: Each group could clear its trail by bringing back as many unnatural objects as possible (for example, beer containers, soda cans, cigarette wrappers, and so on).

- *Silent Appreciation.* This is a small-group walk that is taken in silence. The children might like to imagine that they are in an underwater world and thus unable to speak. They can, however, point out something of interest to a friend and they can also write down or draw (in a small book) anything that is seen, heard, smelled, or felt (for example, birds, animals, leaves, plants, wind, air, rocks, sticks, moss, insects, and so on). Upon returning they share their findings and feelings. The point should be made that silence can heighten their awareness of their surroundings and that loud or insensitive actions (for instance, yelling or picking plants) disturbs the homes (environments) of those whom they are visiting. A discussion can follow about how to better care for land, plants, animals, and each other.

Ralph Ingleton and his staff members at the Forest Valley Outdoor Education Center in Downsview, Ontario, are also experimenting with some interesting outdoor games in hopes of developing children's appreciation for the natural environment, ecology, and each other. I have selected a couple of these games from a large assortment to share with you.

- *Twig Matching.* Each player is given one-half of a twig and then tries to find the person with the other half. After "connecting," the two partners try to identify the type of tree from which the twig came. Variations include connecting carefully divided leaves, dead flower petals, pine needles, fruits, seeds, and so on, and then finding the source from which they came. Edible plants, fruits, and vegetables can be matched up and then eaten by the matching pairs.

Enjoying nature together

- *Creating Birds.* Each player is given a card that shows either a head (and beak), body, wings, or feet of a bird. The object is for the players to put the bird together as it exists or to create a new "unknown" bird. The same game can be played with animals, flowers, trees, and so on.

- *Hunting to See.* A series of "hunt cards" are distributed among the players. Each card presents a written description, a drawing, or a picture of something interesting to find in the outdoors (for example, a seed that travels by wind; food for a bird, a frog, or a squirrel; an animal home; an insect or a plant; soil that feels like clay; a leaf with parallel veins; animal tracks; and so on). Pairs of children, who share several hunt cards, together seek the objects out and then share their finds with the rest of the group.

- *Treasure Walks.* The youngsters go on a short group hike, each searching for her own special treasure (for instance, something beautiful or interesting that she would like to remember). The "treasure" is stored in the child's mind rather than in her pocket. There's no touching, no collecting . . . only looking, admiring, and remembering. At the end of the walk everyone shares her treasure by telling about it.

Games Creation

Creating your own game is the ultimate extension of the cooperative idea (and ideal) and most fully gets across to players what it means to play *together* completely. What follows are two sample games created for children by students in one of my university classes. To devise them, the students worked in pairs or small groups and first decided what they wanted to accomplish with the game and with whom. They then selected, adapted, or made up a game to fulfill these objectives and tried it to see how it worked. How would you get groups you're working (and playing) with to carry out their own ideas?

- *Human Obstacle Course.*

Game Objectives: We wanted to give the children a chance to be creative, with cooperation the most important behavior exhibited throughout the game. The game was to provide fun and enjoyment for the children. All students were to participate. Students were to feel motivated by the game, so that they were eager to play it. Basic skills, such as hopping on one leg, skipping, and crawling, were to be incorporated into the game.

Game Description: The students are asked to find themselves a partner and then find a place in the gym to stand with their partner. Each pair is numbered in a clockwise fashion and asked to create a "human obstacle," the only rule being that they must use each other to do so. The pair of students designated number one starts the game by holding hands and then skipping, running, or jumping (depending on what particular skill is to be learned) to the human obstacles about the room. As they approach each obstacle, the two students creating the obstacle must tell them whether they go over, under, around, or through the obstacle. The pair trying to get through the obstacle must do so together by helping each other. After the first pair of students gets through the fourth or fifth human obstacle, the pair designated pair number two commences the circuit of obstacles. When a pair has completed the entire obstacle course, they assume their original position in the gym and create their own obstacle.

Game Reception: We tried out the game with a class of four-, five-, and six-year-olds. The students really enjoyed the game, since it was a great chance for them to think and be very creative. We're sure they also enjoyed it because they were given the freedom to choose. They listened to the instructions and hurried to take their positions as obstacles. They smiled and laughed a lot, and when a pair had trouble getting through an obstacle, the students forming the obstacle would either help them or simplify their obstacle. They encouraged one another and equally enjoyed playing both parts (that is, forming the obstacles and going through them).

Possible Adjustments or Improvements: Different skills to get around the circuit (for instance, dribbling, passing a ball back and forth, three-legged hop, or piggyback carry) could be incorporated with older children. To increase interaction, the number of people forming an obstacle could be increased to four or five, or the two partners could switch to new partners to make new obstacles. By adapting the difficulty of the skill, the game could be enjoyed by almost any age group.

- *Log Walk.*

Game Objectives: The primary objective was to create a *fun* atmosphere in which group cooperation and initiative would be stimulated.

Game Description: The game is played in groups of about ten people. The game coordinator assigns a number from one to ten to each person standing side by side on a log. Everyone then exchanges places with the person who is the same distance from the end of the log without stepping off it. For example, with ten people on the log, persons one and ten would exchange places, followed by persons two and nine, three and eight, four and seven, and finally five and six.

Game Reception: The game was attempted with a group of ten teen-agers. There was initial confusion within the group and clarifications were sought. Many students then offered suggestions for exchanging places. Within about thirty seconds a concensus on a strategy was reached. Person one would step over person two, who squatted on the log, helped person one by holding his hand for balance, and offered verbal encouragement. This strategy was followed until everybody had exchanged places. The game was met with overall enthusiasm, smiles, jokes, spontaneous laughter, and applause during and after. People physically held others as they passed by and gave verbal encouragement and suggestions, which were readily accepted. The group fun and cooperation that began in the log walk (in an outdoor setting) extended well after the game had ended.

Possible Adjustments: Make the instructions clear at the beginning. For newly formed groups perhaps begin by having players simply exchange places with the person next to them. For additional challenge, find a log that rolls and have the group roll it together on grass or in water while sitting or standing on it. Then try making a position change.

cooperative innovations

This chapter contains a series of alternative programs and approaches that have been introduced to me over the past few years. Some are used for specific groups (for example, older people or the handicapped) or for specific skills (for instance sailing). They demonstrate what excellent work is now going on around the world, and I hope the ideas described here will inspire more thinking and creating on your end.

Saskatchewan Cooperation

One of the most innovative cooperative curricula to which I have been exposed is currently in progress in Canada's province of Saskatchewan. Its major aim is to improve the quality of life for the residents of Saskatchewan, whose heritage reaches back to the pioneers who first settled to clear and farm this land. The Education

Division within the Department of Cooperation and Cooperative Development has made available a variety of resource materials for schools and other organizations in the province (see Resource Section). One of the unique aspects about these materials is that often both the educational content as well as the learning format are cooperative.

At the elementary-school level, the material exposes children to the vital role of cooperation in communicating interpersonally and making the community run. At the high-school level, cooperation is approached in greater depth and expanded to include the role of cooperation and cooperatives in the economic and social life of our society. Lessons cover such topics as learning to live together; communicating with others; group building; working with others; and cooperating for fun, and for family, community, social, and environmental life.

The following activities were extracted from one of their excellent teaching manuals entitled *Cooperation and Community Life* (see Resources section).

- *Internal Cooperation.* Pick a task that we do so often that we can do it effortlessly, without thinking (for example, making a fist, walking, writing, eating). Ask the students to perform one of these acts in slow motion, paying attention to what the muscles do, how the bones move, and whether they are conscious of the messages being transmitted from the brain.

Then have the students repeat the act at regular speed and then again as slowly as possible. How do the parts of the body cooperate? What happens when parts of the body don't cooperate? (Do we miss skills, make errors, experience disease, stress, indigestion?) In the same way that body parts (or minds and bodies) cooperate for smooth and healthy functioning, so can people, teams, and communities.

- *Questions to Pose.* Are you involved in any activities in which competition is not necessary (for example, throwing a frisbee, helping a friend, skipping rope, yoga, creative dance, cross-country skiing)? How do you feel when doing these activities? Are your feelings different from those when performing competitive activities?

- *Slow-Motion Games.* Try playing a game (for example, floor hockey) in time to some slow music. Everything should be in sl—o—w motion. See if the game changes in any way. What changes and adaptations do we need to make in the way we play together?

- *Jug Band.* Collect materials that can be used as instruments (for example, combs and paper for kazoos, tins with stones for rattles, cans for drums, and spoons for clankers). If there are not enough instruments for everyone, have the players share instruments or make vocal sounds that imitate instruments. After players have practiced their instrument or sound, let them choose a simple tune to play. Select a different conductor for each song. What kinds of sounds are produced when instruments cooperate and when they compete?

- *Pot Luck: A Cooperative Meal.* In a pot luck meal, each student brings something to eat that can be shared with others. Students must assist in the preparation of the dish and/or assist in setting up, cooking, and cleaning up. Children's Pot Luck could be tied into a cooperative playday (or picnic outing) that ends with a shared feast.

- *Recreation Places.* Let students work together to identify all the recreational activities and places available in their community. First they can list all the activities they do outside of school, indicate whether they are organized or spontaneous in nature, and note their location. Playing sites or settings for social and entertainment activities can then be marked on a map of the town, city, or community, and the map can be posted in a central area.

To expand on this collective-identification project, small groups of children can prepare and share a report on some of these recreational options (for example, what they offer, who can go, how they treat kids, and how much they cost). In addition, if there are currently unavailable activities in which some students would like to participate, they can be identified. The students can work together and where possible enlist the help of others in the school or community to make one (or some) of these activities available.

Through a project like Recreation Places, youngsters can share ideas and knowledge about something important to them and perhaps work together to effect some positive change.

What Do The Children Think?

My close friend and working colleague, John Partington, is concerned with using children's input in all aspects of their lives. In a study that was completed in 1980, John asked children about their favorite places, the things they liked to do most, and how they would change various dimensions of their lives (for example, their neighborhood parks, sports, schools, homes, other kids, and parents). Their responses were enlightening.

The best times seemed to take place in parks, on beaches, in their own homes, in friends' homes, and while traveling or interacting with other kids. Playing with friends was a favored activity.

Sharing ideas with aboriginal kids

Their suggestions for changing sports included, "Have more even teams," "Have people know that it isn't whether you win or lose, but how you play the game," "Get rid of roughness," "Get rid of violence," "Kick out people who cheat and fight," and "Put all the rough people into one league." Older children also called for more sport facilities and less expensive equipment, while younger children wanted to "make the sports more fun."

Their suggestions for changing school revolved around leaving them some time for play (for example, "Work until lunch and then do something enjoyable the rest of the day," "Have more fun in school," "Have longer recess," "Make the school day shorter," "Have more time in school for homework").

Suggestions for improving parents included such things as "Have them not get so mad at you," "Make them not hurt your feelings," "Have them use active listening," "Make them more understanding," "Give them a truth pill," "Have friendly arguments," "Switch places for a week," "Take their power away," "Make children have the same rights," and "Make them take orders from kids."

For changing other children, the recommendations included "Make them happy, not sad," "Make them friendly," "Have them be nice to each other," and "Make them understanding."

The inescapable conclusion that John draws from this work is, "Children and youth are very concerned about the quality of their social environment. They want people to treat them well, and also to be nicer to each other." He believes that these youth are telling us that love and freedom are much more essential than high-priced facilities and highly organized programs.

Sailing Cooperatively

David Perry, a former All-American sailor, has come up with some great ways to increase kids' enjoyment in sailing. You might find that the ideas and methods he used could be applied effectively in any number of organized programs and activities; for instance, when young skiers practice formations on the slopes. The point is to expose children to a sport in a way that lets them enjoy it both now and as they grow up.

Firsthand experience taught Dave how much of a barrier competition can be to sound learning and enjoyment among junior sailors. As a result, he began to seek out cooperative alternatives. In an article entitled "Improving Your Junior Sailing Program" in *Yachting*, Dave spoke about his innovative program.

> Students who can't keep up experience embarrassment, frustration, withdrawal, alienation, apathy, and often resentment toward the sport. Any creativity or individuality that a student might apply to sailing is therefore stifled for fear of failing, thus turning the entire learning experience into a narrow track of merely learning the skills needed in racing, with winning as the valued and recognized goal. This is not what sailing is about, and is, I feel, why so many kids drop out. However, there is a way to reverse this trend. All that needs to be changed is the orientation, . . . In the cooperative approach the focus is on having kids enjoy their sailing.

In order to prepare for this new cooperatively based program, Dave and his co-instructors sent out a handwritten letter to each of the students. In it he introduced himself and the staff and asked about what the youngsters did and didn't like about their previous program and what they would like to do more of during the coming summer. He urged them to write back and told them he was looking forward to meeting them and having a great summer together.

Out of sixty kids, ages eight to fifteen, he received about forty letters back. Some were seven pages long; others were simple drawings. The suggestions ranged from learning more sailing skills to having a junior dance without chaperones. Dave got a feel for how to set the program up, and best of all, the kids felt much more involved with the success of the summer. "Once under way, every activity and exercise was designed to emphasize cooperation and minimize competitiveness. The kids decorated their clubroom, came up with new names for the club boats, and helped put all the boats in shape for the summer."

On the water, Dave was especially careful to give everyone an equal chance to skipper and crew and tried to avoid always having the same kids sail together. If they were practicing racing, he had them reverse the fleet often, announcing halfway up the beat that it was a race back to the finish. Doing so ensured that everyone got a chance to be at the front and the back of the pack.

Dave's most successful activity was synchronized sailing. The exercises were designed to improve students' sailing skills in an enjoyable way by challenging them to make group formations on the water. They were especially good for teaching precise boat-handling skills and timing without the added distraction and worry of trying to beat other students around the race course.

> The fundamental exercise is "the parade." All boats line up bow to stern as close together as possible. The challenge comes in keeping a straight line without anyone overtaking or losing distance on the boat immediately ahead. The advantage is that each student can experiment with sail trim, and immediately notice the effect in relation to the other boats, without feeling like he is competing. *As the group becomes more cooperatively oriented, the students will actually help each other to sail the boats well, since to make the formations successful they must work as a group.* Kids become much more friendly and tolerant.
>
> With imagination, the variations on this are limitless. The lead boat can take the parade through a series of rapid-fire tacks, long sweeping gybes, or in and out of a crowded mooring area. The group can form a perfect circle, called the "serpentine," or even form letters on the water. These exercises are great to watch and are fun for the kids. Best of all, sailing ability dramatically improves, while adding a new dimension to the sport.

It is interesting to note that Dave also used the parade to introduce beginners to heavier winds and deeper water. He found that they were much more confident sailing with the group. They were too busy concentrating on staying in a straight line to become frightened.

Some other approaches that were very successful in bringing youngsters together to work toward mutually beneficial goals included deciding as a group where they would go on a cruise and learning the parts of the boat together.

> The classic approach is to use a quiz or a relay-race format. However, doing so creates winners and losers within the group and only reinforces competitiveness among the kids. The cooperative approach offers a more fun and effective way. Using a blackboard and some colored chalk, the instructor can have the first child draw one part of the boat, letting the others add on other parts in turn. If a child gets stuck, the instructor or other kids can help him. Result: The child still gets

---

the enjoyment of drawing his own part. In the end the group will have drawn a boat, or some reasonable likeness, which is the result of each individual's input.

As a teaching method this is super. When we used it last summer everyone participated and payed attention. Individual creative input kept morale high, and the kids went so far as to name their design, calling it the S. S. Mess. This became one of the many great times the group could remember and enjoy together. This type of method gives positive momentum to a child's learning experience. An entire group can participate in a winning project.

Cooperative Learning in the Classroom

Elliot Aronson and his colleagues have done a great deal of innovative work on cooperative learning in the classroom. His approach, known as "jigsaw learning," is similar to David Perry's sailing program in that it encourages children to cooperate with one another to attain their educational objectives. Learning takes place in an atmosphere that is challenging without being threatening or anxiety producing.

The learning process itself is cooperative, as opposed to the lesson being studied. The students are taught to work together in small groups and to share information. In essence, each child is given a part of a topic to be studied, and the students fit their pieces together to form a complete "jigsaw" picture. They have to rely on one another for a successful outcome.

Aronson points out the importance of giving all the children the experience of being valuable group members. Initially this is done through a series of team-building activities. One such activity is called the Broken Squares Game, which was created by Alex Bavelas and adapted by Aronson and his co-workers. In this game each member of the group (usually six children) receives six pieces of a six-piece puzzle. The pieces are cut out of the same size cardboard squares and are distributed so that no one player has all the necessary combinations of pieces to complete her square. The objective of the game is for each player to end up with a completed square; the hitch is, you can't talk while you play.

The giving must be initiated by each player by herself. A player cannot simply take a piece from another player, nor can she ask or signal for someone to pass a needed piece to her. Players must become actively helpful in silence. For each group member to end up with a completed puzzle, all group members must notice what pieces their teammates require and reach over to place the needed piece(s) in their hands. Smiles of appreciation are welcomed. For those of you interested in promoting cooperative learning in the classroom, keep in mind that most cooperative games serve as good icebreakers for building a sense of community in the classroom.

Cooperative Games for Handicapped Children

We are all handicapped by our lack of skills in certain situations. Some of us lack the physical skills we might like to have; others lack emotional control skills; and still others are handicapped by a constant need to achieve. The inability to play for the sheer pleasure of the experience and the reluctance to share with others in an open and joyful way are probably our greatest common cultural handicaps.

Cooperative games are particularly well suited for children who are attempting either to overcome handicaps or build on their strengths. This is largely because the games are easily adapted to the needs of players rather than the players' having to adapt to the needs of the game. A certain level of personal acceptance and a spirit of playfulness is built into the games themselves.

Lucie Joanette and Annette Spirators both work with children who are classified as trainable mentally handicapped (T.M.H.) at École Honore-Mercier in Laval, Quebec. Lucie was first exposed to the concept of cooperative games while doing graduate studies at the University of Ottawa. In her own words she tells me, "A child is a child whoever he may be. Our children, labeled T.M.H. by society, are very normal children with very normal needs. They like to play, to have fun, and to have friends. They don't like to lose any more than any other child likes to lose. Yet competition is forced upon these children, often bringing repeated failures, enemies, and a sense of rejection. At once I fell in love with the spirit of cooperative games—they opened a new channel for me."

Lucie and Annette ask readers who work with T.M.H. children or others labeled handicapped to please pass on their successful cooperative games so that other teachers can benefit from all the new ideas that sprout up. The children—those we have chosen to educate and love—will be the ultimate beneficiaries. Here are some of Lucie and Annette's ideas to get you thinking. The first three are played in a pool, with children who are able to use that environment (with appropriate safety measures).

- *Cooperative Water Polo.* When your children are able to use a pool, they'll love this adaptation of an often too fierce game. Divide the children in two teams of equal strength. The game has two objectives. First, players must make three passes before scoring; second, for those who can count, players should try to end with an even score. When the count is uneven, one of the teachers can arrange things so that it ends even (for example, by joining in the play, setting up players, switching sides, and so on). Part of the goal is to move the ball toward the deep end, so children will swim for it, and at times the teacher will hold the ball tightly and have all the children huddled around him trying to get a ride or find the ball. Make sure that every player gets the ball and takes an active part in the game. At the end of the game everyone shakes hands and congratulates one another.

- *Tipping the Boat.* The goal is to turn over a boat in a pool. We use a rubber boat (dinghy) from the Army surplus store. It is very difficult to tip, and so the children really have to combine their effort to succeed. For added excitement one child can lie down in the bottom of the boat and hold on tight, while the others work hard to tip it. Another possibility is for all the children to start off in the water and try to help one another get into the dinghy without tipping.

- *Whirlpool.* Players form one large circle near one corner of the pool, join hands, and move the circle around by walking as briskly as possible. As the water begins to ripple and the current begins to build up, children take turns breaking off and floating with the moving water away from the circle.

- *Touching Colors.* Children begin the game by sitting down on the floor. The teacher calls out one color that the children then try to find and touch on another child. The teacher can call out colors being worn by a shy or nonparticipating child. To help the children identify colors, the teacher holds in her hands a ribbon of the color called—it works!

- *Animal Actions.* Children are divided into two groups that face each other. One group decides on an animal to imitate. The teacher can help by suggesting an animal or a way to do an imitation. All members of that group imitate the animal and move toward the other group.

  As soon as members of the other group guess which animal is being imitated, they all call out its name and start to imitate the animal too. The groups then switch positions.

- *Lions' Tails.* Players are paired off. One member of each pair begins the game with one end of a rope tucked inside the back of his pants and the other end hanging down on the floor like a lion's tail. On a signal his partner chases him and tries to step on the end of his tail. The tail is alternated back and forth between partners over the course of the game.

  To make the game more enjoyable and easier, attach a beanbag, a sandbag (wallet size), or a balloon to the end of the rope. This makes the lion's tail explosive. The children can play Lions' Tails for a long time!

- *Big Snake.* Children pair off and lie on their stomachs. One partner holds on to the ankles of her partner. They move around on their bellies and try to attach onto other pairs, ending up making one giant snake, all hooked together. The little and big snakes can go backward and roll over. Try the game in shallow water for an added treat.

- *Partner Stand-up.* Partners sit down facing each other with their feet flat on the ground and knees bent. They hold hands, and both try to stand up at the same time. When they succeed, they sit down again, still holding hands. For additional fun and challenge, let them hold on to a basketball-size ball that is placed between them for the stand-up.

- *Row Boat.* In the same seated position and maintaining a handhold if possible, one partner extends his legs while the other bends hers. Some very flexible partners can both extend legs together and then bend legs together.

- *Leaning Up and Down.* Children pair off and stand facing each other. They extend both hands so that palms are touching. They then interlock fingers and move their feet slightly back; they must not move again. Leaning in against one another, they start pushing themselves up and down, from a standing position to a kneeling position and then back up to a standing position.

- *Cooperative Feet, Arms, and Bodies.* Children find a partner and have their inside ankles tied together (as for a three-legged venture). They then try to move around, either on commands (for example, forward, backward, sideways, down, up) or on their own. You can also tie pairs by the inside arms, back to back with both arms bound, or waist to waist. Make sure the ties are made of thick soft material like wide strips of thick terry cloth. It is also possible to try to stay together as if tied by an imaginary rope.

- *Human Tunnel.* Children lie down on their backs in a line with their knees bent. The first child crawls under the knees (through the tunnel) and assumes a knee-bent position at the end of the tunnel. Then the next child does the same; the process continues until everyone has gone through the tunnel.

- *Blanket Rock.* One child lies on a sturdy blanket or rug, and the others arrange themselves around the edge and get a secure grip. They gently rock her back and forth sideways, swing her forward and backward, lift her up and down, cover and uncover her with the edges of the blanket, and so on.

  Ask children to bring their own blankets—they're precious tools, and can be used in lots of cooperative ways.

- *The Giant Caterpillar.* Together the children build a caterpillar course in the gym with all kinds of obstacles (for example, gym mats over boxes and benches and other obstacles that represent mountains, streams, and so on). Then they connect into fours, on knees and hands, holding the ankles of the one in front of them, and attempt to negotiate all the obstacles. For more fun and challenge they can cover themselves—all but the leader's head—with a blanket. They each take turns being leader.

- *Human Shape.* Children divide into two groups. One group decides on a shape to imitate—say, a crocodile or an ice-cream cone. Together they make the shape, and then the other group tries to guess what it is. Once they guess (or get close), it is their turn to create a shape of their choice. This game is a *great* success with older children.

MAINSTREAMING WITH COOPERATIVE GAMES

Mainstreaming refers to the integration of so called handicapped children and so called normal children. I have received feedback from various corners of North America indicating that cooperative games work extremely well in the mainstreaming process. This is largely because the games are so adaptable and allow youngsters to use their skills or strengths in a helpful way.

Michel Villeneuve created a modified soccer game as a means of integrating a physically handicapped child into a regular class. This child could spin around well but could not move forward and backward or from side to side very well. He played as a goalie in front of two marker cones about thirty feet (ten meters) away from the wall and three feet (one meter) apart. Goals could be scored by kicking the ball into the goal area from either the front or back. Protecting the net required good spinning ability and a limited necessity to move sideways, especially when two or more balls were in play. This adaptation enabled the child to play a semicooperative game on an equal footing with the others.

When Bill Michaelis played tag games with kids in electric wheelchairs, each of the wheelchair taggers were paired with a mobile tagger (for extended reach). The boundaries were shrunk and all the mobile runners (who were not taggers) hopped. The result: a balanced, fun game in which no one had an unfair advantage over another. These changes were arrived at by consulting with the entire group of players.

David Moses, from Fenton, Michigan, has been attempting to integrate the cooperative-games concept into CYO camps. He is concerned that most children's games played in the woods are of the "good guy" versus "bad buy" variety, or hide-and-seek. Here are a few options with which he has been experimenting to bring children of mixed abilities together.

- *Adopt-a-Friend.* Some of the sessions at camp include mentally impaired or exceptional children's attending along with "normal" campers. "Normal" kids adopt some of the mentally impaired kids and go through the normal camp routine: archery, nature activities, games, and so on. It is beautiful to see the cooperation.

- *Sucker's Creek.* This is an absolute festival of fun if you've got access to a river or a creek. Find a place where the bank is high enough and muddy enough to have some great adventures moving around in the mud—but no throwing mud! If another section is claylike, wet it down and go sliding down into the creek. Getting back up again is cooperation stretched to the limits.

Cooperative Games for Senior Citizens

Village elders have traditionally been looked to for their wisdom and vast reserve of experience. Today we all too often fail to draw on their reserves of knowledge or share with them our new games. The spirit of co-op games seems right for elderly people. Few want dull conditioning exercise, nor are they most interested in strenuous or distressful competition. The social aspect of play is what draws most of them out and holds them in. Improved health and fitness is a by-product and adds to their motivation for playing.

Many games in the first *Cooperative Sports & Games Book* as well as in this book are well suited to village elders who still have a spark of playfulness; special favorites are Puzzled Partners, Beach Ball Balance, and Human Sculptures. In Musical Percussion, each person is given or finds a music maker (for example, a tambourine, shaker, or pot). One person goes to the front of the group to "lead" the orchestra, using gestures only. The music makers can remain stationary, move around as a unit, or play to accompany the dance of their fellow playmates.

The ingenuity comes in your method of first introducing the games to your group. Select a few games that sound interesting to try or have the participants select some themselves. If at all possible, try to bring in a group of very young children (five or six years old) to play together with their older friends. Few sights are as warming as seeing a group of children join with a group of elderly people in cooperative play.

Some modifications of various contemporary sports suggested by active elders were outlined in the Alberta Parks and Recreation *Senior Citizen Sports and Games Manual* (1978). Included were some of the following:

- *Volleyball.*

    Increase the numbers of players per side from six to nine in order to reduce the area of movement required for each player.
    Vary the height of the net to the skill level of the group.
    Use a ball that is lighter than a volleyball so that it stays in the air longer and is softer for safety.

Have a floating service line rather than a specific spot from which to serve.
Take as many time-outs as needed.

- *Field Hockey.*

  Play with six players per side or adjust as seems necessary.
  Shorten the duration of the game.
  Reduce the playing field by half to cut down on the amount of running necessary.
  Replace regulation hard ball with softer rubber or plastic ball.
  Eliminate offside rules.
  If the ball goes over the goal line, it is pushed back in from the point where it crossed the line.
  The stick cannot be raised above the waist.
  The ball cannot be raised into the air.
  Body contact is prohibitied . . . unless it's of an affectionate nature.
  Game can be played at a fast walk (or a half-run).
  Ball must be passed three times before making a shot at the net.
  For safety, use goal markers or posts made of soft flexible material.

- *Water Polo.*

  Number of players adaptable.
  Play across shallow end of pool.
  Shorten game time (for example, four five-minute periods).
  Use rubberized ball with a circumference of about 7 inches (17 cm) for easier handling.
  A goal is scored by *placing* (rather than throwing) the ball over the goal line between the two posts.
  Players move in the water by walking or running slowly (rather than swimming).
  After taking three steps while in possession of the ball, a player must pass it to a teammate.
  The water should be warmish (80 to 85°F; 27° to 29°C).
  No physical contact allowed.

party and other inside games

Over the years we have had many parents ask us for games for parties—especially for birthday parties—that will change tears to cheers. Sally Olsen, editor of our *Cooperative Games Newsletter* (see the Resources section), has collected and adapted a whole series of cooperative activities that we feel are worthy of children's celebrations. A few of those activities, primarily for the three-to-seven age group, are presented below.

- *Cooperative Cadeau (Something for Everyone).* Fill one box with enough little gifts to allow one for each child attending the party (for example, fourteen little books, marbles, plastic rings, candies, cookies, or pieces of a puzzle). Wrap the box in newspaper so that there are at least as many layers of wrapping as there are children. The children sit in a circle and pass the parcel around clockwise to music. They can sing a short song or you can have someone at the record player to turn the music on and off. When the music is turned off or they come to the end of the short song, the person holding the parcel gets to take off *one* layer. Some people put a prize, such as party hat or another funny prize, in every layer. Older children sometimes like jokes, which they can read out to the group, written on each layer of paper.

Each time the music starts again, the parcel continues around the circle until the music stops. If a child has already had a turn at unwrapping a layer, she chooses someone who has not yet had a turn. The child who removes the final layer of wrapping has the honor of passing the gifts around to all the other children.

• *Sharing Cookies.* Here's a simple but effective method to help two- and three-year-olds share their favorite cookies at parties. When you put the cookie batter on the cookie sheet, instead of separating each cookie, place two teaspoonfuls right next to each other with no space in between. The two cookies will then bake together like "Siamese twins" and will have a small line down the middle, which makes for easy splitting. You can show the child where to break her cookie in order to share it with a friend. If you enjoy baking cookies in fancy shapes, try making gingerbread people in pairs or trios, holding hands. Make the cookies according to your recipe, and when putting them on the cookie sheet, overlap their hands and press down slightly. A little bit of raw egg dabbed on the ends of the connecting hands will help cement their relationship, at least long enough for the children to share their pair.

• *Pairing for Sharing.* To pair the children for games or cookie sharing, cut large pictures of animals or familiar cartoon characters in half, so that they are easy to match. If you do this two or three times during the party, each child will have a picture puzzle to take home with him after the party.

• *Cooperative Musical Cushions.* Place half the number of cushions (or pillows) as there are children in a circle formation on the floor. The children begin sitting on the floor in pairs, with two sharing one cushion. When the music is played or a short song is sung, one cushion is removed as the children skip around the circle all in the same direction. When the music is stopped, they all sit down sharing the remaining cushions. Continue until only one or two cushions are left. It probably won't be possible for everyone to sit on it, but as long as everyone is touching either the cushion or someone else who is touching the cushion, everyone wins.

• *Big Turnip.* This is a familiar folktale known in the Slavic countries as well as in China. It is a story about a monstrously overgrown turnip that by harvest time requires the cooperative pulling of grandfather, grandmother, little boy and girl, and all the farm animals to unearth it. Tell the story first (if possible, holding up a picture for the children to see from the children's book called *The Turnip*, by Janing Domansky; see the Resources section). Then have each child in the group choose which part they would like to be. There are always enough parts to go around because you can have all sorts of farm animals or two or three of each kind, if needed. A bird is usually the last animal whose final cooperative effort helps unearth the turnip. You can play without any props, or you can provide a wig and cane for grandmother and grandfather and masks for the animals; they help set the atmosphere but they are not necessary. We often choose the tallest person present for the turnip and cover him with a sheet or have him hold up a handful of green strips for leaves. When grandfather comes to pull the turnip out of the turnip patch, he holds the "turnip" by the hand and *pretends* to pull (otherwise all that pulling might hurt the poor turnip's shoulder). Grandmother comes along and holds on to grandfather's waist and *pretends* to pull, and so on with the little boy and girl and all the animals. Finally the bird comes, and this time everyone does pull. They will pull the turnip up to his feet, and usually everyone falls down in a merry heap. Pass around *small* pieces of raw turnip plus carrot sticks and celery sticks to make a sharing feast at the end of the play.

- *Balloon Fortunes.* Write a "fortune" for each child on a small piece of paper; then roll each one up and slip it into a balloon, and blow all the balloons up. The fortunes are actually instructions that encourage cooperative play (for example, "Make an elephant using everyone as a part of it"; "Find a friend who had the same thing as you for breakfast and shake hands"). For younger children, instead of a fortune insert a picture of an animal, which partners or everyone can then imitate. Give each person a balloon that they pop in turn by sitting on it or by letting someone else (another willing child or adult) sit on it. They then carry out what the fortune says.

  Another option is to play musical balloons like hot potato. The balloons are passed around in a seated circle, and the person holding the balloon when the music stops sits on it to pop it or passes it on to a friend to pop. She then retrieves the fortune, which everyone acts out. For the last fortune, save a balloon that instructs everyone to go to the table for a special treat.

- *Buckets Galore.* Collect a variety of buckets and containers, everything from a small tin can to a mop bucket to a peach basket. Collect all the balls you have in the house and try to match them up with the buckets, so that large balls go in the large buckets and small balls in the small buckets. (If you need more balls, have the children make some paper balls when they arrive.) Let the children line up in parallel lines across from a partner. Partners take turns holding the bucket and trying to bounce the ball into it. The objective is for the ball to bounce once on the floor before bouncing into the bucket. Balls that don't bounce can be tossed directly into the bucket. After each partner has had two or three tries at one bucket station, everyone switches (for example, partners move one station to the right, with the last set of partners in the line moving to the front of the line). All partners now have a different bucket and a different ball. A friend who tried this game with a group of eight- to twelve-year-olds at her son's birthday party reported that they found the game very challenging and at the end didn't even ask, "Who won?" An alternate way to play this game is to take

Parachutes can come inside, too

turns trying to bounce the ball into a bucket that is placed on the floor between two partners, or for one person to throw the ball over his head—backward—with his partner trying to catch it in the bucket.

Buckets Galore also works well with paper bags (for example, grocery bags) and cardboard boxes. Pairs of players spread out around the room in random order and toss a ball into their partner's hand-held bag or box. Balls can be tossed (or caught) frontward, backward, sideways, under the legs, over the head, or in whatever way desired and are not necessarily restricted to landing in your own partner's box. More people can be involved in the exchanges, and some pairs may choose to each have a ball and a catching bag for more active exchanges.

● *Parting with Gifts.* Some children have difficulty giving away "their" gift to the birthday child. Here's one way to turn the giving process into a game. One at a time, each guest hides her gift somewhere in the room. One child (or pair of children) then tries to find the hidden gift. When the searcher finds the gift, she gives it to the birthday child. The children who are not actively searching for the hidden gift can help the searcher(s) by making the group hum louder and louder if the child is getting near the gift and softer and softer as she moves away from it. As the birthday child opens one gift, another searcher (or pair of searchers) begins to look for another gift with the humming help of the group. The last present hidden can be a package that contains small trinkets or goodies for everyone. The birthday child can find this one and distribute the goodies to all of her friends.

Martin Strube has developed an alternative version of Monopoly, using the standard game board. First, wealth and roles are distributed arbitrarily in sealed envelopes at the beginning of the game. Thus, instead of being given an equal start, some players find themselves in the role of worker with a few hundred dollars and no property, while others find themselves in the role of manager with thousands of dollars and several properties. This beginning, he feels, is more in line with reality and may help some recognize the plight of others. A variety of new rules within the game allows greater interaction and negotiation among players than those for the standard game. As pointed out by Martin, "The cooperative element comes into play at such times as players with poor or underprivileged starting assets begin to recognize the commonness of their plight and begin to sort out joint strategies. . . . By including ready-built houses and factories in the sealed envelope distributions, it becomes more apparent sooner who the wealthy people are, and issues of housing and employment arise that much faster."

cooperative parachute and earth ball activities

Parachute Games

When we spread the parachute canopy on the ground or on the floor, people come over full of curiosity. "What is it?" "Is it a real chute?" "Did someone jump out of a plane with it?" "What is the hole in the center for?" There is no need for loud hailers, megaphones, or whistles to gather the people around. The sheer size of a parachute attracts attention.

With a friendly invitation to try our games, people naturally space themselves out around the circle formed by the canopy. There seems to be no more cooperative way of communicating with a group of people than in a circle. A circle puts all members of the group on an equal footing. They will listen to the leader until they have the idea of what to do, and then they will start making suggestions, giving ideas, sharing the leadership. Perhaps it is the lack of a defined place for the leader to stand and be recognized, such as a lectern or a pulpit, but soon the group starts to participate, from the smallest or shyest to the loudest or tallest.

Parachute games provide for the maximum participation by all members of the group. The very dynamics of moving the parachute means that cooperation is a must, and parachute activities reinforce this ideal by being more fun and successful when everyone cooperates. Each child has a meaningful role to play within the games and is partially responsible for their successful outcome. People feel free to create new games and to experiment with ideas without fear of having to fight officials or tradition for a rule change. But best of all, parachute games are loads of fun!

WHERE TO GET A PARACHUTE

Look in the Yellow Pages of your telephone book under "Parachutes." In larger cities, there are usually one or two sky-diving clubs that might have a limited number of used parachutes, often with rips and tears in them and large vents in the side that need repair. Patching them up is not too difficult a job if someone in your group has a portable sewing machine and a bit of space to spread the chute out. Try to repair the tears with a French seam, as this seems to hold up the longest.

The closest military outpost or surplus store might have used cargo parachutes. Caution: Don't get a parachute that has wide ribs that look like a spider's web. These chutes are very heavy and will not have enough silk for you to inflate them. Look for a large circular piece of material, cut and stitched together in a pie shape with a hole in the center.

If no parachutes are available (they seem to be in short supply in Canada, since they are shipped to the Arctic to use as temporary tents over machinery that has to be worked on in the field), one can be made out of light nylon sails or nylon material. Borrow a chute (from a school, for example) long enough to make a pattern; cut the nylon into a pie-shaped circle with the series of "pie slices" sewn together with a French seam. Cut a hole 12 inches (30 cm) in diameter in the middle, and sew a rope around the outer edge of the circle for grip. Make the chute at least 12 feet (4 meters) in diameter for multipurpose uses. Make sure a hole is left in the center or the chute will not "loft" successfully and fill with air.

Special parachutes made for the gym can be obtained through certain sports equipment supply outlets. These parachutes have a rope sewn around the edge for a better grip. See the list of suppliers in the Resources section.

PLAYING SAFELY WITH THE CHUTE

People of all ages seem to enjoy cooperative parachute games, and the excitement of the group mounts very quickly whether they are watching the chute fill with air or hiding under it. Start with the canopy placed flat on the floor or ground, with all the participants sitting comfortably around the edge and after every game, bring the canopy down to the floor again. Doing so guarantees that everyone can see everyone else and that everyone can hear instructions, ask questions, or contribute an idea. Bringing the parachute down to the ground is particularly important when playing with a mixed age group. Young children get frustrated when the parachute is held too high and they can't see or hear the action.

As the group becomes more familiar with the parachute you can use the "fruitbasket" position between each game. All the participants stand, hold the parachute with both hands at the chest level of the smallest participant, and allow the canopy to touch the floor or ground in the center, thus forming the "fruitbasket."

Try to avoid fatigue by stopping the game while the youngest or smallest is still enjoying it. Don't ask the players to shake the chute up and down for too long. Plan some quiet activities between the more active ones, or take a break from the parachute and play a game like nonelimination Hot Potato or Sing a Song. People seem to enjoy sitting in a circle right on the soft and silky material.

For games that involve a large number of people going under or on top of the chute, first choose small groups, perhaps two or three people, until everyone understands the idea of the game. If some children bump or crash into others, usually a reminder to the whole group about taking care not to hurt others is enough to rectify the situation. If not, standing beside the child who is crashing into others will usually stop this activity. With younger children it helps to take their hands as partners and show them how to do the activity safely. If older children persist in bumping into one another even after a positive explanation, change the game to one that does not require such active movement or ask them to try the same activity in slow motion. This will solve the problem temporarily and perhaps the spirit of cooperation will win them over in the end.

When first playing ball games with the parachute, consider assigning certain children the task of retrieving the balls when they fall off the chute; otherwise you may have half the group under the parachute fighting over who is to throw the ball back onto the chute.

If playing with the parachute outside, try to play in a grassy area. Falls on the pavement hurt, and crawling games on pavement wear out knees. The only problem with playing on loose dirt is that dirt can get on the chute, and when the parachute is inflated, the dirt will fly out and might get in someone's eyes.

Inflating the chute

INFLATING THE CHUTE

To inflate the parachute, everyone squats around the edge, holding it with both hands. A signal is given and all the participants stand up, raising the chute above their heads until their arms are fully extended. The chute will fill with air and look like a giant umbrella. To deflate the chute, everyone, still holding the edge with both hands, squats down and brings the entire edge to the ground. Air will be trapped in the canopy but will gradually spill out the center hole and deflate the parachute. If you want to get it down quickly, everyone has to pull strongly on the edge away from the center hole.

A starting signal is often needed for the games. We use the traditional "One, two, three—go!" adapting to French, German, Spanish, Russian, and Chinese, depending on what languages the group knows. After a particularly long and tiring day, we seemed to regain our strength when we started counting off in German.

Some games require only a few people at a time to do a task, although everyone has some role to play in all the games. If only one person is needed, we usually start with the person at some central point (for example, to the right of or directly opposite the leader) and work our way around the circle until everyone who wants a turn has had one.

GAMES FOR PRESCHOOLERS AND KINDERGARTEN CHILDREN

- *Chuting Stars.* It generally takes at least fifteen little kids to handle the chute successfully by themselves. In this game, the children (with adult helpers) grasp the edge of the chute, raise it to waist height, and gently move it up and down. Small groups of children walk, skip, or run under the chute as it floats. If there are enough adults to hold the chute, all the children can go under it. To change the expression of movement, tell the children a story about lions who move *quickly*, turtles who move *slowly*, robots who move *jerkily*, elephants who move *heavily*, or fish who swim *smoothly*. They will take it from there. If some children seem afraid to go under the chute, encourage them to go under in pairs or small groups, hand in hand, or simply let them hold on to the edge and help make the chute go up and down for the other children. When all the children have had a chance to run under (at their own pace), bring the chute down to the ground. You have to give the children a few minutes warning that you will be bringing it flat to the ground. Not everyone will come out even with this friendly warning. In a few minutes it gets quite hot and perhaps lonely under the chute, though. It is fun for the children around the chute to count the "bumps" and see them get fewer and fewer as the children pop out the sides—like counting down for a rocket takeoff, 10–9–8–7–6 . . .

You can make an exit tunnel by pulling the edge up from the ground in line with the telltale bump. The rest of the chute can remain flat. After peeking down the tunnel and inviting the child to crawl out, move your body to the side so that the child will see just an open space at the end of his tunnel, unless of course the child would prefer to keep your smiling face in sight.

- *Walking on Water, Waves, Bubbles, or Clouds.* Half the children get on top of the chute. The rest of the children and the adults make waves for the children on top to walk, run or crawl across. This is done by grasping the chute and moving your arms up and down with a gentle motion. The waves grow stronger as the imaginary wind picks up; soon you will have a storm and eventually a hurricane as you move your arms swiftly from head to toe. This is good exercise but cannot be kept up for very long. The wind gradually dies down and the waves become softer and lighter until the "pond" is as still as glass. When the waves grow larger, some of these young children may dive (belly flop) into a wave if they do not understand that there is nothing but air between them and the hard ground. They probably won't do it a second time, as it hurts, but a warning beforehand will sometimes prevent them from doing it the first time. Roll back the parachute a bit, show them the floor, and remind them that it is hard underneath. During the activity they can pretend they are walking across the tops of the clouds or that they are trying to break the bubbles of air you make. When they have enjoyed these activities for a long time, ask everyone to find a place on the floor around the chute.

Walking on waves

• *Revolving Sit-ups.* Players sit on the ground around the chute with their legs underneath it, toes toward the middle, and the chute pulled taut. While still holding on to the edge of the chute, players lie back and then pull themselves up using the taut parachute to help. Repeat this several times in a row. Usually the members of the group naturally get into a harmonious synchronization in which the people on one side end up helping the people on the other side, thus making for a cooperative sit-up. Continue for as many sit-ups as you want the group to do, but be careful not to overdo it. People will usually stop by themselves when they have had enough. If people have back problems, have them bend their knees and keep their feet flat on the ground when they put their legs under the chute.

• *Silk House.* Children sit around the chute, hold on to the outside edge, and crawl all the way under it. While still facing the center, they pull the parachute material behind their backs and tuck it under their bottoms. Once the whole group is sitting around the edge in this manner you can start playing "underwater" games. You could talk about how it would feel to be in the tummy of a whale or to be a jellyfish, or if this is what it would look like if you were in an igloo on a sunny day.

When everyone is seated with their legs flat on the floor, ask the children to rock the Silk House by pushing back gently on the material with their backs. You can get the rocking house to move in a circular way by indicating the direction players should lean as they rock. Rock one way, and then reverse the direction for a while.

On a warm day a parachute will get very hot underneath, and so you will not want to stay under there too long. However, if you are playing on a cold day, the air under the parachute will warm up and be nice and cozy. One particular cold, windy day, we spent the entire afternoon playing and eating under the parachute. We rocked the Silk House, played Nonelimination Hot Potato, passed around a joke, and ate watermelon under the chute.

• *Ring Games.* Ring games are successful without a parachute, but when you add one you add some excitement. Preschoolers will ask to play these games over and over. Players hold the chute with their right or left hands (as the leader designates) and walk around the circle chanting or singing a rhyme. "Ring around the Rosy" is one almost everyone knows:

> Ring around the rosy,
> A pocket full of posies,
> Hush-a, Hush-a,
> All fall down!

The children all fall down on the last verse, making the chute flat. To get up again we have another rhyme:

> Down in the garden,
> Picking buttercups,
> Along comes the bee,
> Buzz-z-z-z-z-z-z-
> And we all jump up!

The children flap the parachute quickly when we say, "Buzz-z-z-z-z," like a bee's wings moving quickly, and we all jump up on the last line. Another way to get up after "All fall down!" is to count down like a rocket launch: 10–9–8–7–6 . . . until "Blast off!" when everyone raises the parachute above their heads.

There are many more ring games that can be used with the parachute. Edith Fowke's book *Sally Go Round the Sun* is full of Canadian favorites.

• *Air Conditioning.* The children lie on their backs on the floor under the chute, with their heads pointed toward the hole in the center (or in that general direction). The adults and perhaps a few children remain outside with the parachute at waist level and begin to make waves by moving their arms up and down gently. This will give a lovely fan to those below and, if done gently, will be soothing to little ones who have played hard and may be getting tired. Once the children have had a nice long Air Conditioning, adults usually go under and let the children give them a good flap. They seem to enjoy it as much as we do.

- *Name Game.* Several children are chosen to go under the chute and hide. One person is asked to chant the name of one of the children hiding under the chute. The group joins the chant, "Ka-tie, Ka-tie, Ka-tie," until Katie pops out of the hole in the center. Katie then comes out to the side and helps the group chant the name of another child hiding underneath, "Jim-my, Jim-my, Jim-my," until Jimmy pops out of the hole, and so on until all the hiding ones have had a turn. Another group of children then goes under until everyone has had his moment in the sun.
    Another version of this game is played in conjunction with the following chant:

    Where is Katie?
    Where is Katie?
    Here she is! (Katie pops out of the hole)
    Here she is!
    How are you today, Ma'am (Sir)? (The group makes a slight bow towards Katie)
    Very well, I thank you. (Katie answers the group)
    Run and hide. (Katie pops down the hole)
    Run and hide.

- *Funny Faces.* The children inflate the parachute, take one step toward the center, stick their heads underneath, and wrap the parachute around their heads and under their chins like a woman's headscarf. They begin to make funny faces or share a giggle as they kneel down and then lie down stretched out on their stomachs. Under the chute is a circle of heads; outside the chute, a circle of bodies. The chute will eventually deflate, but there is plenty of time to smile at your friends around the circle.

- *Mountain.* Make a mountain of air by inflating the parachute, and quickly pull it down to the ground in front of you; then kneel on the outside edge. Once the mountain has been made and you are sure no one is underneath the chute, allow two or three children to climb the mountain on their hands and knees. They will squish all the air out of the hole by the time they arrive at the center. Warn the children about meeting other climbers coming from the opposite side of the mountain. If they are too enthusiastic about climbing, they may bump heads with someone coming from the other side. Have the children come back to the edge of the parachute by asking them to come down to the bottom of the mountain. Choose a few more children for the next mountain climb, and continue until everyone has had a turn.

You can make a great "mountain" out-of-doors on a windy day with just four big people. Ask two of the larger children or adults to kneel on the far side of the parachute facing the wind. They should be about 15 feet (5 meters) apart. Two other adults or older children then grasp the edge of the chute nearest the wind and hold it up as high as they can. The parachute will fill with wind and expand, making a huge mountain of air. (The four big people will form a square, with two kneeling and two standing.) The children, who have been waiting at the bottom of the mountain (between the kneeling adults), now begin the climb. The climbers will push some of the air out in front of them, but the standing adults also have to let down their edge gradually until the children reach the top of the mountain, making the parachute completely flat.

This mountain-making is really fun for the children. What they seem to enjoy most is the wind's blowing the soft material in their face and around their bodies, and completely enveloping them as they move up the billowing mountain. Before long they go back to the bottom of the mountain to let the wind fill the chute again.

- *Giant Doughnut.* One child hides under the chute near the center and is told to stand up straight with her arms by her sides. The rest of the children inflate the "doughnut" and then try to bring the center hole right down over the center person's head.

- *Collective Peek-a-Boo.* Several children sit on the parachute. The rest gather together and pull up the sides of the chute, covering the sitting children. Someone shouts, "Peek-a-boo!" and the children pull the edge out, exposing the sitting children. This sounds simple, but preschoolers love the game. The leader must be careful that the sitting children do not become entangled in the material or frightened to be covered in this way. The outside circle of people must not step forward too much, or they may tread on tiny fingers and feet under the material.

- *Popcorn.* Fill the giant pan (chute) with unpopped popping corn. Socks stuffed with foam, nerf balls, badminton birds, and beach balls work well. Tell the children that the pan is getting hot and that the corn is starting to pop, then flick and flap the chute to get the kernels moving. Allow several children to become popcorn pickers with the responsibility of retrieving the popcorn that flies out of the "pan" and onto the "floor." If children have never seen popcorn pop, you may want to let them see the real thing before getting out the chute.

A variation of this game can be used on special occasions. Let the children help you wrap up crackers, small chunks of cheese, or pieces of fruit like slices of apple or whole grapes in foil or paper. Make sure each child has her name on two wrappers. Put the goodies on the chute and let the kids pop them all off. Once they are all popped off, the children collect them from the floor. They try to find the person whose name is on the wrapper, make exchanges, and finally eat the goodies together. Remind the children that there are two pieces each, and any extras they find should be shared with those who do not have two.

GAMES FOR ELEMENTARY-SCHOOL-AGE CHILDREN

Elementary-school-age children actually like most of the games described in the preschool section, but you may have to change the names to make them appealing. "Peek-a-Boo" will be accepted when called Tidal Wave or Fish Bowl, with all the fish in the middle spilling out when the sides are let down. They can also make wave patterns as well as play games. In Walking on Water, for example, older children can produce a very coordinated and cooperative wave by dividing into three groups. While the first group moves the parachute up, the second group moves the parachute halfway down to the floor, and the third group brings the material all the way down to the floor. By alternating their positions they can produce a very fluid motion.

- *Chute Exercises.* Whether you do sit-ups, toe touches, squat thrusts, rowing, buttock's walk, or stride jumps, exercises take on a new light when done together around a parachute. Hold on to the chute throughout the exercise. Ask the children to inflate the parachute, bring it down to the floor as is done in Mountain, and see how many exercises they can do before the chute deflates.

- *Umbrella.* When the parachute is spread out on the floor, the children squat around the edge and hold it with both hands. On a signal, they all stand up, raise their arms as high as possible, and let the chute fill with air. You're trying to fill it with so much air that it will look like a giant's umbrella; don't worry if this doesn't happen the first time. Let the parachute fall with the natural movement of air spilling out the sides and through the center hole, until it is flat on the floor and the children are once again squatting around the edges. If you want to expel the air quickly, everyone has to pull the chute down and out. Variations of Umbrella include making it while kneeling, squatting, or sitting. Once the children have been successful in creating the umbrella it can be used for a number of games.

- *Umbrella Exchange.* The children count off from one to three or from one to five (if you have more than forty players). On a signal, the whole group inflates .the parachute and someone calls out a number. All the people with that number then run under the parachute to the opposite side before the chute falls softly to the ground. The group's job is to keep the chute up in the air until everyone has made it safely to the other side. This can be accomplished by letting the parachute deflate on its own or by keeping the arms raised slightly until the last person has made the exchange. Mid-chute collisions are a potential problem in this game. If you encourage children to take a slightly rounded route under the chute, most bumping will be avoided.

Another version of Umbrella Exchange uses different kinds of calls instead of numbers: "Everyone with sandals on, change places"; "Everyone with blue eyes, exchange"; "Everyone with brown, green, gray, or mixed-color eyes, change places." Soon you will have the group thinking up ideas: "Everyone who likes pizza"; "Everyone with black underwear" (we once had two people running under on that call, accompanied by much laughter); "Everyone who has not exchanged yet." Every once in a while, choose something that almost everyone has or has done: "Everyone who has ever lost a front tooth." Doing so causes minor chaos, as there will probably not be enough people to hold up the chute and the material will fall down on everyone. If the group is friendly and careful, you'll usually produce laughter with the chaos. If the group is an aggressive one, save the call until they have learned more cooperative habits.

- *Two-Parachute Exchange.* You can play the same exchange games with two groups, each of which has its own parachute. When the call is made, children run under their own parachute to the outside edge of the other parachute.

- *Umbrella Hug.* Certain players are chosen to move as described in Umbrella Exchange, but when they run under the parachute, they meet in the middle, hug, and return to their places. You can hug one or more people or even get together in one big "squishy" hug. This game works well with the youngest children as well as with co-ed teen-age and adults groups. Some elementary-school-age children may prefer to shake or slap one another's hands when they run into the center.

- *Balloon.* The children inflate the parachute and take two or three giant steps toward the center. Thus the balloon shape will form. When the balloon gives out, they take two steps back to their original position.

- *Drifting Cloud.* First the children must have mastered the art of letting go at the same time. If done properly, the parachute will hang suspended for a few seconds before gently drifting down on top of them. Ending a game by making a Drifting Cloud is a nice way to finish up.

- *Mountain Roll.* The children count off (as in Umbrella Exchange) and then make a "Mountain" as described in the preschool section. When their group number is called, they do forward rolls to get on the parachute and backward rolls to get off. If the whole group rolls together, they can roll while still holding on to the edge of the chute.

• *Lean In and Out.*   For this game you need enough children to comfortably hold hands around the chute. Children number off in twos all around the circle. They then make a "mountain," kneeling around the edge. This time, though, they all join hands, and on a signal, all the number ones lean backward (keeping their torsos as stiff and straight as possible) and all the number twos lean toward the center. The number twos are held back from falling on their faces by the counterbalancing of the number ones. On a signal, they can change direction so that the number ones move forward and the number twos lean backward. The signal can be given a number of times in a row—slowly. Continue for as long as it takes the "mountain" to deflate. The game can also be played in small groups without a chute in either a standing or kneeling position (see Leaning Ring).

• *Hot Dog, Mustard, and Relish.*   The children are divided into groups of three, with the names "Hot dog," "Mustard," and "Relish," and distributed evenly around the chute. They hold the chute at waist level with both hands. When the group's name is called, all those players let go and run around the outside of the parachute. The leader must specify the direction in which they are to run (right, left, clockwise, or counter-clockwise). When the first "Hot dogs" near their original starting point, the other players inflate the chute. The "Hot dogs" run under the inflated parachute, go to the center, and either hug or huddle in a group shouting, "Hot dog!" before returning to their original position. A good safety rule in this game is that if any of the children running around the circle want to pass a teammate running in front of them, they must do it on the outside. But this is not a race. Ideally, everyone should arrive in the middle around the same time.

• *Beanbag Pile.*   Wallet-size beanbags or blocks of three or four different colors are distributed randomly to all the children. When the parachute is inflated, a color is called, and all those children holding that color beanbag or block run under the chute to the center and pile their beanbags or blocks in a tower. The next color group called can try to make the tower taller. The game continues until all the colors have been called.

• *Wagon Wheel.*   Play this one in a large room with no obstructions around the walls. The parachute is held at waist level and is pulled taut, with everyone's leaning back slightly to keep the tension on the material. The "wheel" then moves in a circular motion around the walls. The backs of two or three children (the bottom of the wheel) touch the wall momentarily as the "wheel" spins along the wall. The fun increases as the speed picks up and the children feel the momentum of the "wheel" pulling them around. However, it's important to keep to a controlled speed limit and a quick response to the signal "Stop!" in case a child should trip. For smaller "wheels," children can spread themselves around any circular material sturdy enough to hold up to their pull.

- *Spinning Wheel.* This game requires the children to grasp the chute tightly as before, but with their right hands only; they then face forward (they will be looking at the back of the child in front of them). They walk, dance, run, hop, or skip forward, always keeping the chute taut. On a signal, they can turn and move in the opposite direction, changing to the left-hand grip. For more exercise and challenge have the children count off by threes. When their number is called, they let go of the chute and run completely around it in the same direction it is moving and slip back into their original spot. This is especially appealing when done to music.

- *Igloo.* Players grasp the edge of the chute with a crossover grip (right hand over the left with palms down). They then swing the parachute over their heads while turning their bodies to the right, so that they face outward. They bring the edge to the ground in front of them. (Everyone will now be on the inside of the chute facing the silk.) This forms the "igloo." To get out of the "igloo," they reverse the procedure, turning to the left and swinging the chute over their heads. They will end up in their original position with the crossover grip. This task takes a lot of demonstration and considerable patience to learn. Even adults have needed four or five tries before they were able to accomplish it. There were many people hopelessly entangled in the silk— hopelessly because they were laughing so hard they couldn't move to untangle themselves or others.

- *Jellyfish.* After playing Silk House (page 212) and rocking on the floor for a while, have everyone stand up with the parachute still wrapped around their backs and held to their bottoms. The "jellyfish" can stand in place and undulate for a while, and then directions can be given to move in a circle. Sidestep to the right and then the left. Try to move the fish around the room. This requires slow movement, as some of the children will be walking backward, some sideways, and some forward. Go slowly so that the children moving backward can keep their balance.

  This undulating creature could be anything the children desire, from an amoeba to a centipede or some wild space creature. The creature can decide what kind of a collective noise it should make.

- *Birds and Worms.* This is actually a semicooperative game. Two groups work together while a third tries to catch some of them. It's a good game to ease the transition between cooperative games and low-key competition. You need at least two dozen players.

  Choose a smooth clean floor or a soft grassy area on which to play. Depending on

Birds and Worms

the size of the parachute, choose two or three children to go on top of it. These children are the "birds" of Birds and Worms, the "cats" of Cats and Mice, or the "fishermen" of Fishermen and Sharks, depending on the group's whims. You could even have the "officers" of the Empire searching for the "rebels," if you want to use the *Star Wars* characters. Six or eight children are then made "worms" (or whatever) and hide beneath the chute. The rest of the group arrange themselves around the edge of the chute.

The "birds" crawl around on the parachute *on their knees*, looking for the "worms" hiding underneath. The "worms" *belly crawl* under the parachute and try to avoid being touched by the "birds." When a "bird" finds a "worm," the "bird" pats the "worm's" bottom or top (depending on which end is encountered first) and then goes on to find another "worm." When touched, the "worm" rolls out to the side of the parachute, and whoever is at the spot where he rolls out becomes the next "worm," replenishing the supply. "Birds" should get quite full after two or three "worms," at which point they too crawl off the chute and have someone from the side replace them. You could set a limit of two "worms" to a "bird" if you want the children to change positions quickly. Continue until all the children have had a turn as either a "bird" or a "worm." The obvious safety rule is that the "birds" must pat gently if squished and battered "worms" are to be avoided.

Now for the cooperative part. The people around the edge of the chute have the important job of hiding the "worms" from the "birds" by raising and lowering the chute, making waves that will hide the worms. Everyone is involved in something while waiting her turn to go under or on the chute. For a little variety or perhaps fair play, reverse roles. Let the people under the chute try to catch those on top. Eight little "worms" can do a good job tracking down two or three "birds."

- *Claws.* Players hold the parachute waist high while one—the giant "crab"—gets under it. As he moves around under the chute, he bends over and pushes his head or hand into the material, so that you can see the spiny bump on his back. Whenever he gets the urge, the "crab" clamps onto the leg of someone around the outside of the chute. That persons yells, "Crabs!" She then slips under the chute to join him. Each of them then clamp onto a person of their choice; they yell and more "crabs" join in under the chute. This continues until everyone has become a "crab"—the chute that now drapes over all the players forms the shell of the biggest "crab" you've ever seen.

- *Ball Roll.* Players hold the parachute at waist level. A large ball—a soccer ball, a beach ball, a medicine ball, or even an earth ball—is placed on top of it. The goal of the game is to roll the ball around the edge of the parachute first in one direction and then in the other. Some people will have to lift the parachute as the people in front of them lower their edge. A well-synchronized group can really get that ball rolling!

  An alternative game is to try to roll a smaller ball through the hole in the center of the chute. This can be difficult but worth the effort. For added challenge try Ball Roll or any of the parachute games with players grasping the chute with only one hand.

- *Bull's-Eye.* Players number off from one to three around the chute. Four baskets of tennis balls or small rubber balls are placed on the floor behind the players. The players hold the parachute at waist level and the leader calls a number. If number one is called, all the number ones leave their place at the edge of the parachute, get a ball, and try to shoot it through the center hole. If the ball does not make it through the hole, the players still holding on try to shake it in. When the last ball (or any designated ball) has been shaken down the hole, the players shout, "Bull's-eye!" and inflate the chute. All the number ones run under the parachute to retrieve their balls and place them back in the original baskets. The leader calls another number until everyone has had a turn.

- *Hot Ball.* The players hold the chute at waist level. Beanbags, tennis balls, or stuffed socks are handed to four (or more) individual players at distances around the parachute. On a signal, the objects are passed from hand to hand around the circle. Children usually pass with one hand and hold onto the chute with the other. When the call "Hot ball!" is made, the players inflate the chute, and the players holding the objects exchange places under it.

- *Ten-Second Parachute Formations.*   In this game the players around the chute count off by fours. The chute then is inflated and one number is called as a signal for that group to run to the center of the chute. The remaining players close the mushroomed chute over the center group by placing the edge on the ground in front of them. They then count to ten (or perhaps a little longer in the beginning) and inflate the chute to see what kind of formation the center group has created. All kinds of interesting formations (lying, sitting, and standing) are uncovered. It would be great if cooperative decisions in some bureaucracies and meetings could be made as quickly.

- *Can You Do Things Together?*   This game has an infinite number of variations. The common thread running through the different activities is that the children must perform a task or act out a motion together with one or more friends while all are still holding on to the parachute. For example:

> Can you be really tall?
> Can you be really small? Wide? Narrow?
> Can you do a round thing together?
> Can you do a square thing? Triangular? Octagonal?
> Can you skip with your friends around the parachute?
> Can you all move the parachute to the wall together?
> Can you make a fort with your friends and all get in it?
> Can you make a tunnel and crawl through? To the center? All the way across?
> Can you row a boat while holding onto the edge of the chute?
> With your back stuck to a partner, can you move the parachute?
> Can you all meet in the middle of the parachute?

GAMES FOR MIXED-AGE GROUPS

Some of the most pleasant times we have had playing cooperative games have started with parachutes. On, say, picnics for church groups, parent/teacher associations, clubs, nursery schools, and organizations of all sorts, you might have adults of all sizes and shapes, while the children range from a baby in daddy's backpack to teen-agers. When you have such a variety of ages and skill levels, cooperative games are more fun than competitive ones for the children, while the children's playfulness seems to rub off on the adults around them. Tensions just disappear.

Again, you can play most of the games described in the previous two sections with any mixed-age group. Umbrella Exchange and Silk House are good ones with which to start. Here are some others that call for a strong hand and a strong back to make them work. Whatever their role, you'll find everyone playing in them full of laughter, too.

- *Tail Swing.* This game is based on the spontaneous drag-them-around-the-floor idea children love. Just spread the parachute out on a smooth surface and let the children crawl all over and under it. Eventually some dad or big sister will be persuaded to grab an end and start pulling the children about. The more people pulling the chute, the better the ride. If a couple of children lie on the chute and the rest pull, the parachute will twirl in a circle and the child on the end will get a wild ride. Make sure that the floor is clear of obstructions and that you don't twirl the chute near the walls.

- *Rock-a-Bye Baby.* This game usually appeals to the preschoolers and is a gentler version of the next game. Two children lie down on their backs on the parachute, away from the center hole and away from each other. You need enough strong people around the edge of the chute to hold onto each rib (that is, the stitching that comes from the center hole to the edge). Other children can hold onto the edge between the stitching. You can also roll up the edge a little way so that everyone gets a good grip. The group, on a signal, raises the children off the ground and swings them gently back and forth in a rocking motion. Singing the tune "Rock-a-Bye Baby" once through usually gives them a long enough turn. This game may take a fair amount of time as every young child will want a turn, and then another, and another—sometimes past the time when the adults are tired!

- *Rock and Roll.* Fold the parachute in half, using the center hole as the dividing line. Placing the parachute flat on the ground and asking half the group to bring its edge to the opposite side seems to be the most efficient way to do this. You have now a half-pie shape. The adults can space themselves around this shape, making sure they get a secure grip on a rib. People along the double edge will have to hold two pieces of material. It is best to roll the edge up so that the bottom piece of material doesn't fall on the floor and get tangled around people's feet.
  One child at a time lies down on the chute parallel to the folded edge. The group, on a signal, raises the child off the ground. One side then lifts the edge of the parachute while the other side lowers its edge. The child, who is asked to lie rigid with her arms by her sides, will start to roll toward the lowered edge. Before she can get to the edge that side lifts its edge as the opposite side begins to lower its. The child will then roll back and forth across the parachute for as long as the group decides her turn will last. Try it with a ball before putting a person in the folded-over chute.

When the group has mastered the art of Rock and Roll with one child, they can put two children on the chute by spreading them out at opposite ends. As the children do not have much control over their rolling, don't let them start out too close together.

• *Parachute Toss.* Have everyone stand around the chute and roll up the edge so that they have a good grip, but leave the chute on the ground. Place a stuffed doll (preferably one of those big soft ones stuffed with clothing, with a pillow head) in the center of the chute. On the signal "One, two, three—go!" everyone pulls back on the chute at the same time to propel the doll into the air. Children will scream with delight as they watch Miss Sky-High soar into the air. Some children will be tempted to climb onto the chute themselves for a view from the top. Unless you have had specific instruction for the gentle art of propelling little people safely with a parachute, forget it. Parachutes were not built for tossing people. For that you need the right group and the right equipment—see Blanket Toss for more instructions.

• *Growing Mushrooms.* Children are alternated between adults around the edge of the chute, with everyone holding on tightly. On a signal, the adults inflate the parachute, raising the sides slightly (between waist and chest height). This action will lift the smaller children off the ground and give them a ride. Let them down gently. You can raise the sides a little higher each time, but smaller hands cannot hold on very long before dropping, and we don't want little mushrooms with broken stems.

Parachute-Balloon Toss

Sitting inside the Silk House

- *Rock-a-my-soul.* This is a play-while-you-sing game. If you don't know the tune to the spiritual, just chant the words together.

Rock-a-my-soul in the bosom of Abraham.	(Group skips around in time to the music
Rock-a-my-soul in the bosom of Abraham.	or chant.)
Rock-a-my-soul in the bosom of Abraham.	
O, Rock-a-my-soul!	
So high you can't get over it,	(Inflate the chute as for Growing Mushrooms.)
So low you can't get under it,	(Lower the chute to the ground gently.)
So wide you can't get around it,	(Stretch the chute as taut as possible.)
(You) Gotta go in through the door.	(Everyone run into the center, still holding the chute so that it wraps around everyone.)

- *Water Coming In.* Adults make giant waves by raising the edge as far up as they can (not all together) and then bringing the edge down to the ground (essentially doing toe-touching exercises). The children pretend to swim *under* the parachute, but when a giant wave comes down on them, they have to squat down as low as they can. When the wave rises (chute inflates), they can continue swimming across to the other side.

PUTTING THE CHUTE AWAY

After the last chute activity we usually ask all players to roll their edge toward the hole in the middle. Within ten to fifteen seconds everyone meets in the center, and the chute is in a nice little bundle. Another cooperative victory! You can also simply inflate the chute and let it float down to the floor, then stuff it in a bag or a box, like tucking the floating cloud away for another day.

Earth Ball Games

Earth ball games (played with a giant heavy canvas ball) are increasingly popular—but few people realize that they can be very dangerous. The sheer size of the ball can lead to problems: Children can sprain wrists, fall down, get rolled over, or be pushed aside in a frenzy, particularly if the game is, or becomes, competitive. As a result, we use earth balls only for a few specific games, almost always ones in which the children remain stationary and the balls move, thus reducing the chances of injury. We also recommend using smaller balls for children.

If you do organize an event for children or mixed-age groups, try using large beach balls instead of earth balls in the same games. For example, Collective-Score Volleyball and Blanketball (outlined in the first *Cooperative Sports & Games Book*) can be played safely and enjoyably by children with just beach balls. For games that involve rolling the ball, try inner tubes.

If you do have an earth ball and are looking for a few games that may allow you to make the best cooperative use of your equipment, consider the following.

• *Ball Roll on Chute.*   This is one of the best cooperative activities you can introduce with an earth ball. You'll need a parachute as well as a ball. Place the ball on the parachute (held waist high) and roll it around the edge of the chute so that it just misses peoples' fingers. If you do not have a parachute, the children can roll the ball around a circle on the ground so that it just misses their toes.

• *Train Roll.*   Players lie on their backs in a circle, with their heads toward the center. The earth ball is first rolled around the circle over their tummies, moved by the players' arms. The players can then bend their knees and raise their arms to form a "train track" on which the earth ball rolls. Helpers are needed on the inside and the outside of the circle to keep the train on the track. Helpers must be careful not to step on any of the participants.

You can play a variation in which the tracks are formed by a straight line of children lying on their backs. Young children seem to enjoy the feeling of a big ball's rolling over their tummies and making a noise as the ball makes contact. Ask the children if they can make a roller coaster for the ball to go over. They can use their imaginations,

Earth ball fun

or you can start them off by having alternate children lying and kneeling so that the ball will go up and down like a roller coaster.

• *Back Rub.* Have you ever felt like you have the world on your shoulders? This game really gives you that feeling, but in a good way. Participants line up in two lines, back to back. They then bend forward so that they are bottom to bottom, forming a stand-up track for the ball. The earth ball is hoisted onto their backs by two helpers and rolled down the line. A nice but momentary back rub results. You can roll the ball up and down the line a few times or form a continuing line by running to the end of the line immediately after the ball has passed over your back.

A variation of this game that is a little more relaxing begins with players lying on their stomachs in a circle, with heads toward the center. They put their hands by their sides and their shoulders touch those of their neighbors. Other players stand in a circle around the lying-down players' feet. One person stands in the center of the circle. The standing people gently roll the earth ball over the backs of the other players. The speed of the ball can be increased by increasing the number of people who stand around the circle and keep it moving. The person in the center also helps to guide the ball on its circular path. Don't forget to change places frequently.

- *Feet Up.* Participants lie on their backs in a straight line. Then every other person turns to lie in the opposite direction. The line will still be straight but people will be hip to hip facing different directions. On a signal, the players put their legs in the air and the earth ball is hoisted onto their feet. They try to shuffle it down the line without dropping or kicking it off. Helpers are needed to run down the sides to keep the ball on the feet. Make the return trip a few times. Helpers have to be careful not to step on anyone.

- *Earth Ball Pass.* Players stand in two lines facing each other. With arms outstretched upward, they pass the ball down the line—no wild tosses, please. As the ball passes a player he runs to the end of the line and prepares to take the ball again. Don't use a very large earth ball that can hurt the children's wrists; with a moderate-size ball the game can be safe *and* fun.

- *Caterpillar over the Huge Mountain.* In our original version of this game, children connected to one another by grasping ankles and crawling over a small "mountain" (for example, a bench over which a mat is draped). The earth ball version is similar except that the "mountain" is much much higher. Consequently, six reliable spotters (preferably adults) are needed to guide the children over the ball and to catch them as they descend toward the earth.

To get going, the children form a line and the first person in the line presses her chest against the ball with her arms stretched forward. Two spotters, one on either side of the starting point for the first child, roll the ball forward slowly so that the child is carried to the top of the ball. At this point the next child in line grasps the first child's ankles and will be pulled up onto the ball just by holding onto her ankles. However, when he gets to the top of the ball he must let go of the first child's ankles so that the spotters catching the first child can allow her to swing her feet to the ground. It is the job of the first two spotters to help get the children up on the ball securely and to control the speed at which the ball moves forward.

Four additional spotters stand ready to receive children on the other side of the ball. These people catch each child as he comes riding over the top of the ball. They work in pairs. The first two spotters grasp the first child by the upper arm and under the armpit as he comes over the top of the ball. By lifting up on the child's arms and taking some of his weight, they allow him to swing his feet under himself to a standing position on the ground. As the first two spotters carry the first child forward off the ball, the second two move in to grasp the second child by the upper arm and armpit and prepare to ease him off the ball. The four catchers continue exchanging places as the children come over the ball. After each child has had her turn, she can return to the back of the line for another.

Caterpillar over the Huge Mountain

It's crucial to use responsible spotters—and to stop as soon as they get tired (usually long before the children do). If the ball gets moving too fast or spotters are not able to catch a child, she can take a pretty good dive right into the ground. However, if the ball is moved very slowly, if it is stopped momentarily to ensure that catchers have the top child's arms, and if children are reminded to let go of the ankles of the child in front of them as they reach the top of the ball, the game can be a lot of fun. Variations played in shallow water have great possibilities.

• *Controlled Group Maneuvers.* A group of about ten people try to maneuver the big ball through an obstacle course *without the use of their hands.* Some of the obstacles (for example, small hurdles) require lifting the ball as well as pushing it around markers, up ramps, or into little gullies. Since you're restricted in how you move the ball, you need to maintain tight control of it—usually by increasing the level of cooperation. Slowing the pace also makes the game safer.

• *Sitting on Top of the World.* At the end of the session, undo the air valve and let everyone who can fit sit and lie over the earth ball to "squish" all the air out. The earth ball will gradually deflate and bring people closer and closer. You might spend the last minutes of the day discussing what was fun and what could be changed for more fun.

moving on

Some people want to be famous,
Some people want to be wise
I want to be like my grandfather
With laughlines framing my eyes
"Goals," by Paul Teskey

What gentle children lose as they move into a "modern age" is their humanity. Therefore, the greatest need in education lies in promoting cooperation, personal responsibility, and humanistic cultural values.

In the area of children's games, when one compares what was with what has come to be, there is one striking observation. Organized competitive games, primarily those promoted by professional sport interests, have almost completely replaced the traditional games in virtually all cultures, even where games usually drew on cooperation for their energy.

Before all traces of sharing and cooperative skills disappear, we need to reassess their important place in our lives and our children's lives. To reintroduce and maintain original playful orientations in children's games, I offer these specific recommendations. Try to keep them in mind as you set up playdays and supervise recesses, organize parties, establish teams and leagues, and enjoy physical play with your own friends and family. You'll notice a difference in yourself—and those around you:

- Encourage child input and rule adaptation so that games are played in a cooperative way:

  Everyone plays.

  No one is left out (or on the sidelines).

  No physical contact of a destructive nature (for example, hitting or tackling) is allowed.

  The smiles in the games become the priority.

- Introduce an elder-to-child approach, in which each child asks his grandparent or other older adult to teach him a game that she played when a young child. Older adults can also teach children how to make their own playthings.

- Introduce a child-to-child approach, in which older children learn cooperative games and teach them to younger children.

- Encourage children to make up new games within human value structures (for example, cooperation, sharing, involvement, having fun).

- Introduce (or make up) more games whose goal is to have older children help younger children.

- Use as many cooperative games as possible, and where competitive games are used, introduce simple cooperative rules or rituals to keep them in perspective.

- Become more proficient at picking out and pointing out the good things your children do. Catch them being good (aaah, gotcha!).

- Help your children set personal goals that are realistic and achievable, such as self-improvement in a variety of skill areas.

- Play with your children and encourage other adults to do likewise. Barriers are broken and lines of communication are opened when you enter their world of play. This is particularly evident when you are able to laugh together or play together to reach a common goal.

- Talk with your children about their likes and dislikes and about their suggestions for improving games and sports.

- Encourage your children to talk with you about what you want them to get out of the sport experience. See *Every Kid Can Win* for specific questions children can ask their parents.

- If your children play organized sports, encourage them to tell you how they would like you to behave before, during, and after their play.

- When your children come home after having played a game, instead of asking, "Did you win?" ask, "Did you have fun? Did you learn anything?"

- Through your actions help your children to believe that your acceptance of them as valued people has nothing to do with a score in a game.

Every time I hear about another person, program, or book that recognizes the value of people, I feel good inside. It makes me believe that something is beginning to take hold. I am optimistic about some of the exciting developments I have witnessed in cooperative play and games over the past ten years. I am also realistic enough to know that we are fighting an uphill battle. There are no magical solutions here, only everyday people like you and me. If constructive change is to occur, it will come as a result of our everyday interaction with our children, our families, and those who try to run our lives. Only a concerted cooperative effort will enable us to surmount the obstacles and allow our grandchildren to experience the real potential of humanity.

My good friend, Cal Botterill, has a sensitive and talented four-year-old son (Jason), who loves sports. Cal has promoted the playful part of games right from the beginning. He always asks Jason about enjoyment and fun . . . never anything about winning. Not long ago, the university hockey team that Cal coaches won an important game. When Cal returned home he told Jason that his team had won. Jason replied, "Dad, you're forgetting one thing. . . . Did they enjoy themselves?"

In your personal quest for positive change remember the ancient Chinese proverb, "If we are all of one heart and mind, we can change clay into gold."

appendix a

Growing up Sane: Thoughts on Raising Healthy Children

An extensive study by Marion Yarrow attributes the primary difference in empathy among young children (in North America) to the intensity with which parents convey the message not to hurt or otherwise harm others. Forceful or dramatic responses to hurting others, such as, "Look what you did!" and "You must never poke anyone's eyes," along with explanations as to why, seem to nurture a child's concern and responsibility for the welfare of others. Neutral, calmly reasoned responses, such as "Mary is hurt now," have little or no altruistic effect.

Another important factor that is directly related to young children's empathy toward others is the parents' gestures of love toward their own children (for example, hugs and kisses, soothing words, and other demonstrations of caring, understanding, and support). It is the overall message communicated about the value of other people that is most important of all in nurturing cooperation and empathy.

When visiting an aboriginal preschool in Australia, I noticed that the aboriginal mothers attempted to turn "incidents" of conflict or distress into lessons of sharing. If there was a conflict over a toy, they made an effort to show the children how they could share the toy. Their white counterparts separated the children, giving each one a toy, or removed the toy, and thereby inadvertently took away an excellent opportunity for cooperative learning.

The simple but profound wisdom of the aboriginal people is now gaining support from researchers in industrialized societies. One such study demonstrated that by having children practice sharing after a disruptive action, you get a threefold increase in sharing toys (Barton and Osborne, 1978).

Because potential conflicts among young children can provide such a beautiful opportunity to teach cooperative skills, I have tried to take advantage of these occasions in my own life and work. Let me give you some examples.

Len (twenty months old) was scooting around on his miniature scooter car. When he got off the car, Anouk (nineteen months old) began to approach it. Immediately he jumped back on the car. Anouk continued to play with some building blocks. Len again got off the car and this time climbed on his mother's knees. Anouk looked up, saw the car free, and walked toward it. Len quickly slipped off his mother's knees and, just as Anouk arrived, jumped back on the car.

What would you do in a situation like this? Take Len off the car and let Anouk have a turn? Leave Len on the car and give Anouk something else with which to play? Separate the two children, giving each of them something else with which to play? Put away the car and let each find something else with which to play?

What I did was leave Len on the car and lift Anouk onto the car directly behind him (like two riding on a motorcycle). I then pushed the car back and forth around the room. Anouk wrapped her arms around Len and hung on as we wheeled around the room.

They both laughed and giggled. I then lifted Len to the back and slid Anouk into the driver's seat. Again I pushed them around the room to their great delight. Then I stopped and sat down. Together they continued to move the car around as a unit by pushing on the floor with their feet. This enabled me to turn a situation of potential conflict into a constructive lesson in sharing, and I was able to do so in a way that avoided tears and increased both children's fun.

Another example arose when Anouk and Alex wanted to play with the same toy car at the same time. I sat them both down facing each other, with their legs apart, and guided them through a car-sharing game. I placed Anouk's hand on top of the car and rolled the car to Alex, and then I repeated the same process with Alex, pushing the car to Anouk. I guided the exchange about ten times, being sure to tell each of them how great they were doing. By this time they were squealing and enjoying the process on their own, and so I moved away.

On another occasion, two one-year-olds were arguing over a can that was filled with wooden blocks. I gently took the can and dumped out all the blocks between the children. I made sure that some blocks dropped directly in front of each child. I then began to put some blocks back into the can and they followed my example. All three of us filled the can and then took turns dumping the blocks out for everyone to fill again. I have found container-filling games in general (for example, with sand, pebbles, or water) go over well with young children and promote the idea of cooperative play.

Cooperative responses can also be tied into everyday food sharing and minor incidents of distress. For example, if one child falls down, another child can be encouraged to help him up.

Children in cooperative cultures grow in the midst of many playmates. In order for any child to practice and perfect social interaction skills, she needs the opportunity to interact with other children in constructive ways. The earlier this contact begins, the better. By age three, children in cooperative cultures share and help one another with some regularity. The high value placed on loving and caring for one another comes from a variety of sources, including stories, songs, dance, play, games, and people. By providing collective-play areas and cooperative playthings, these children begin with a history of living and sharing with other children.

Nursery-school teachers almost everywhere are extremely interested in promoting healthy interaction among children. In the wintertime Chinese nursery-school children often wear coats or jackets that button up the back. Since they cannot reach their own buttons, they are encouraged to help one another, and each gains from the process. In Canada we do not have coats that button up the back, but we do have snowsuits (which zip up from toe to neck) and snow boots that are sometimes hard to get off alone. Children could be encouraged to help one another with this important daily function for mutual benefit. There are many such cooperative activities that foster mutual social development and could be tied into our homes, school, and play.

I find it unfortunate that many modern-day parents do not experience intensive everyday interaction with their children. They miss much of the joy of learning that is written all over the child's face when he begins to roll over, crawl, stand, walk, make sounds, open cupboards, watch birds, explore flowers. Each step in discovering the world brings new joy and excitement to young children and observant parents. I also find it unfortunate that our culture is not designed in a way that encourages families to do things together. Activities are often segregated by age. Children are not welcomed in many social settings ("No dogs or children"), whether they be public or private gatherings. Exactly who is invited to dinner or to a party? I recently received a wedding invitation that indicated the couple's preference that children under five not attend. I went to a movie with my eight-month-old daughter sleeping in my arms and was refused entry at the door. The law was read to me. She must be eighteen years old to get in (even if sound asleep). "Them's the rules." I went back another day and noted that the film had a few nude dancing scenes. It is interesting that she would have been admitted to a theater across the street that was showing a film filled with war and killing (general admission). I never could figure that out.

I know that both parents and children can benefit by having a break from each other from time to time. We all need time for ourselves. However, children also benefit a great deal from being included in as many outings as possible, regardless of normal bedtime. Celebrations and feasts in more technologically primitive societies are never for adults only. The children also have something to celebrate. In fact, in Papua New Guinea we were invited to a feast in honor of the birth of a baby. Pigs were roasted, vegetables were brought in from the gardens, and food was shared by all. The children ran around freely. Young children learn from these experiences— about themselves, about others, and about how people function in different social settings. Perhaps most important is that they learn that they are important enough for you to want to bring them along.

In far northern Arctic settlements, even if the traditional dances and celebrations continue all night, you can be sure that babies and youngsters of all ages will be there all night. *Everyone* is there and everyone is welcome. In Chinese communes and factories, babies and young children often accompany their mothers to work, sometimes staying on their backs and sometimes being left in collective nurseries (with collective cribs and playpens) where mothers visit periodically during the day to breastfeed and cuddle. In many traditional cultures babies accompany their parents who are working in the garden. There is much less segregation of children from the daily routines and ongoing social events that make up life.

Good parenting is the toughest job in the world. We cannot possibly provide everything we might like for our children because many situations are beyond our immediate control. But some of us are very fortunate for having had parents who really cared.

In order to bring out the humanness in your own children here are some things you might consider:

> Positively recognize and respond to your child's gestures of giving.
> Emphatically demonstrate your dissatisfaction with hitting or otherwise hurting others.
> Let children practice ways to share in order to increase harmony or prevent disruptive acts.
> Let children experience shared mutually beneficial solutions in situations of potential conflict.
> Discuss the problems and bad feelings that surface when people behave in an inconsiderate way (whether in a supermarket, on TV, or in a game).

Do everything in your power to ensure that your child's first exposures to preschool leaders, elementary-school teachers, and community coaches reflect the kind of values that you feel are important.

Carefully select family activities, community events, and television programs that support the value of people and empathy toward others.

Freely demonstrate your gestures of love to your own children and expose them to as many considerate and loving people as possible.

Remember also that quality play experiences provide ample opportunity to nurture acts of caring, understanding, and mutual support. These can occur between you and your own child, you and your child's friends, your child and other children, or your child and other adults. Through play you can clearly demonstrate (or model) sharing, acceptance of others, and empathy for others. You can also clearly and powerfully convey the message that children must not hurt others.

Our cooperative learning programs in preschool and kindergarten have helped us to influence positively children's cooperative and empathetic responses, even for those who were initially considered retarded in their development in this area.

Continuing to Communicate

In order to fulfill the common goal established in cooperative games or competitive team games in a mutually satisfying way, *communication* is essential. Sometimes it is verbal; more often it is nonverbal, requiring youngsters to tune into the signals being sent by their playmates.

Communication can be encouraged before, during, and after games. People feel and function better when they feel accepted and have an opportunity to share ideas, discuss problems, present suggestions, and give one another support. When you begin to sense that other people have feelings that are touched by your actions and become concerned about their feelings of inclusion or exclusion, you know you are becoming more fully human. When people begin to let down their barriers and share themselves, I feel really connected to them.

Open communication is as important for preventing problems as it is for solving them. However, being responsive to other peoples' needs or feelings is difficult if you do not know what they are. Harmony among people begins with developing the skills to feel what others are feeling and helping them to feel what you are feeling.

Stress Control

If we expose children to stressful situations, it is my feeling that we have a responsibility to teach them how to cope constructively with that stress. It is never too early to begin to transmit these kinds of lessons.

As a first step toward anxiety control, we can teach children to become aware of their personal signs that accompany the onslaught of anxiety (for example, physical sensations and self-talk). We can help them become conscious of the things they say to themselves when they get nervous and when the nervousness goes away. In short, we can help them to cope with anxiety, to constructively deal with anger or frustration, and to channel aggression in more positive ways. There is ample opportunity to practice, refine, and test the effectiveness of various self-control strategies during competitive games and sport. The new challenge becomes one of feeling the way you want to feel, behaving the way you would like to behave, and learning what you would like to learn before, within, and after the game.

Teaching children to tune in to their bodies and to relax should be a part of every competitive sports program. In the long run, the relaxation may turn out to be more important than the activity.

MUTUAL RELAXATION EXERCISES (PAIRS SHARE)

Children and youths have some very interesting and effective ways of dealing with stress. If they can share their stress-control techniques with other children, everyone can benefit. A good introductory exercise in stress control is to split the children into groups of two or three and let them share their answers to the questions below. If adults are part of the group the matching of a child with an adult works well:

1. *Personal Signals of Anxiety*—When you get nervous or uptight, what do you feel in your body? For example, do some parts feel tense? If so, which parts? Do you get a funny feeling (butterflies) in your stomach? Sweaty palms?
2. *Anxious Situations*—When do you get most anxious (for example, competitions, exams, in front of groups, when an adult yells)?
3. *Ways of Coping*—When you get uptight is there anything you can do to make the feeling go away (or reduce it)? What has worked best for you? In this question you are attempting to bring out the child's most effective coping strategy(ies).

After the children have explored their answers to these questions with their partners, have them regroup to share some responses with the larger group. Doing so will help them realize that everyone gets nervous sometimes and that it is possible to control your own anxiety level. It will also provide them with some additional coping strategies that might work for them.

End the session with some relaxation exercises. Tell the children that one of the many ways of reducing anxiety is through the use of physical relaxation. To relax you have to cooperate with your own body, with your own muscles. You have to tell your muscles to relax. You have to tell yourself to become calm, like a lake without a ripple.

Children can work together in pairs to help each other relax. A relaxation script can be read (see *In Pursuit of Excellence* for script), or children can draw upon their own ingenuity and personal experience to help their partner relax. A specific relaxation procedure can also be communicated to the entire group at once.

Children can be encouraged to practice relaxation and be given time to do so when you are with them. They can also be encouraged to try to recreate the relaxed and calm feelings before, within, or after stressful events. Whenever their signals of anxiety begin to surface, they should ask their bodies to cooperate by using words like "calm" and "relax." Other problems such as the loss and control of temper can be handled by following similar procedures.

appendix b

Alternative Hockey

Martin Strube works with the Social Education Project (15 Harwoods Road, Watford, England). He has been involved in developing some interesting alternative approaches to games, including this set of rules for an Alternative Hockey League.

Alternative Hockey differs from the traditional game in a number of ways. To begin with, points are not earned by winning or losing—they are earned by showing up for a match. These "showing up" points are the only ones recorded and are assigned to a player's home street, village, or town. Let's say five players from Village A, three from B, one from C, and two from D attend a match jointly arranged by a player from Village E and one of the six players from Village F. The two players who arranged the game, having done most of the initial telephone calling to negotiate both a time and a place, act as captains (or convenors). Essentially their task is to meet on the

---

pitch and to agree on the best distribution of players in the interests of a balanced encounter. This means that out of the six "teams" and eighteen players assembled, two "sides" of equal playing capacity will emerge. One "side" might consist of three players from Village A, one from B, two from D, one from E, and two from F. The remainder of the players would then make up the other "side."

The goals scored in the game are not noted, for the match points are already determined (that is, five for Village A, three for B, one for C, two for D, one for E plus two for organizing (three altogether), and six for F plus two for organizing (eight altogether). After the match, these points are totaled up and telephoned into a central league registrar. At the end of the year, a newsletter appears with the final standing and a good bit of commentary from participants. The winning "team" is duly noted and lauded, as are the efforts of all the other teams in the league. Remember though that scores come strictly from showing up or organizing a match.

The whole business of established or well-funded teams dominating leagues is out of the question unless they are well represented at the grass-roots level. And even then, domination of the league doesn't necessarily mean domination of matches. Preoccupation with the score dies hard, but new Alternative Hockey players find the relevance diminishing as they note the prevailing lack of concern. More time is spent in appreciating dexterity, accuracy, or the chance emergence of strategy. Age and sex barriers are discarded, and intensity of play tends to vary with who has the ball; one quite often sees a six-year-old making good headway up the field while some of the older players take the opportunity to catch their breaths. Players over seventy quite often find their niches playing specific areas of the field rather than trying to keep up with the to-and-fro of play. The game in action is thus quite reminiscent of some of the better aspects of ice hockey and is, in fact, based to a certain extent on one of the originator's experiences of that sport.

After the match, one of the organizers (or "promoters") usually gives a tea (actually a little feast). This has come to be a fairly important aspect of the sport—so much so that there is a movement afoot to ensure that good teas are accredited points.

Here are the specific rules for Alternative Hockey:

1. A "convenor" is anyone wishing to organize a match.
2. One convenor must contact another to arrange time, place, and tea for his or her team.
3. At the time and the place, the convenors stand discreetly to the side of the warm-up exercises and arrange the "teams" into "sides" (no less than three to a side; no more than thirty) so as to distribute best the various qualities of the assembled players for a "balanced encounter."
4. Goals are set up approximately 8 feet wide (2.4 meters) and a minimum of 75 feet (23 meters) apart plus 5 feet (1.5 meters) more for every two players above the minimum. Goal height is the shoulder height of the goalkeeper of the moment.

---

5. The game is started with a face-off at center field between two opposing players. The ball is thrown between them by one of the convenors, and each tries to gain possession and pass to his own side. At the start, each side occupies its own half of the field.

6. Playing time is not less than one hour. Occasionally, a "half time" is called and ends are changed.

7. The ball is inflated rubber—18 to 20 inches (42 cm) in circumference.

8. The sticks are of the walking variety (canes)—inverted of course.

9. The ball may be struck with a stick, hand, head, or foot, but it may not be held except by a goalkeeper, who must immediately throw.

10. The stick should not be used above the shoulder. High balls should be played by hand and "wild swings" should be frowned upon.

11. Don't keep any running score.

12. Out of bounds does not exist except when a goal has been scored—at which time the defending side may pick up the ball and, in no great hurry, put the ball into play from their own goal mouth.

13. Field positions are disregarded in the normal sense (it is not even necessary to have a full-time goalkeeper); however, sides quite often try to determine strategies, which might involve some positional play during the course of a match.

14. At a suitable time (after at least one hour's play), if the consensus among the players is that the game must end, a cry of "last goal" is raised—at which time it is agreed that the next goal will terminate the match. It is understood that a "last goal" must be one of much verve and finesse.

15. At the conclusion of the proceedings (usually over a snack or tea), the convenors determine the game points. Each convenor earns three points for his or her team. Each other player earns one point for his or her team.

A sample game report that appeared in the *Alternative Hockey (AH) Newssheet* follows:

And now . . . the first AH report from Clwyd. November 26th 1978—a historic date in the annals of AH, the inaugural match in Clwyd, North Wales. Promoted by North Watford Knockers and newcomers Satin Wanderers. The game took place on a snow-covered pitch under a cold gray sky. There was plenty of action and excitement enhanced by the slippery surface. Soon people were peeling off scarves and jackets as the steam began to rise. The majority of the players were new to Alternative Hockey but quickly grasped the spirit of the game and played with zest and humor. A fine tea was hosted by the Satin Wanderers and there was much talk of the next match, possible dates and venues. The Clwyd situation is clearly very optimistic.

(At the conclusion of this article was a list of points that each "team" member was awarded for showing up and/or acting as convenor.)

The last time I heard from Martin Strube, Alternative Hockey was going strong and two new rules were under serious consideration, the most important of which was to award one point for a cooked cake or dish at an Alternative Hockey post-game meal and for providing tea.

appendix c

The Second Annual Grapefruit Cup

This was the brainchild of one of my former students, Dan Murphy. The following information was extracted from his announcement for the 1980 Grapefruit Cup. The Grapefruit Cup is an annual cooperative hockey game held on Ramsey Lake in the Gatineau Park, Quebec.

Equipment

Each player must bring a shovel in order to help clear a playing surface on the lake and for general ice maintenance.

Games are played on ice in boots or running shoes to allow for less stability and more wide-open play.

Boots are recommended for snow removal, while running shoes are recommended for game play.

Broomball shoes (made specifically for good traction on ice) are not permitted. Normal hockey sticks will help.

Every player must bring either a fresh grapefruit or a six-ounce grapefruit can, which will be smashed into regulation size for use as a puck.

Each player must bring two sweaters, scarves, or jerseys: one red and another blue.

Each player must bring an old hockey sock, with two rubber bands (to keep the sock up).

Rules

Switch

Players will be split randomly and evenly into two teams.

One team will wear red sweaters, while the other will wear blue.

Any player scoring a goal must switch sweaters to that of the opposite team, and start playing for them.

Goaltenders are not required, but if they are used, the goal size must be increased at least two times that of regulation size.

Two-Legged Hockey

Players will be divided into pairs, and these pairs will be divided into two teams.

Hockey socks will be worn on the shared leg.

Players must be paired with the opposite sex (where possible).

Normal hockey rules apply.

About twenty university students (ten females and ten males) showed up for the Second Annual Grapefruit Cup, which was *not* broadcast live on TV. A variety of sticks were used in the game, including hockey sticks, brooms, broomsticks, and dead branches. One person who was unable to locate a fresh grapefruit brought along a small can of frozen grapefruit juice. A variety of pucks were tried, including an empty paint can that was taped in case it hit anyone. People with broomsticks could place the ends inside the can and propel it, as in floor hockey or ringette.

Players tried a variety of options, including "switch," "two-legged hockey," and a "normal" game played in a cooperative and fun manner. Finally the guys played against the women and got wiped. Dan, a former university football player and coach, contends that it was because the women used hockey sticks and the men used broomsticks, but deep down he knows they were outclassed. It was all played in good spirit and everyone had a really good time.

resources

Equipment Suppliers

By writing to the following equipment suppliers you can obtain catalogs and price lists for such items as recreational parachutes, earth balls, scooter boards, sponge balls, beanbags, frisbies, hula hoops, beach balls, and so on. Include a self-addressed, stamped envelope for speedier service.

Brault et Bouthillier (full line of equipment)
700, rue Beaumont
Montréal, P.Q.
H3N 1V5
Canada

New Games Foundation (parachutes and earth balls)
P.O. Box 7901
San Francisco, California 94120
U.S.A.

Niagara Parachutes Ltd. (parachutes)
8407 Stanley Avenue
P.O. Box 927
Niagara Falls, Ontario
L2A 6V8
Canada

Program Aids, Inc. (full line of equipment)
161 MacQuesten Parkway
Mount Vernon, New York 10550
U.S.A.

Ravens Industries, Inc. (parachutes, earth balls)
P.O. Box 1007
Sioux Falls, South Dakota 57101
U.S.A.

Tremac Industries Ltd. (parachutes)
5357, 25th Avenue
Vernon, British Columbia
V1T 7A5
Canada

U.S. Games, Inc. (full line of equipment)
Box EG 874
1511 North Harbor City Boulevard
Melbourne, Florida 32935
U.S.A.

Recommended Readings

EXCLUSIVELY COOPERATIVE

There are few books or articles of a practical nature that are exclusively cooperative. What follows is a list of my most recent recommended publications within this domain. The basic content within each of these writings reflects a concern for the overall development of cooperative people and humanistic values.

Aarons, A., and H. Hawes. *Child-to-Child*. MacMillan Press Ltd. (4 Little Essex Street, London WC2R, England), 1979. (In Canada, Gage Publishers, Commander Boulevard, Agincourt, Ontario, M1S 3C7, Canada.)

Aronson, E.; Blaney, N.; Stephan, C.; Sikes, J.; and Snapp, M. *The Jigsaw Classroom.* Sage Publications (275 South Beverly Drive, Beverly Hills, California 90212), 1978.

Cooperation and Community Life—A Teacher's Resource Manual (1980) and *Cooperative Outlooks*, (1980). Saskatchewan Department of Cooperation and Cooperative Development (2055 Albert Street, Regina, Saskatchewan, S4P 3V7, Canada).

Cooperative Games Newsletter. Sally Olsen, editor (18 Bedale Drive, Nepean, Ontario, K2H 5M1, Canada).

Deacove, J. *Cooperative Parlor Games.* Family Pastimes (R.R. #4, Perth, Ontario, K7H 3C6, Canada).

Deacove, J. *Sports Manual of Cooperative Recreation.* Family Pastimes (R.R. #4, Perth, Ontario, K7H 3C6, Canada), 1978. (Good for many ideas of turning traditional sports into cooperative ventures.)

Deacove, J. *Supplement to Games Manual of Noncompetitive Games.* Family Pastimes (R.R. #4, Perth, Ontario, K7H 3C6, Canada), 1980.

* Orlick, T. *The Cooperative Sports & Games Book*, Pantheon Books (201 East 50th Street, New York, New York 10022), 1978.

Orlick, T. *Winning Through Cooperation—Competitive Insanity: Cooperative Alternatives.* Hawkins and Associates Inc. (804 D Street N.E., Suite 100, Washington, D.C. 20002), 1978.

Perry, D. "Improving Your Junior Sailing Program: Cooperation—Not Competition— The Key to Teaching Kids to Sail." Part I and Part II. *Yachting* (1 Park Avenue, New York, New York 10016), April and May 1978.

Playing Cooperatively: Another Way to Win. Saskatchewan Department of Cooperation and Cooperative Development (2055 Albert Street, Regina, Saskatchewan, S4P 3V7, Canada), 1980.

Poutre, N. *Cooperative Activities.* Kimbo Educational Records and Activities (Box 246, Deal, New York 07723), 1973. (Booklet for simple co-op exercises done to music.)

Provost, P., and Villeneuve, J. *Jouons ensemble: Jeux et sport cooperatifs.* Les Editions de L'Homme (955 rue Amherst, Montreal, Quebec, H2L 3K4 Canada), 1980.

Stevenson, H. *Balancing*, Argenta Friends School Press (Argenta, British Columbia, V0G 1B0, Canada), 1980. (For a variety of excellent cooperative balancing activities.)

Weinstein, M. and Goodman, J. *Play Fair: Everybody's Guide to Noncompetitive Play.* Impact Publishers (P.O. Box 1094, San Luis Obispo, California 93406), 1980. (For some excellent cooperative games to create a sense of community.)

---

* In Canada, all of my books can be obtained promptly by writing to the Coaching Association of Canada, 333 River Road, Ottawa, Ontario K1L 8B9, Canada.

WITH EXCLUSIVELY COOPERATIVE SECTIONS

The following books include very good practical sections or chapters that are exclusively cooperative in orientation.

Dearling, A., and Armstrong, H. *The Youth Games Book*. I.T. Resource Center (21 Atholl Crescent, Edinburgh, Scotland), 1980. (See chapter on group relationship games.)

Johnson, D.W., and Johnson, R. *Learning Together and Alone: Cooperation, Competition, and Individualization*. Prentice-Hall (Englewood Cliffs, New Jersey 07632), 1975.

Orlick, T. *In Pursuit of Excellence*. Coaching Association of Canada (333 River Road, Ottawa, Ontario K1L 8B9, Canada), 1980. (See chapter "Team Harmony"; in U.S.A. available from Human Kinetics Publishers, Box 5076, Champaign, Illinois 61820.)

Orlick, T., and Botterill, C. *Every Kid Can Win*. Nelson-Hall Publishers (111 North Canal Street, Chicago, Illinois 60606), 1979. (See chapter "What Do You Feel?")

Sharon, Lois, and Bram [singing group]. *Elephant Jam: A Trunkful of Musical Fun for the Whole Family*. McGraw-Hill Ryerson Ltd. (330 Progress Avenue, Scarborough, Ontario, M1P 2Z5, Canada), 1980. (See sections on clapping games, circle games, and dancing games.)

Torbert, M. *Follow Me: A Handbook of Movement Activities for Children*. Prentice-Hall (Englewood Cliffs, New Jersey 07632), 1980. (See chapter "Social Growth.") Can be obtained promptly by writing to L. G. Advisors, Box 175, Bala Cynwyd, Pennsylvania 19004.)

ADDITIONAL READINGS

Additional reference material from which you can extract some good cooperative activities or ideas include:

Armstrong, A. *Maori Games and Hakas: Instructions, Words and Action*. A.H. and A. W. Reed Publishers (182 Wakefield Street, Wellington, New Zealand), 1964. (For complete instructions on a variety of Maori stick games with traditional chants.)

Barton, E., and Osborne, J. "The Development of Classroom Sharing by a Teacher Using Positive Practice." *Behavior Modification*, 2, 231–250, 1978.

Best, E. *The Maori as He Was*, R. E. Owen, Government Printer (Wellington, New Zealand), 1924, 1952.

Butler, G., and Karetak, J. *Inuit Games*. Keewatin Inuit Association (Rankin Inlet, Northwest Territories, X0C 0G0, Canada), 1980.

Capp, J. "Games for Aboriginal Children." Unpublished manuscript (Areyonga School, Areyonga, Northern Territory, Australia), 1977.

A Child's Model for Adult Games. Ontario Ministry of Culture and Recreation Resource Center (9th Floor, 77 Bloor Street West, Toronto, Ontario, M7A 2R9, Canada), 1979.

The Child in Australian Aboriginal Societies. National Museum of Victoria (Melbourne, Australia), 1979.

Contact Quarterly. (P.O. Box 603, Northhampton, Massachusetts 01061). (For some very cooperative current forms of dance.)

Creative Playgrounds. Creative Playgrounds Inc. (719 Yonge Street, Toronto, Ontario, M4Y 2B5, Canada), ND.

Domanska, J. *The Turnip*. Macmillan (866 Third Avenue, New York, New York 10022), 1969. (To accompany the game Big Turnip.)

Elstner, F. *Spielmit*. Deutschen Sportbunds (Otto-Fleck-Schneise 12 6000 Frankfurt, Federal Republic of Germany), 1979.

Fabian, L.; Ross, M.; and Harwick, B. "Recreational Sports: How Every Player Wins." University of Pittsburgh, (Intramural Sports, University of Pittsburgh, Pittsburgh, Pennsylvania), 1980.

Fluegelman, Andrew, *More New Games*. New Games Foundation (P.O. Box 7901, San Francisco, California 94120), 1981.

Fowke, E. *Sally Go Round the Sun*. Macmillan (866 Third Avenue, New York, New York 10022), 1971. (See "Singing Ring Games.")

Games for Recreation. McWilson Recreational Services of Australia (P.O. Box 246, Lane Cove, N.S.W. 2066, Australia), 1978.

Gapes, C. *New Games for Community*. Board of Education, Uniting Church (P.O. Box E179, St. James, N.S.W. 2000 Australia), 1978.

Harris, F. *Games*. (Eastern Cooperative Recreation School, 1700 B. Franklin Pkwy, #601 Philadelphia, Pennsylvania 19103, or Can-ed Media Ltd., Suite #1, 185 Spadina Avenue, Toronto, Ontario, M5T 2C6, Canada), 1976.

Hogan, P. *Playgrounds for Free*. The M.I.T. Press (26 Carleton Street, Cambridge, Massachusetts 02142), 1974.

Level I and II Theory—Coaching Certification Manual. Coaching Association of Canada (333 River Road, Ottawa, Ontario K1L 8B9 Canada), 1979. (See sections on sport psychology and group goal setting.)

Life: Be in It with New Games. Department of Youth, Sport and Recreation, Marland House (570 Bourke Street, Melbourne 3000, Victoria, Australia), 1976. (Some good co-op games can be extracted from this manual.)

Michaelis, B. "Creating the Playful Space: "It" power—A Game Detergent." Unpublished paper (California State Polytechnic University, Pomona, California), 1979.

Michaelis, B. "Learning through Noncompetitive Activities and Play." *Learning Magazine Press* (Palo Alto, California), 1977.

Morris, D. *Elementary Physical Education: Toward Inclusion.* Brighton Publishing Company (P.O. Box 6235, Salt Lake City, Utah 84106), 1980.

Mulac, M. E. *Fun and Games.* Collier Books (866 Third Avenue, New York, New York 10022), 1956.

Newton, J. *Village Games of Papua New Guinea.* Expressive Arts Department, Goroka Teachers College (Goroka, Papua New Guinea), 1974.

Partington, J. T. "Children's Perspectives in Recreation Planning." *Recreation Canada* (CPRA, 333 River Road, Ottawa, Ontario, K1L 8B9, Canada) December 1980.

Permainan Masa Lapang Malaysia (Malaysian Pastime Games, Books 1 and 2). National Unity Board (c/o The Prime Minister's Department, Kuala Lumpur, Malaysia), 1976.

Physical Education and Sports Games. Beijing Institute for Physical Culture and Sport (Beijing 100084; People's Republic of China), 1979. (Available only in Chinese, but illustrations help non–Chinese.)

Pines, M. "Good Samaritans at Age Two." *Psychology Today* (P.O. Box 2990, Boulder, Colorado 80323), June 1979.

Play Spaces for Preschoolers: Design Guidelines for the Development of Preschool Play Spaces in Residential Environments (NHA 5138). Canada Mortgage and Housing Corporation (ICOM National Office, Montreal Road, Ottawa, Ontario K1A 0P7 Canada), 1978.

Players Manual 1 and 2 (1980), *Coaching, A New Look* (1978), and *A Family Approach to Youth Sports* (1978), YMCA Youth Sports Development (1750E Boulder Street, Colorado Springs, Colorado, 80909).

Reed, A. W. *Games the Maoris Played.* Reed Publishers, 182 Wakefield Street, Wellington, New Zealand), 1964.

Roleasmalik, P.M. *Traditional Games of Papua New Guinea.* PNG Ministry of Education, Science and Culture (Cultural Activities, Box 2051, Konedobu, Papua New Guinea), 1979.

Senior Citizens Sports and Games Manual. Alberta Recreation and Parks Department (Recreation Development Division, ARPD, Edmonton, Alberta, Canada), 1978.

Silverstein, S. *Where the Sidewalk Ends: The Poems and Drawings of Shel Silverstein.* Harper & Row, 10 East 53rd Street, New York, New York 10022), 1974.

Zuk, W. *Eskimo Games.* Curriculum Division, Department of Education, Government of the Northwest Territories (Yellowknife, Northwest Territories, Canada), 1973.

Recommended Films

I use the following excellent films in my university classes, as well as in various cooperative-games workshops, to stimulate thought on the need for alternatives and possible directions for the future:

Tuktu and the Indoor Games (14 minutes, 1967), *Northern Games* (25 minutes, 1982), *It's Winning That Counts* (55 minutes, 1975), *Les Vrai Perdants* (The Real Losers) (93 minutes, 1978). All available from the National Film Board of Canada—Film Library, 150 Kent Street, Ottawa, Ontario, K1A 0M9, Canada.

Two Ball Games (30 minutes, 1975). Department of Psychology, Cornell University, Ithaca, New York 14850.

What Price Victory (17 minutes, 1972). North American distributor—Daniel A. Segal Productions, 19433 Pacific Coast Highway, Malibu, California 90265.

Recommended Records

"Alternative Child," on the album *Gold Turkey—National Lampoon.* (Columbia Records, 1121 Leslie Street, Don Mills, Ontario, M3C 2J9, Canada).

"Comment Ça Va?" (by Edith Butler), on the album *Asteur qu'on est la.* (SIP Records, 2039 Crescent, Suite 6, Montreal, Quebec, Canada. (To accompany the game *Comment Ça Va?*)

Educaring (KEA 9060), *Clap, Snap, Tap* (AR 48), *Parachute Activities with Folk Dance Music* (KEA 9090), *Cooperative Activities* (KEA 9005). (In Canada, available from Van Nostrand Reinhold Ltd, 1410 Birchmont Road, Scarborough, Ontario, M1P 2E7. In U.S.A., available from Kimbo Educational Records, P.O. Box 477, 14 North Third Avenue, Long Beach, New Jersey 07740.)

"Flowers Are Red" and "Why Do Little Girls?" (by Harry Chapin), on the album *Living Room Suite.* (WEA Music of Canada, 1810 Birchmount Road, Scarborough, Ontario, Canada.)

Further Resource Material

For one of the most extensive cooperative curriculums ever developed for use in schools write to:

Education Coordinator
Saskatchewan Cooperation
5th Floor, 2055 Albert Street
Regina, Saskatchewan
S4P 3V7
Canada

Sweden's Nic Nilsson, president of the International Playground Association, is currently promoting a global concept of peace education for children. Among other things, he uses cooperative games to help in working toward this goal. Nic was influential in the decision to ban "war toys" altogether in his own country, as well as in Norway. He is a strong backer of an international youth movement known as Unga Ornar (Young Eagles), which attempts to integrate children's perspectives in a democratic way. Some of their goals as outlined in their Program of Action are presented below:

> For Unga Ornar the concept of carrying on their activities in a democratic form is not just a question of democracy in the technical sense but a question of a way of life and an attitude toward others. To help and support, instead of to win or to beat; to cooperate with, instead of working against; to look at things critically instead of accepting them uncritically; to try to understand, instead of to judge— all these, in our view, are part of the concept of working democratically.

By developing activities on an alternative basis to rivalry, and more particularly by the encouragement of creative activity, this group feels that they can teach children to think critically and function cooperatively and thereby equip themselves to bring about a better society. If you wish to contact Nic for more detailed information, write to:

Nic Nilsson,
Humlegardsgatan 17
S-114 46 Stockholm
Sweden

Photography Credits

Unless otherwise noted, all photographs were taken by the author.
Grateful acknowledgment is made to the following for supplying or allowing us to use photographs:

Rick Cendali: pages 76, 93
The Citizen, Ottawa, Canada: page 79
Patrick Hall, Saskatchewan Cooperation and Cooperative Development: pages 84, 91, 96, 98, and 206
Ky Aulis Nyqvist & Company, Kasamkatu 34, 130 Helsinki 13: page 45 (© Ky Aulis Nyqvist & Company)
Sylvie Lavoie: page 183
Nils John Vorenlind/Tiofoto AB: pages 63 and 186 (© Nils John Vorenlind/Tiofoto AB)
Rod and Sally Olsen: pages 10, 14, 55, 65, 83, 173, 177, and 224
Ron Orlick: page 35
Bernie Swords: page 73
Saskatchewan Cooperation and Cooperative Development: pages 8 and 36
Michel Villeneuve: pages 146 and 167
Ian Robertson: page 190

And grateful acknowledgment is made to Vic MacKenzie for the artwork on pp. 129 and 174.

index

About the Author

Terry Orlick is a professor and researcher in the psychology of sport and physical activity at the University of Ottawa. A graduate of Syracuse University, the College of William & Mary, and the University of Alberta, he is also a former Eastern intercollegiate and NCAA regional gymnastics champion. In recent years, he has been very active in developing and promoting cooperative game programs in schools and daycare centers throughout the world. His other works include *Every Kid Can Win, Winning Through Cooperation: Competitive Insanity, Cooperative Alternatives, The Pursuit of Excellence*, and *The Cooperative Sports & Games Book*.